Debt by Dysfunction

The 2033 Fiscal Crisis Hiding in Plain Sight

Karina Vunnam

Creative Nudge Press

Debt by Dysfunction: The 2033 Fiscal Crisis Hiding in Plain Sight

Written by Karina Vunnam

Copyright © 2026 by Karina Vunnam

All rights reserved.

Published by Creative Nudge Press, LLC

First Edition, 2026

For permission requests

Creative Nudge Press

2108 N St

Sacramento

contact@creativenudge.net

DebtByDysfunction.com.

Library of Congress Cataloging-in-Publication Data

Vunnam, Karina

Debt by Dysfunction: The 2033 Fiscal Crisis Hiding in Plain Sight / Karina Vunnam

978-1-966193-26-5 (paperback)

978-1-966193-27-2 (hardback)

1. Fiscal policy—United States

2. Social security—United States—Finance

3. Economic forecasting

4. Debt—United States

5. Political economy

Printed in the United States of America

10 9 8 7 6 5 4 3 2 1

Contents

Author's Note

This book is the product of over a year of research into a topic that demands care. I am a Stanford-trained economist with no financial products to sell, no political agenda, and no institutional constraints preventing candor. The United States faces a fiscal crisis that is neither speculative nor partisan. It is documented in official government projections that anyone can verify. My goal is not to be incendiary. It is to be useful.

Parts I and IV present the problem and explain why political solutions remain elusive. Parts II and III are where I walk the most difficult line: describing how the crisis may unfold and what individuals can do to prepare. I have done my best to ground these sections in historical precedent and current data rather than speculation, while acknowledging the inherent uncertainty in any forward-looking analysis.

The data cutoff for this book is December 15, 2025. All citations can be found in the Notes section at the end of each chapter.

This book draws substantially from my research paper: *The 2033 Social Security Deadline: Statutory Depletion as a Distinct Mechanism of Fiscal Crisis* published on November 20, 2025, available at SSRN: https://ssrn.com/abstract=5849942.

An interactive companion to this book, including timelines, data visualizations, and additional resources, is available at DebtByDysfunction.com.

I hope I am wrong about what follows. But the numbers suggest I am not.

Introduction

In 2033, the Old-Age and Survivors Insurance Trust Fund will run out of money.[1] This is not a prediction. It is a statutory deadline, documented in the Social Security Administration's 2025 Trustees Report and confirmed by Congressional Budget Office projections.[2] When the fund depletes, federal law mandates that benefits be reduced to match incoming payroll tax revenue.

The magnitude of this cut worsened significantly in the year between the 2024 and 2025 Trustees Reports. The 2024 report projected a 21 percent reduction.[3] One year later, following passage of the Social Security Fairness Act in January 2025, which restored benefits to certain public employees without any corresponding revenue to pay for them, the 2025 report increased the projected cut to 23 percent.[4] Independent analysis incorporating additional 2025 legislation estimates the cut will reach 24 percent.[5] This deterioration, occurring in a single year due to legislation that increased benefits without funding them, exemplifies the fiscal dysfunction this book documents. More than 74 million Americans will face this reduction.[6]

A typical dual-earning couple retiring in 2033 will lose approximately $18,400 annually, while a single-income couple faces a $13,800 reduction.[7] For context, the average Social Security retirement benefit in 2024 was $1,924 per month, or $23,088 annually.[8] A 24 percent reduction transforms that into

$1,462 per month: $462 less every month for rent, groceries, medications, utilities.

This reduction is automatic unless Congress acts. Congress will not act. The required fix to stabilize the national debt, a combination of tax increases and spending cuts totaling approximately $9.0 trillion in deficit reduction over the next decade, exceeds any politically survivable threshold for either party.[9] We know this because a similar crisis in 1983 required bipartisan compromise on a problem half this magnitude.[10] Today's political environment cannot replicate that achievement.[11]

This is the first crisis. There are two others, and they converge in the same narrow window.

By 2027, federal net interest costs will exceed all non-defense discretionary spending.[12] The government will spend more servicing debt than funding infrastructure, education, scientific research, national parks, courts, and federal operations combined. Interest payments will consume 22.2 percent of federal revenue by 2035, transforming debt service into what functions as a third entitlement program, one that buys nothing, builds nothing, and crowds out the capacity for any future investment or crisis response.[13]

Simultaneously, the United States carries federal debt at approximately 100 percent of GDP, with projections showing it will surpass the World War II record in 2029 and reach 118 percent by 2035.[14] Unlike the post-war period, when a young population, robust growth, and slashed defense spending created rapid deleveraging, today's trajectory combines an aging population, slower growth, and structural deficits with no foreseeable reversal.[15]

The dollar's reserve currency status provides a buffer. Approximately 56 percent of global foreign exchange reserves are held in dollars, and U.S. Treasury securities remain the benchmark for risk-free assets.[16] This privilege allows the United States to borrow at lower rates than fiscal fundamentals alone would justify. But this protection depends on institutional credibility and political stability.[17] One major shock, whether a debt ceiling default, repeated political brinksmanship, or visible interference with Federal Reserve independence, could trigger a rapid shift in market confidence, converting a slow structural deterioration into an acute crisis.

These three forces, entitlement insolvency, interest cost explosion, and confidence vulnerability, are not sequential. They are converging.

So why haven't you heard about this?

The data exists in Congressional Budget Office reports, Social Security Administration actuarial tables, International Monetary Fund analyses, and Federal Reserve research papers. These are not fringe sources. They are the official projections produced by the institutions responsible for monitoring U.S. fiscal health. The numbers are public. The implications are clear. Yet sustained public discourse about this convergence remains largely absent.

The silence is not conspiracy. It is rational.

Politicians operate on electoral cycles of two to six years. A crisis with a seven-year timeline and solutions requiring immediate, severe political pain presents a simple calculation: the cost of reform is certain and arrives before the next election, while the cost of inaction lands on a successor.[18] Media organizations operate on engagement economics, where complex, slow-moving crises cannot compete for attention against immediate stories.[19] Economic experts face career penalties for early warnings; being correct but premature carries nearly the same professional cost as being wrong.[20] Financial advisors face legal liability for recommendations that cause clients to act on dire predictions.[21] And sovereign debt markets exhibit confidence-dependent equilibria, meaning those responsible for financial stability have powerful incentives not to undermine confidence by warning too credibly.[22]

Every actor is individually optimizing for survival within their constraints. Collectively, they produce what game theorists call a Nash equilibrium: a stable state where no individual benefits from changing their behavior, even though the collective outcome is catastrophic.[23] The first person to break from silence pays the highest cost, ensuring gridlock until crisis makes the status quo untenable.

This is what I call rational dysfunction: individually sensible behavior producing collectively disastrous outcomes.

The dysfunction is documented. The projections are public. The collision is coming. This book exists to synthesize official data that policymakers, economists, and financial professionals see but cannot publicly discuss in its full implications.

Part I examines the evidence. The 2033 Social Security deadline. The interest cost explosion already underway. The confidence dynamics that could accelerate the timeline. Every projection comes from official sources. This section also explains why every actor with knowledge of this data faces structural incentives to remain silent.

Part II details how crisis actually unfolds. Not sudden collapse, but progressive deterioration. The 1930s Great Depression produced 25 percent unemployment without triggering civil war.[24] Social order is more resilient than apocalyptic narratives suggest. But the United States today differs from the 1930s in critical ways: an aging rather than young population, urban concentration rather than rural distribution, and massive entitlement obligations rather than fiscal flexibility.[25] This section traces a realistic timeline from 2025 through 2040, showing how fiscal stress transmits into economic contraction, municipal breakdown, and geographic stratification.

Part III addresses preparation. Geographic positioning, financial diversification, skill acquisition, psychological readiness. What constitutes realistic preparation versus counterproductive anxiety. Where you live, what you own, and what you know how to do will matter more than they have in living memory.

Part IV examines the solutions we are not choosing. The math is solvable. Every policy lever exists. The 1983 Social Security fix proved comprehensive reform is possible.[26] But that crisis was half this magnitude with lower political polarization and revenue tools that have since been exhausted. Today's requirement of $9.0 trillion in deficit reduction creates electoral annihilation risk for any party that proposes it.[27] Both parties need each other to pass reform. Neither can trust the other. The result is guaranteed gridlock until external crisis forces action under the worst possible conditions.[28]

The 2033 deadline provides a fixed point. Seven years is enough time for those who take this analysis seriously to make meaningful adjustments. It is also short enough that we will know relatively soon whether the analysis was accurate.

Understanding the mechanism matters. If crisis unfolds as projected, people with frameworks for understanding what is happening will make better decisions than those operating in confusion. And if political miracles occur and reform actually passes, then the worst outcomes can still be avoided, though nothing in current political dynamics suggests that path is likely.

The data is public. The math is clear. The collision is coming.

Let's examine exactly how.

INTRODUCTION NOTES

1. Social Security Administration, "A Summary of the 2025 Annual Reports," June 2025, https://www.ssa.gov/oact/TRSUM/index.html. ("The Old-Age and Survivors Insurance (OASI) Trust Fund will be able to pay 100 percent of total scheduled benefits until 2033.")

2. Congressional Budget Office, "CBO's 2024 Long-Term Projections for Social Security," June 2024, https://www.cbo.gov/publication/60679. ("In CBO's projections, the balance of the Old-Age and Survivors Insurance Trust Fund is exhausted in fiscal year 2033.")

3. Social Security Administration, "A Summary of the 2024 Annual Reports," May 2024, https://www.ssa.gov/oact/TRSUM/2024/index.html. ("At that time, the fund's reserves will become depleted and continuing program income will be sufficient to pay 79 percent of scheduled benefits.")

4. Social Security Administration, "A Summary of the 2025 Annual Reports," June 2025, https://www.ssa.gov/oact/TRSUM/index.html. ("At that time, the fund's reserves will become depleted and continuing program income will be sufficient to pay 77 percent of total scheduled benefits.") The report notes: "The projected long-term finances of the combined OASDI fund worsened this year primarily due to three factors. First, the Social Security Fairness Act, as enacted on January 5, 2025, repealed the Windfall Elimination and Government Pension Offset provisions of the Social Security Act."

5. Committee for a Responsible Federal Budget, "As Social Security Turns 90, It's Racing Towards Insolvency," August 14, 2025, https://www.crfb.org/blogs/social-security-turns-90-its-racing-towards-insolvency. ("all current and new retired beneficiaries, regardless of age or income, will face an across-the-board 24 percent

benefit cut when the retirement trust fund is depleted in 2032.")
CRFB's analysis incorporates both the Social Security Fairness Act
($200 billion cost over ten years) and the One Big Beautiful Bill Act
($169 billion cost over ten years), which reduced Social Security rev-
enue from income taxation of benefits.

6. Social Security Administration, "Monthly Statistical Snapshot," August 2025, https://www.ssa.gov/policy/docs/quickfacts/stat_snapsh
   ot/. Table 1 shows 74,521,000 total beneficiaries receiving Social Security, Supplemental Security Income (SSI), or both as of August
   2025.

7. Committee for a Responsible Federal Budget, "As Social Security
   Turns 90, It's Racing Towards Insolvency," August 14, 2025. ("we
   estimate a typical couple retiring shortly after the trust fund runs out
   will face an $18,400 benefit cut... a typical single-earner couple would
   face a $13,800 cut.")

8. Social Security Administration, "Monthly Statistical Snapshot," October 2024, https://www.ssa.gov/policy/docs/quickfacts/stat_snaps
   hot/2024-10.html. Table 2 shows average monthly benefit for retired
   workers was $1,924.35 as of October 2024.

9. Committee for a Responsible Federal Budget, "Meeting Fiscal Goals Under CBO's January 2025 Baseline," January 29,
   2025, https://www.crfb.org/blogs/meeting-fiscal-goals-under-cbos
   -january-2025-baseline. ("Stabilizing debt over the next decade at its
   current share of the economy would require $9.0 trillion of deficit re-
   duction relative to the Congressional Budget Office's (CBO) January
   2025 baseline.")

10. Louise   Sheiner   and   Georgia   Nabors,   "Social   Securi-
    ty: Today's Financing Challenge Is at Least Double
    What It Was in 1983," Brookings Institution, September

18, 2023, https://www.brookings.edu/articles/social-security-toda ys-financing-challenge-is-at-least-double-what-it-was-in-1983/. ("the changes that are required to put Social Security on a stable footing over the next 75 years are significantly larger than they were in 1983... the required adjustments to revenues and/or benefits are twice as large today.")

11. Shanto Iyengar et al., "The Origins and Consequences of Affective Polarization in the United States," Annual Review of Political Science 22 (2019): 129-146, https://doi.org/10.1146/annurev-polisci-05111 7-073034.

12. Congressional Budget Office, "The Budget and Economic Outlook: 2025 to 2035," January 2025, https://www.cbo.gov/publication/61 172. ("Interest costs exceed outlays for defense from 2025 to 2035 and exceed outlays for nondefense discretionary programs from 2027 to 2035.")

13. Peter G. Peterson Foundation, "Any Way You Look at It, Interest Costs on the National Debt Will Soon Be at an All-Time High," February 2025, https://www.pgpf.org/article/any-way-you-look-at-it-interest -costs-on-the-national-debt-will-soon-be-at-an-all-time-high. ("As a share of federal revenues, federal interest payments would rise to 18.4 percent this year... and would climb to 22.2 percent by 2035.")

14. Congressional Budget Office, "The Budget and Economic Outlook: 2025 to 2035," January 2025, https://www.cbo.gov/publication/61 172. ("Federal debt held by the public rises from 100 percent of GDP this year to 118 percent in 2035, surpassing its previous high of 106 percent of GDP in 1946.")

15. Congressional Budget Office, "The Long-Term Budget Outlook: 2025 to 2055," March 2025, https://www.cbo.gov/publication/61270.

16. International Monetary Fund, "Currency Composition of Official Foreign Exchange Reserves (COFER)," Q2 2025 data release, October 2025, https://data.imf.org/en/news/october%201%202025%20cofer. ("The share of US dollar holdings in the allocated reserves decreased to 56.32 percent.")

17. Council on Foreign Relations, "The Dollar: The World's Reserve Currency," updated 2024, https://www.cfr.org/backgrounder/dollar-worlds-reserve-currency.

18. William G. Gale and Alan J. Auerbach, "Fiscal Myopia," Urban Institute and Urban-Brookings Tax Policy Center, September 30, 2013, https://www.urban.org/sites/default/files/publication/23176/1001698-Fiscal-Myopia.PDF.

19. Tom Cunningham et al., "Ranking by Engagement and Non-Engagement Signals: Learnings from Industry," Annals of the New York Academy of Sciences (2025), https://nyaspubs.onlinelibrary.wiley.com/doi/10.1111/nyas.15399.

20. Stephen Mihm, "Dr. Doom," New York Times Magazine, August 15, 2008, https://www.nytimes.com/2008/08/17/magazine/17pessimist-t.html.

21. Financial Industry Regulatory Authority (FINRA), "Suitability," Rule 2111, https://www.finra.org/rules-guidance/rulebooks/finra-rules/2111.

22. Paul De Grauwe, "The Governance of a Fragile Eurozone," CEPS Working Document No. 346, May 2011, https://aei.pitt.edu/31741/1/WD_346_De_Grauwe_on_Eurozone_Governance-1.pdf.

23. John Nash, "Non-Cooperative Games," Annals of Mathematics 54, no. 2 (1951): 286-295, https://www.jstor.org/stable/1969529. The application to fiscal policy gridlock is the author's synthesis.

24. Congressional Research Service, "Unemployment During the Great Depression," Report R40655, https://www.everycrsreport.com/rep orts/R40655.html. ("The unemployment rate rose from 3.2% in 1929 to 24.9% in 1933 during the Great Depression's more severe first do wnturn.")

25. Robert D. Putnam, *Bowling Alone: The Collapse and Revival of American Community* (New York: Simon & Schuster, 2000).

26. Social Security Administration, "Report of the National Commission on Social Security Reform," January 1983, https://www.ssa.gov/his tory/reports/gspan.html.

27. Committee for a Responsible Federal Budget, "Meeting Fiscal Goals Under CBO's January 2025 Baseline," January 29, 2025, https://www.crfb.org/blogs/meeting-fiscal-goals-under-cbos -january-2025-baseline.

28. On March 28, 2012, a bipartisan budget proposal based on the Simpson-Bowles framework (the Cooper-LaTourette amendment) was brought to a vote in the House and defeated 382-38 (House Roll Call 145). See Charles J. Lewis, "Himes Predicts Action on Debt After Election," CT Insider, March 29, 2012, https://www.ctinsider.com/local/article/himes-predicts-actio n-on-debt-after-election-3445605.php.

PART I

What's Coming

(And Why You Haven't Heard About It)

Chapter 1
The 2033 Deadline

S ocial Security was designed to be untouchable. When Franklin Roosevelt signed the Social Security Act in 1935, he insisted on a dedicated payroll tax rather than general revenue funding. "We put those payroll contributions there so as to give the contributors a legal, moral, and political right to collect their pensions," Roosevelt later explained. "With those taxes in there, no damn politician can ever scrap my social security program."[1]

The design worked. For ninety years, Social Security has operated as a self-contained system: workers pay in through payroll taxes, the money goes into dedicated trust funds, and benefits are paid out from those funds. The program exists outside the annual appropriations process that governs most federal spending. Congress does not vote each year on whether to fund Social Security. The benefits flow automatically, protected from the political battles that determine funding for defense, education, infrastructure, and everything else the federal government does.

This architectural independence made Social Security the most successful and durable social program in American history. It also created a ticking time bomb.

Because Social Security operates from dedicated trust funds rather than general revenue, the program faces a constraint that other government spending does not: when the trust funds run out of money, benefits must be cut to match incoming revenue. This is not a policy choice. It is statutory law. The Social Security Act does not authorize the program to spend money it does not have.[2] Unlike the rest of the federal government, which can deficit spend indefinitely by borrowing, Social Security must balance its books. When the Old-Age and Survivors Insurance Trust Fund depletes its reserves, the law requires that benefits be reduced to whatever level current payroll tax revenue can support.

This is what makes 2033 different from every other fiscal projection. When the Congressional Budget Office warns that debt will reach 180 percent of GDP by 2050, that is a projection that depends on dozens of assumptions and policy choices that could change. When economists warn about unsustainable deficits, they are describing trends that Congress could theoretically reverse through legislation. But 2033 is not a projection of what might happen if trends continue. It is a statutory deadline written into the structure of the program itself. The trust fund will deplete. The cuts will occur automatically. Congress does not need to vote for them to happen. Congress would need to vote to prevent them.

The Social Security Administration's 2025 Trustees Report confirms the timeline: the Old-Age and Survivors Insurance Trust Fund will be able to pay full scheduled benefits only until 2033.[3] The Congressional Budget Office independently projects the same exhaustion date.[4] When that date arrives, benefits will automatically be reduced to match incoming payroll tax revenue, a cut of approximately 24 percent affecting more than 74 million Americans.[5]

The magnitude of this cut has worsened significantly in recent years. The 2024 Trustees Report projected a 21 percent reduction.[6] One year later, following passage of the Social Security Fairness Act in January 2025, which restored benefits to certain public employees without any corresponding revenue to pay for them, the 2025 report increased the projected cut to 23 percent.[3] Independent analysis incorporating additional 2025 legislation estimates the cut will reach 24 percent.[5] This deterioration, occurring in a single year due to legislation that expanded benefits without funding them, demonstrates the political dynamic this book documents: even as the crisis approaches, the political system continues making it worse.

What does a 24 percent cut mean for actual retirees? A typical dual-earning couple retiring in 2033 will lose approximately $18,400 annually, while a single-income couple faces a $13,800 reduction.[7] The average Social Security retirement benefit in 2024 was $1,924 per month, or $23,088 annually.[8] A 24 percent reduction transforms that into $1,462 per month. That is $462 less every month for rent, groceries, medications, utilities. For elderly Americans who depend on Social Security for the majority of their income. This is not an adjustment. It is a crisis.

The demographic mathematics driving this insolvency are locked in and irreversible. Social Security is a pay-as-you-go system: current workers pay taxes that fund current retirees' benefits. The system's solvency depends on maintaining a sustainable ratio between those paying in and those drawing out. In 1950, there were 16.5 workers paying into the system for every beneficiary receiving payments.[9] By 2013, that ratio had collapsed to 2.8 workers per beneficiary.[9] Current projections show it declining further to 2.1 workers per beneficiary by 2100.[10]

This collapse reflects two demographic forces that no policy can reverse. The first is the Baby Boom retirement wave. Americans born between 1946 and 1964, the largest generation in the nation's history, began reaching retirement age in 2011. Every day for the next decade, approximately 10,000 Baby Boomers will turn 65.[11] This is not a temporary surge that will pass. It is a permanent expansion of the beneficiary population that will persist for decades as this generation ages through their retirement years.

The second force is persistently low fertility. The United States Total Fertility Rate, the average number of children born per woman over her lifetime, currently stands at approximately 1.66 births per woman.[12] This is well below the replacement rate of 2.1 required to maintain population size without immigration. Fewer births today means fewer workers tomorrow, which means less payroll tax revenue to support a growing retiree population.

The policy community is planning based on assumptions that may prove optimistic. The Social Security Administration assumes the fertility rate will gradually recover to 1.90 children per woman by 2060, a projection extended by ten years in the 2025 report, reflecting slower-than-hoped demographic rec overy.13 The Congressional Budget Office is less optimistic, projecting fertility will remain at 1.60 through 2055, identical to the SSA's high-cost scenario used to illustrate unfavorable conditions.[14] If the CBO projection proves accurate, the crisis accelerates. Persistent low fertility means fewer future workers, lower payroll tax revenue, and a larger financing gap than official projections suggest.

Measured over a 75-year horizon, Social Security faces an actuarial deficit of 3.82 percent of taxable payroll, the largest shortfall since 1977.[15] Measured over an infinite horizon to assess true perpetual sustainability, the unfunded obligation totals $72.8 trillion in present value, up from $65.9 trillion reported just two years earlier.[16] This represents the total amount by which promised benefits exceed projected revenues extending indefinitely into the future. These are not numbers that gradual economic growth will erase. They are structural gaps that require deliberate policy changes to close.

The last time Social Security faced a crisis of this nature, the political system rose to meet it. In 1983, with the trust fund months from insolvency, President Reagan and House Speaker Tip O'Neill negotiated a comprehensive reform package. The solution combined payroll tax increases, a gradual rise in the retirement age from 65 to 67, delayed cost-of-living adjustments, and the introduction of income taxation on Social Security benefits for higher earners.[17] The legislation passed with strong bipartisan support and was projected to keep the program solvent for 75 years.

That fix addressed a problem half the current magnitude.[18] The required adjustment in 1983 was equivalent to 1.82 percent of taxable payroll. Today's gap is 3.82 percent, more than double. The easy revenue tools available in 1983, such as expanding coverage to federal employees and introducing benefit taxation, have already been used. The retirement age increase enacted then is fully phased in. What remains are the politically toxic options: further tax increases, further benefit cuts, or both.

Achieving 75-year solvency now requires the equivalent of at least a 29 percent increase in payroll taxes, a 22 percent reduction in benefits, or some combination of both.[19] Consider what this means in practice. The current combined employer-employee payroll tax rate for Social Security is 12.4 percent of wages up to the taxable maximum of $176,100.20 A 29 percent increase would raise the rate to approximately 16 percent, an additional 3.6 percentage points split between workers and employers. For a worker earning $60,000 annually, this translates to roughly $1,100 more per year in payroll taxes, with their employer paying an equal amount. Alternatively, a 22 percent benefit reduction means the average monthly benefit of $1,924 drops to approximately $1,501, a loss of over $420 per month, or more than $5,000 annually.

The policy options that politicians frequently cite as obvious solutions fail to close the gap. Eliminating the payroll tax cap entirely, requiring high earners to pay Social Security taxes on all wages rather than just the first $176,100, would close only approximately 61 percent of the 75-year funding gap.[21] Raising the full retirement age from 67 to 68 would eliminate only 14 percent of the shortfall.[21] No single policy adjustment is sufficient. Every credible proposal requires combining tax increases with benefit reductions, simultaneously alienating both parties' core constituencies.

The political system has already demonstrated its inability to pass such reforms. When a modified version of the bipartisan Simpson-Bowles deficit reduction plan came to a vote in the House in March 2012, it was rejected 382 to 38.22 The original commission, created by President Obama in 2010, had proposed $2.6 trillion in revenue increases and $2.9 trillion in spending cuts over ten years, a nearly balanced approach to deficit reduction.23 Even within the commission itself, the plan failed to achieve the 14-vote supermajority required to send formal recommendations to Congress. Republican members objected to tax increases. Democratic members objected to entitlement cuts. When a modified version reached the House floor, only 22 Democrats and 16 Republicans voted yes.[22]

This was not a failure of policy design. It was proof that the political system cannot pass reforms requiring both parties to accept pain their respective bases reject. The $9.0 trillion in deficit reduction now required to stabilize federal finances is more than triple the scale Simpson-Bowles proposed.[24] The political system that rejected that plan will not pass reforms three times larger.

The structural obstacles are quantifiable. Among voters aged 50 and older, 90 percent say Social Security is very important to them, making it a single-issue voting priority for millions of Americans.[25] This demographic is not a minority constituency. Voters aged 50 and older accounted for 55 percent of the electorate in competitive congressional districts in the 2024 election and 61 percent in the 2022 midterms.[26] In the districts that determine control of Congress, older voters are not just a significant voting bloc. They are the majority.

Any legislator proposing benefit cuts faces immediate electoral consequences. When Republican candidates in 2014 attempted to defend positions on Social Security reform, Democratic attack ads weaponized their support for bipartisan fiscal commissions, mocking the "once-revered, supposedly bipartisan Simpson-Bowles deficit proposal" as a controversial plan that raises the retirement age.[27] The party that proposes reforms becomes the party that loses elections. The party that attacks those reforms wins.

This creates a stable equilibrium of inaction. The Democratic base will not accept benefit cuts to Social Security. The Republican base will not accept tax increases of sufficient scale to close the gap. Both parties require the other to pass comprehensive reform, as neither possesses the votes alone. Yet neither can trust that the other will not weaponize compromise positions in the next election cycle. Every politician optimizing for re-election makes the individually rational choice to avoid the issue. The aggregation of these rational individual choices produces collective paralysis.

When 2033 arrives and the trust fund depletes, Congress will face three options, none of them good.

The first option is to allow the automatic 24 percent benefit cuts to take effect as required by law. This would immediately reduce income for 74 million Americans, including current retirees who have no time to adjust their financial plans. Social Security benefits generated $2.6 trillion in total economic output and supported $1.6 trillion in GDP in 2023.[28] A sudden 24 percent reduction represents a massive negative shock to consumer demand, with effects amplified during periods of economic stress.[29] The political fallout would be immediate and severe.

The second option is to authorize emergency transfers from the General Fund to cover the shortfall and maintain scheduled benefits. This avoids immediate benefit cuts but accelerates the broader fiscal crisis. Social Security already accounts for 48 percent of the projected increase in the primary budget deficit over the next decade, more than any other program.[30] Emergency General Fund transfers would add trillions to federal borrowing while destroying the political consensus around Social Security as an earned benefit program financed by dedicated taxes. Once benefits are covered by general revenues, the program becomes vulnerable to annual appropriations battles and broader deficit reduction pressures.

The third option is to implement emergency tax increases or benefit reductions sufficient to restore solvency. This represents managed crisis response rather than proactive reform, with adjustments larger than if enacted earlier because each year of delay increases the required correction. Immediate changes on the scale necessary would impose severe hardship on current retirees who lack time to compensate, or drag down economic growth through sudden tax increases.

The most likely outcome is emergency borrowing, the second option, which kicks the problem five to ten years further down the road. This choice minimizes immediate political pain while making the eventual reckoning worse. It requires only a single emergency authorization rather than the sustained coalition necessary for comprehensive reform. Future Congresses can tell themselves they will address the underlying problem before the borrowed money runs out. They will face the same incentive structure that prevents action today, now with a larger problem and fewer options.

Every year of inaction makes the required adjustment geometrically larger. At current debt levels of approximately 100 percent of GDP, stabilizing the debt-to-GDP ratio requires achieving a primary deficit of roughly 2 percent of GDP, difficult but feasible.[31] If action is delayed until debt reaches 180 percent of GDP, projected for the early 2050s under current trajectories, stabilization requires achieving a primary surplus of approximately 1 percent of GDP.[31] This 3 percentage point swing represents an enormous increase in the political and economic pain required.

The worker-to-beneficiary ratio will not improve. Fertility rates show no signs of recovering to replacement level. The Baby Boom generation will not un-retire. The electoral math that makes Social Security reform politically suicidal will not change as long as voters aged 50 and older represent the majority of the electorate in competitive districts.

Roosevelt designed Social Security to be untouchable, and he succeeded beyond his imagining. The program's independence from annual appropriations protected it from "damn politicians" for nine decades. But that same independence now guarantees a crisis that politicians cannot prevent through inaction. The automatic cuts are written into law. The deadline is statutory. In 2033, more than 74 million Americans will receive notice that their benefits are being reduced, not because Congress voted for cuts, but because the architecture Roosevelt built to protect the program will finally enforce the constraints he embedded within it.

The question is not whether the crisis will arrive. The question is what happens when it does.

CHAPTER 1 NOTES

1. Arthur M. Schlesinger Jr., *The Age of Roosevelt: The Coming of the New Deal* (Boston: Houghton Mifflin, 1958), 308-309. Roosevelt's quote about "no damn politician" is widely attributed and appears in multiple historical accounts of Social Security's founding.

2. Social Security Administration, "Compilation of the Social Security Laws: Title II—Federal Old-Age, Survivors, and Disability Insurance Benefits," https://www.ssa.gov/OP_Home/ssact/title02/0201. htm. The Social Security Act authorizes benefit payments only from the trust funds, with no provision for general revenue transfers absent specific congressional authorization.

3. Social Security Administration, "A Summary of the 2025 Annual Reports," June 2025, https://www.ssa.gov/oact/TRSUM/index.ht ml. ("The Old-Age and Survivors Insurance (OASI) Trust Fund will be able to pay 100 percent of total scheduled benefits until 2033." Also notes: "The projected long-term finances of the combined OASDI fund worsened this year primarily due to three factors. First, the Social Security Fairness Act, as enacted on January 5, 2025, repealed the Windfall Elimination and Government Pension Offset provisions of the Social Security Act.")

4. Congressional Budget Office, "CBO's 2024 Long-Term Projections for Social Security," June 2024, https://www.cbo.gov/publication/6 0679. ("In CBO's projections, the balance of the Old-Age and Survivors Insurance Trust Fund is exhausted in fiscal year 2033.")

5. Committee for a Responsible Federal Budget, "As Social Security Turns 90, It's Racing Towards Insolvency," August 14, 2025, https://www.crfb.org/blogs/social-security-turns-90-its-racin g-towards-insolvency. ("all current and new retired beneficiaries, re-

gardless of age or income, will face an across-the-board 24 percent benefit cut when the retirement trust fund is depleted.") Social Security Administration, "Monthly Statistical Snapshot," August 2025, https://www.ssa.gov/policy/docs/quickfacts/stat_snapshot/. (Table 1 shows 74,521,000 total beneficiaries)

6. Social Security Administration, "A Summary of the 2024 Annual Reports," May 2024, https://www.ssa.gov/oact/TRSUM/2024/ind ex.html. ("At that time, the fund's reserves will become depleted and continuing program income will be sufficient to pay 79 percent of scheduled benefits.")

7. Committee for a Responsible Federal Budget, "As Social Security Turns 90, It's Racing Towards Insolvency," August 14, 2025. ("we estimate a typical couple retiring shortly after the trust fund runs out will face an $18,400 benefit cut... a typical single-earner couple would face a $13,800 cut.")

8. Social Security Administration, "Monthly Statistical Snapshot," October 2024, https://www.ssa.gov/policy/docs/quickfacts/stat_snaps hot/2024-10.html. Table 2 shows average monthly benefit for retired workers was $1,924.35 as of October 2024.

9. Social Security Administration, Office of the Chief Actuary, "Table I V.B3. Covered Workers and Beneficiaries, Calendar Years 1945-2100," 2025 Annual Social Security Trustees Report, https://www.ssa.gov /oact/TR/2025/index.html. Historical data shows 16.5 workers per beneficiary in 1950, declining to 2.8 in 2013.

10. Social Security Administration, Office of the Chief Actuary, "Table I V.B3. Covered Workers and Beneficiaries, Calendar Years 1945-2100," 2025 Annual Social Security Trustees Report. The 2100 projection shows 228,446 thousand workers and 110,313 thousand beneficiaries, yielding 2.1 workers per beneficiary.

11. Pew Research Center, "Baby Boomers Retire," December 2010, https://www.pewresearch.org/short-reads/2010/12/29/baby-boomers-retire/. ("On January 1, 2011, the oldest Baby Boomers will turn 65. Every day for the next 19 years, about 10,000 more will cross that threshold.")

12. Centers for Disease Control and Prevention, "Births: Provisional Data for 2022," Vital Statistics Rapid Release Report No. 28, May 2023, https://www.cdc.gov/nchs/data/vsrr/vsrr028.pdf. ("The total fertility rate (TFR) for the United States in 2022 was 1,665.0 births per 1,000 women, essentially unchanged from 2021.")

13. Social Security Administration, "V.A. Demographic Assumptions," 2025 OASDI Trustees Report, https://www.ssa.gov/oact/TR/2025/V_A_demo.html. ("Under the intermediate assumptions, the total fertility rate (TFR) is assumed to rise gradually from current levels to 1.90 children per woman by 2060, and remain at that level thereafter.")

14. Congressional Budget Office, "The Demographic Outlook: 2025 to 2055," March 2025, https://www.cbo.gov/publication/61164. CBO projects fertility "continuing at 1.60 children per woman, well below replacement level, through 2055," without the modest recovery that SSA assumes.

15. Committee for a Responsible Federal Budget, "Analysis of the 2025 Social Security Trustees' Report," June 18, 2025, https://www.crfb.org/papers/analysis-2025-social-security-trustees-report. ("The 2025 Trustees project a 75-year actuarial deficit of 3.82 percent of taxable payroll, up from 3.61 percent in last year's report.")

16. Social Security Administration, "Table VI.F1. Present Values of OASDI Cost Less Non-interest Income and Unfunded Obligations for Program Participants," 2025 OASDI Trustees Report, htt

ps://www.ssa.gov/oact/TR/2025/VI_F_infinite.html. ("The OASDI open-group unfunded obligation over the infinite horizon is $72.8 trillion in present value.") Compare to 2023 Trustees Report, Table VI.F1, https://www.ssa.gov/oact/tr/2023/VI_F_infinite.html, which showed $65.9 trillion.

17. Social Security Administration, "Report of the National Commission on Social Security Reform," January 1983, https://www.ssa.gov/history/reports/gspan.html. See also Social Security Administration, "Summary of P.L. 98-21, Social Security Amendments of 1983," https://www.ssa.gov/history/1983amend.html.

18. Louise Sheiner and Georgia Nabors, "Social Security: Today's Financing Challenge Is at Least Double What It Was in 1983," Brookings Institution, September 18, 2023, https://www.brookings.edu/articles/social-security-todays-financing-challenge-is-at-least-double-what-it-was-in-1983/. ("the changes that are required to put Social Security on a stable footing over the next 75 years are significantly larger than they were in 1983... the required adjustments to revenues and/or benefits are twice as large today.")

19. Committee for a Responsible Federal Budget, "Analysis of the 2025 Social Security Trustees' Report," June 18, 2025. ("A plan to restore solvency will require the equivalent of at least a 22 percent reduction in benefits for current and future beneficiaries, a 29 percent increase in payroll taxes, or some combination of the two.")

20. Social Security Administration, "2025 Social Security Changes," https://www.ssa.gov/news/press/factsheets/colafacts2025.pdf. The 2025 taxable maximum is $176,100. The combined employer-employee Social Security tax rate is 12.4 percent (6.2 percent each).

21. Program for Public Consultation, "Social Security Reform Re-

port," University of Maryland School of Public Policy, September 2022, https://publicconsultation.org/wp-content/uploads/2022/09/Social_Security_2022_Report.pdf. The report finds that making all wages above $400,000 subject to the payroll tax eliminates 61 percent of the shortfall, while raising the retirement age from 67 to 68 eliminates only 14 percent.

22. Charles J. Lewis, "Himes Predicts Action on Debt After Election," CT Insider, March 29, 2012, https://www.ctinsider.com/local/article/himes-predicts-action-on-debt-after-election-3445605.php. ("Lawmakers voted 382-38 against the debt plan that was closely modeled on the 2010 recommendations of the Simpson-Bowles commission... The 38 'aye' votes included 22 Democrats and 16 Republicans.")

23. Richard Kogan, "What Was Actually in Bowles-Simpson, And How Can We Compare it With Other Plans?," Center on Budget and Policy Priorities, October 2, 2012, https://www.cbpp.org/research/what-was-actually-in-bowles-simpson-and-how-can-we-compare-it-with-other-plans. ("The plan proposed $2.6 trillion in revenue increases and $2.9 trillion in spending cuts over ten years.")

24. Committee for a Responsible Federal Budget, "Meeting Fiscal Goals Under CBO's January 2025 Baseline," January 29, 2025, https://www.crfb.org/blogs/meeting-fiscal-goals-under-cbos-january-2025-baseline. ("Stabilizing debt over the next decade at its current share of the economy would require $9.0 trillion of deficit reduction.")

25. AARP Research Center, "Social Security 2024 Survey of Voters Ages 50+," November 2024, https://www.aarp.org/pri/topics/voter-research/politics/voter-preferences-2024-battleground-states/. ("Around 90% said they would be more likely to vote for a candidate who pledged to make sure workers get the Social Security they paid into.")

26. AARP, "New AARP Post-Election Poll of Competitive Congressional Districts Shows Older Voters Prioritized Economic Concerns," news release, November 15, 2024, https://www.prnewswire.com/news-releases/new-aarp-post-election-poll-of-competitive-congressional-districts-shows-older-voters-prioritized-economic-concerns-302307272.html. ("Voters ages 50 and older were key in the 2024 election. Data shows that across the country, older voters made up 55% of the electorate.") See also AARP, "AARP Poll of 63 Most Competitive Congressional Districts Shows Older Voters Were the Deciders in 2022," news release, November 17, 2022. ("Overall, voters 50+ accounted for 61% of the electorate in these key districts.")

27. Brian Faler, "The Ghost of Simpson-Bowles," Politico, October 25, 2014, https://www.politico.com/story/2014/10/the-ghost-of-simpson-bowles-haunts-2014-112199.

28. National Institute on Retirement Security, "New Research Finds Social Security Has a Strong Economic Impact," 2024, https://www.nirsonline.org/articles/new-research-economic-impact-social-security/. ("Social Security benefits play a powerful role in supporting the U.S. economy, generating $2.6 trillion in total economic output and supporting more than 12 million American jobs in 2023 alone.")

29. National Bureau of Economic Research, "How Powerful Are Fiscal Multipliers in Recessions?," NBER Reporter 2015, no. 2, https://www.nber.org/reporter/2015number2/how-powerful-are-fiscal-multipliers-recessions.

30. Bipartisan Policy Center, "Failing to Fix Social Security Would Prove the Credit Rating Agencies Right," accessed November 2025, https://bipartisanpolicy.org/article/failing-to-fix-social-security-would-prove-the-credit-rating-agencies-right/. ("Social Securi-

ty plays a major role in driving this crowd-out, accounting for 48% of the increase in the primary budget deficit over the next 10 years—more than any other program.")

31. Vanguard, "Assessing U.S. Fiscal Space," December 2023, https://corporate.vanguard.com/content/dam/corp/public-p olicy/policy-research/assessing_us_fiscal_space_122023.pdf. ("At to-day's debt level of close to 100% of GDP, a 2% primary budget deficit would be sufficient to keep debt on a sustainable path... if the government were to wait until debt is closer to 180% of GDP... a 1% surplus would be required.")

Chapter 2

The Interest Rate Trap

In 2027, the federal government will spend more on interest payments than on everything it actually does. Not more than defense, though that threshold has already been crossed.1 More than all non-defense discretionary spending combined: infrastructure, scientific research, education grants, federal courts, national parks, the State Department, the Justice Department, homeland security, veterans' healthcare, environmental protection, food safety, transportation, and the basic operations of the federal government.[1] Interest payments will exceed the cost of all of it.

This is not a distant projection. It is eighteen months away.

The money flowing to creditors in 2027 will build no roads, fund no research, educate no children, protect no environment, secure no borders. It will compensate bondholders for past borrowing. And it will keep growing, year after year, consuming an ever-larger share of federal revenue while the government's capacity to invest in the future or respond to crises steadily erodes.

This is the Type B Crisis: the slow strangulation of government capacity that operates on a different timeline than Social Security's 2033 deadline but arrives sooner and persists longer. While Chapter 1 documented the statutory collision awaiting in 2033, this chapter examines what is already destroying the federal government's ability to invest, respond to crises, or maintain basic functions. The crowding out has begun.

Federal spending divides into three categories. Mandatory spending, primarily Social Security and Medicare, currently consumes approximately 41 percent of the federal budget.[2] These programs operate under permanent appropriations, paying benefits to anyone who qualifies regardless of annual budget constraints. Defense spending accounts for roughly 15 percent.[2] That leaves the remainder for everything else: other mandatory programs, discretionary spending divided between defense support functions and non-defense priorities, plus net interest payments that are growing faster than any other category.

Interest costs currently represent 13 percent of federal spending and rising rapidly.[2] Unlike Social Security or Medicare, which provide retirement security and healthcare, interest payments deliver nothing. They do not build roads, fund research, educate children, protect the environment, or enhance national security. They compensate creditors for past borrowing. And they are about to become the second-largest item in the federal budget.

Net interest costs reached $970 billion in fiscal year 2025, representing 18.4 percent of federal revenue, already exceeding the previous historical peak set in 1991.[3] Over the coming decade, cumulative interest payments will total $13.8 trillion.[3] By 2035, interest costs will consume 4.1 percent of GDP and 22.2 percent of all federal revenue.[1] For context, the previous post-war peak for interest costs as a share of GDP was 3.2 percent, reached in 1991.[3] Today's interest burden will exceed that crisis peak by 28 percent despite interest rates being far lower, because the debt itself is vastly larger.

The current federal debt held by the public stands at approximately 100 percent of GDP, or roughly $29.6 trillion in nominal terms.[4] This metric excludes intragovernmental debt, the Treasury securities held by Social Security and other trust funds, focusing only on what the government owes to external creditors: domestic and foreign individuals, businesses, pension funds, and central banks. It is this external debt that generates interest costs and requires market financing.

The trajectory from here is relentless. The Congressional Budget Office projects federal debt will reach 118 percent of GDP by 2035 and 156 percent by 2055.[5] Cumulative deficits over the 2025-2034 period alone will total approximately $20 trillion.[6] This projection assumes no recessions, no wars, no pandemics, no financial crises, events that historically arrive with regularity and require fiscal responses that add trillions to debt overnight. The baseline is optimistic, and reality consistently proves worse.

In 2029, federal debt will surpass 107 percent of GDP, exceeding the previous all-time high of 106 percent reached in 1946 at the conclusion of World War II.[5] That milestone matters symbolically, but the comparison reveals how structurally different the current crisis is from past episodes of high debt.

The post-war debt was a temporary spike caused by extraordinary wartime spending. Defense outlays had consumed 37 percent of GDP at the war's peak.[7] Once hostilities ceased, defense spending collapsed to 5 percent of GDP by 1950.[7] This dramatic reduction, combined with strong economic growth driven by a young, expanding population and productivity gains from wartime technological development, allowed the government to run primary surpluses. Debt fell from 106 percent of GDP in 1946 to 23 percent by 1974, a decline achieved through economic expansion making the debt relatively smaller without requiring explicit paydown.[7]

Today's debt cannot be resolved through the post-war playbook because none of the conditions that made that resolution possible exist now. Current defense spending stands at approximately 3 percent of GDP, already near historical peacetime lows given contemporary geopolitical threats.[8] There is no 32-percentage-point cushion to cut as there was in 1946. The population is aging rather than young, with the Baby Boom generation entering retirement and fertility rates well below replacement level. Economic growth is projected to average 3.7 percent nominal GDP growth over 2025-2055, compared to the 4.8 percent average achieved from 1995-2024.[9] Most critically, the current debt is driven by structural primary deficits projected to persist indefinitely, averaging 2.1 percent of GDP by 2035.[1] The government is not running temporary wartime deficits that will naturally reverse with peace. It is running permanent deficits driven by demographics and entitlement commitments that grow automatically as the population ages.

The mechanics of debt accumulation under current conditions create a self-reinforcing cycle. High debt generates high interest payments. High interest payments increase the deficit. Larger deficits require more borrowing. More borrowing raises the debt stock. Higher debt produces even larger interest payments. The loop accelerates unless interrupted by policy changes that either dramatically reduce spending or substantially increase revenue.

Whether this cycle becomes a death spiral depends on the relationship between two variables: the average interest rate paid on federal debt (r) and the nominal rate of economic growth (g). When economic growth exceeds the interest rate (g > r), the debt-to-GDP ratio can decline naturally even with modest primary deficits, because the economy grows faster than the debt burden. When interest rates exceed growth (r > g), the debt ratio rises automatically unless the government runs primary surpluses large enough to offset the differential.

From 1995 through 2024, the United States enjoyed favorable conditions with average nominal GDP growth of 4.8 percent and average interest rates of 3.7 percent.[9] This 1.1 percentage point advantage meant economic expansion gradually reduced the relative debt burden, providing fiscal breathing room. The Congressional Budget Office projects this relationship reverses over 2025-2055, with average interest rates of 3.8 percent and average growth of 3.7 percent.[9] By 2045, interest rates officially exceed growth rates on a sustained basis.[4]

Once r exceeds g, the mathematics of debt sustainability change fundamentally. The United States can no longer grow out of its debt through economic expansion alone. Stabilizing the debt-to-GDP ratio requires running primary surpluses sufficient to counteract the automatic growth driven by interest accumulation. The current primary deficit of 2.1 percent of GDP moves in the opposite direction.[1] The gap between where fiscal policy stands and where it needs to be is enormous and growing.

The cost of delay is exponential, not linear. If comprehensive fiscal reform begins in 2025, the required average primary surplus to stabilize debt over 2025-2099 is 4.3 percent of GDP.[10] If reform is delayed by one decade until 2035, the required average primary surplus over 2035-2099 rises to 5.1 percent of GDP.[10] The 0.8 percentage point difference represents the permanent annual penalty exacted by ten years of inaction. In 2025 dollars, this equals approximately $200 billion per year forever, the cost borne by all future generations because current policymakers deferred necessary adjustments.

At current debt levels of approximately 100 percent of GDP, stabilizing the debt-to-GDP ratio requires cumulative deficit reduction of $9.0 trillion over 2025-2035.[11] This demand proves politically impossible, as Chapter 1 documented through the Simpson-Bowles precedent. If action is delayed until debt reaches 180 percent of GDP, projected for the post-2050 period under current law, stabilization requires achieving a primary surplus of approximately 1 percent of GDP.[12] The swing from the current 2.1 percent primary deficit to a 1 percent surplus represents a 3.1 percentage point adjustment. Implementing this swing would require either eliminating Medicare and Medicaid entirely while simultaneously raising income taxes by 30 percent, or some equivalent combination of draconian spending cuts and massive tax increases. Measures of that magnitude are incompatible with the electoral incentives of a democratic system.

The debt trajectory is also acutely vulnerable to interest rate fluctuations. With nearly $30 trillion in debt outstanding, small changes in borrowing costs translate to massive fiscal impacts. The Congressional Budget Office estimates that if interest rates were just 0.1 percentage point higher across the yield curve each year than currently projected, cumulative deficits over 2026-2035 would increase by $351 billion.[13] A mere ten-basis-point shift in rates, the kind of movement that occurs routinely in bond markets, costs the equivalent of three years of NASA's entire budget.

This sensitivity creates exposure to events beyond policymakers' control. Federal Reserve decisions about monetary policy directly affect short-term rates and indirectly influence long-term rates. Global inflation dynamics, which no single nation controls, determine the real return creditors demand. Geopolitical shocks that increase risk premiums on U.S. debt would immediately raise borrowing costs. A loss of confidence in dollar reserve status, explored in Chapter 3, would trigger a repricing of Treasury securities that could add trillions to interest costs within months. The fiscal trajectory operates within a narrow corridor bounded by favorable assumptions about future interest rates, and deviations from that corridor produce catastrophic outcomes.

The crowding out of discretionary spending is not metaphorical. It is arithmetic, documented in budget tables and inevitable under current law. In 2027, interest costs will exceed total non-defense discretionary spending for the first time.[1] From that year forward, the federal government will face a stark choice: cut discretionary programs to offset rising interest costs, or allow total spending to grow and accelerate the debt spiral. Under current projections, policymakers choose the latter, allowing both interest and mandatory spending to grow while discretionary spending shrinks as a share of the economy.

What gets crowded out is the capacity for investment in the future and response to crises in the present. Infrastructure spending, already inadequate relative to maintenance needs, faces further reductions. The American Society of Civil Engineers estimates $2.6 trillion in unfunded infrastructure needs for roads, bridges, water systems, and public transit over the next decade.[14] Federal funding moves in the opposite direction. Scientific research funding through the National Institutes of Health, National Science Foundation, and Department of Energy faces flat or declining real budgets at precisely the moment technological competition with China intensifies. Education grants that support low-income college students and funding for K-12 schools in disadvantaged districts become targets for deficit reduction.

The federal court system, operating with chronic understaffing and deferred maintenance on aging facilities, receives no relief. National parks, which generated $50.3 billion in economic activity in 2022 through tourism, deteriorate as deferred maintenance backlogs grow.[15] The State Department, responsible for diplomatic engagement and foreign aid that supports American interests globally, sees budgets cut while adversaries expand influence. Environmental protection, food safety inspection, transportation infrastructure, veterans' healthcare, homeland security: every function funded through discretionary appropriations competes for a shrinking pool of available resources while interest payments consume an ever-larger share of federal revenue.

More consequentially, the elimination of fiscal space destroys the government's capacity to respond to crises. The 2008 financial crisis required the Troubled Asset Relief Program, quantitative easing, and fiscal stimulus totaling trillions of dollars to prevent economic collapse. Federal debt stood at 35 percent of GDP in 2007, providing enormous room for emergency borrowing.[16] The COVID-19 pandemic prompted $5 trillion in emergency spending for healthcare response, unemployment support, business assistance, and vaccine development. Debt increased from 79 percent of GDP in 2019 to 100 percent by 2020, an expansion possible only because fiscal space existed.[16]

By 2027, with debt at 106 percent of GDP and interest costs consuming 22 percent of revenue, that space no longer exists. The next recession, and recessions arrive regularly with ten occurring since 1950, will find a federal government unable to mount a robust fiscal response. Automatic stabilizers like unemployment insurance will still function, but discretionary stimulus spending, infrastructure investment to create jobs, or emergency assistance to failing industries becomes politically and economically impossible when the starting point is already maximum sustainable debt and interest costs that crowd out everything else.

The same constraint applies to military contingencies. A major conflict requiring sustained defense expenditures would force impossible choices between military necessity and fiscal sustainability. Historically, wars have been financed through temporary debt accumulation followed by peacetime reduction. That playbook assumes starting from a position of fiscal health. Beginning from 100 percent debt-to-GDP with structural primary deficits leaves no margin for additional borrowing without triggering a confidence crisis.

Natural disasters, which are increasing in frequency and severity due to climate change, generate federal assistance costs averaging $100 billion annually in recent years.[17] Hurricane Katrina in 2005 cost approximately $160 billion in federal aid. Hurricane Sandy in 2012 required $65 billion. The 2017 hurricane season (Harvey, Irma, and Maria) exceeded $120 billion in federal disaster relief. By 2027, these costs must be absorbed within a discretionary budget already underwater from interest crowding out, forcing either inadequate disaster response or additional borrowing that worsens the spiral.

Interest payments buy nothing. They do not educate children, cure diseases, build transportation networks, protect the environment, ensure food safety, maintain courts, or secure borders. They compensate creditors for past consumption and past borrowing. Unlike Social Security, which provides retirement income and supports consumer spending that generates economic activity, or Medicare, which provides healthcare and indirectly supports the medical sector, interest payments represent pure transfer to bondholders that exits the domestic economy when foreign creditors are involved. Approximately 32 percent of U.S. debt is held by foreign entities, meaning roughly $310 billion in annual interest flows abroad, providing no domestic economic benefit.[18]

By 2035, when interest costs reach 22.2 percent of federal revenue, the government will have transformed into a debt-servicing machine that also happens to mail Social Security checks and fund Medicare. Everything else, the discretionary functions that define what government does beyond transfer payments, will have become residual, funded only after mandatory obligations and interest costs are satisfied. This is not governance. It is debt maintenance.

The permanence of this situation distinguishes it from Social Security's 2033 deadline. That crisis features a statutory trigger requiring Congressional action. The trust fund depletes, automatic cuts occur, political pressure forces a response. The timeline is fixed, creating a forcing mechanism that compels eventual policy change even if inadequate or implemented under duress.

Interest crowding out operates on no such timeline. It simply accelerates, year after year, constrained only by the point at which creditors lose confidence and refuse to finance deficits at prevailing rates. Until that confidence evaporates, a potential crisis examined in Chapter 3, the crowding out continues indefinitely, gradually destroying government capacity without triggering political forcing mechanisms that would compel comprehensive reform.

The 2027 crossover, when interest costs exceed all non-defense discretionary spending, will not generate headlines or prompt emergency legislation. It is a threshold crossed quietly in budget tables while policymakers debate other priorities. The erosion becomes normal, accepted, and unremarkable. Infrastructure decays. Research slows. Parks deteriorate. Courts operate short-staffed. Federal employees remain underpaid relative to private sector equivalents, driving talent away from public service. The machinery of government continues functioning but operates at reduced capacity, deferring maintenance, postponing investment, and accumulating hidden costs that will manifest in infrastructure failures, scientific stagnation, and reduced state capacity for decades to come.

This differs from the Social Security crisis not just in timing but in nature. Social Security creates clear winners and losers. Current retirees face 24 percent benefit cuts or workers face massive tax increases. The pain is immediate, concentrated, and politically mobilizing. Interest crowding out disperses pain across years and populations, making it politically inert. No single interest group organizes to demand infrastructure investment or scientific research funding with the intensity that retirees demand Social Security protection. The gradual erosion of discretionary capacity generates no mass protests, no single-issue voting blocs, no political crisis that forces resolution.

Politicians optimize for re-election, not for maintaining long-term governmental capacity. Allowing infrastructure to decay or research funding to stagnate imposes costs years or decades in the future, after current officeholders have moved on. Opposing tax increases or entitlement cuts generates immediate political rewards. The incentive structure ensures the crowding out continues unabated until external events, a recession the government cannot respond to, a disaster it cannot adequately fund, or a military contingency it cannot finance, demonstrate the consequences of lost fiscal capacity.

By then, the damage is structural. Rebuilding governmental capacity after decades of erosion requires not just money but institutional knowledge, personnel pipelines, and physical infrastructure that cannot be reconstituted quickly. The bridges that collapsed due to deferred maintenance cannot be un-collapsed. The diseases that progressed while research funding stagnated remain uncured. The scientific talent that pursued private sector careers because federal research funding dried up does not return to public service. The cost of allowing interest payments to crowd out discretionary spending extends far beyond the decade in which it occurs.

The mathematics are unforgiving. The primary deficit remains at 2.1 percent of GDP in 2035 while interest costs reach 4.1 percent, producing a combined deficit of 6.1 percent of GDP.[1] This level, sustained over time, guarantees accelerating debt accumulation. The relationship between interest rates and growth turns unfavorable by 2045, eliminating the possibility of growing out of debt.[4] The required policy adjustment to stabilize debt grows larger with each year of inaction, while the political capacity to implement that adjustment shows no signs of expanding.

Social Security cuts hit in 2033, a statutory deadline that will force response even if inadequate. Interest costs eclipse government capacity starting in 2027 and accelerate thereafter, a permanent degradation with no forcing mechanism to compel correction. These are not predictions. They are projections based on current law, documented in Congressional Budget Office reports, representing what happens if existing policies continue unchanged.

But there is a third vulnerability, qualitatively different from the first two. Social Security operates on a statutory timeline. Interest crowding out operates on a mathematical trajectory. The third risk operates on confidence: psychological, contingent, impossible to forecast precisely but capable of converting gradual deterioration into acute catastrophe almost overnight. It depends on political stability, institutional credibility, and continued faith in American governance. And recent events suggest none of these can be guaranteed.

CHAPTER 2 NOTES

1. Congressional Budget Office, "The Budget and Economic Outlook: 2025 to 2035," January 2025, https://www.cbo.gov/publication/61172. ("Interest costs exceed outlays for defense from 2025 to 2035 and exceed outlays for nondefense discretionary programs from 2027 to 2035." The report projects net interest at 4.1 percent of GDP by 2035 and primary deficits at 2.1 percent of GDP, yielding total deficits of 6.1 percent of GDP.)

2. U.S. Department of the Treasury, "How much has the U.S. government spent this year?," Fiscal Data, October 2025, https://fiscaldata.treasury.gov/americas-finance-guide/federal-spending/. (FY2025: Medicare 22 percent, Social Security 19 percent, National Defense 15 percent, Net Interest 13 percent, Health 13 percent.)

3. Peter G. Peterson Foundation, "Any Way You Look at It, Interest Costs on the National Debt Will Soon Be at an All-Time High," August 2025, https://www.pgpf.org/article/any-way-you-look-at-it-interest-costs-on-the-national-debt-will-soon-be-at-an-all-time-high/. ("In 2025, the United States paid $970 billion in interest costs... federal interest payments would rise to 18.4 percent by the end of 2025, exceeding the previous high set in 1991. They would reach 22.2 percent by 2035... interest costs would reach 3.2 percent of GDP in 2026, eclipsing the previous high set in 1991. Interest costs would climb to 4.1 percent of GDP by 2035." Cumulative interest costs total $13.8 trillion over the next decade.)

4. Committee for a Responsible Federal Budget, "Analysis of CBO's March 2025 Long-Term Budget Outlook," March 2025, https://www.crfb.org/papers/analysis-cbos-march-2025-long

-term-budget-outlook. ("Federal debt held by the public is approximately 100 percent of GDP in FY 2025" and "under the long-term outlook, the average interest rate will officially exceed economic growth (R>G) by 2045." Current nominal debt is approximately $29.6 trillion.)

5. Congressional Budget Office, "The Long-Term Budget Outlook: 2025 to 2055," March 2025, https://www.cbo.gov/publication/612 70. ("Federal debt held by the public rises from 100 percent of GDP this year to 118 percent in 2035, surpassing its previous high of 106 percent of GDP in 1946... Debt reaches 156 percent of GDP by 2055." The 1946 record of 106 percent GDP is surpassed by 2029 when debt reaches 107 percent GDP.)

6. Congressional Budget Office, "The Budget and Economic Outlook: 2024 to 2034," February 2024, https://www.cbo.gov/publication/5 9710. ("In CBO's projections, federal budget deficits total $20 trillion over the 2025–2034 period.")

7. Peter G. Peterson Foundation, "Why Is the U.S. Fiscal Outlook More Daunting Now than After World War II?," January 2025, https://www.pgpf.org/article/why-is-the-us-fiscal-outloo k-more-daunting-now-than-after-world-war-ii/. ("Between 1942 and 1945, an average of 84 percent of the federal budget was allocated to national defense... After the war, defense spending was drastically reduced from $1.1 trillion in 1945 to $177 billion in 1950... led to a reduction in debt-to-GDP most years through 1974." Defense peaked at 37 percent GDP in 1945 per OMB Historical Table 8.4; fell to 5 percent GDP by 1950; debt fell from 106 percent to 23 percent GDP by 1974 per OMB Historical Table 7.1.)

8. Peter G. Peterson Foundation, "Budget Basics: National Defense," accessed November 2025, https://www.pgpf.org/article/budget-exp lainer-national-defense/. (Chart shows U.S. defense spending at 3.3

percent of GDP in 2023.)

9. Peter G. Peterson Foundation, "What Is R Versus G and Why Does It Matter for the National Debt?," April 2025, https://www.pgpf.org/article/what-is-r-versus-g-and-why-does-it-matter-for-the-national-debt/. (Table: Historical Average 1995-2024: R=3.7 percent, G=4.8 percent; Projected Average 2025-2055: R=3.8 percent, G=3.7 percent. Source: Congressional Budget Office.)

10. U.S. Department of the Treasury, "Financial Report of the United States Government," FY2024, Table 6: Costs of Delaying Fiscal Reform, https://fiscal.treasury.gov/reports-statements/financial-report/mda-unsustainable-fiscal-path.html. ("Immediate reform would require increasing primary surpluses by 4.3 percent of GDP on average between 2025 and 2099... if policy reform is delayed by 10 years, closing the fiscal gap requires increasing the primary surpluses by 5.1 percent of GDP on average between 2035 and 2099.")

11. Committee for a Responsible Federal Budget, "Meeting Fiscal Goals Under CBO's January 2025 Baseline," January 29, 2025, https://www.crfb.org/blogs/meeting-fiscal-goals-under-cbos-january-2025-baseline. ("Stabilizing debt over the next decade at its current share of the economy would require $9.0 trillion of deficit reduction relative to the Congressional Budget Office's (CBO) January 2025 baseline.")

12. Vanguard, "Assessing U.S. Fiscal Space," December 2023, https://corporate.vanguard.com/content/dam/corp/public-policy/policy-research/assessing_us_fiscal_space_122023.pdf. ("At today's debt level of close to 100% of GDP, a 2% primary budget deficit would be sufficient to keep debt on a sustainable path. However, if the government were to wait until debt is closer to 180% of GDP, a level the CBO expects the government to reach shortly after 2050, a

1% surplus would be required.")

13. Congressional Budget Office, "How Changes in Economic Conditions Might Affect the Federal Budget: 2025 to 2035," April 2025, https://www.cbo.gov/publication/61249. ("If all interest rates on Treasury securities were just 0.1 percentage point higher each year than projected in the baseline, the cumulative deficit over the 2026-2035 period would be $351 billion larger than projected.")

14. American Society of Civil Engineers, "2021 Report Card for America's Infrastructure," accessed November 2025, https://infrastructurereportcard.org/. (The report estimates a $2.6 trillion infrastructure investment gap over the decade.)

15. National Park Service, "2022 National Park Visitor Spending Effects," Economic Benefits Report, accessed November 2025, https://www.nps.gov/subjects/socialscience/vse.htm. (National parks generated $50.3 billion in economic output in 2022.)

16. Federal Reserve Bank of St. Louis, "Federal Debt Held by the Public as Percent of Gross Domestic Product," FRED Economic Data, updated November 2025, https://fred.stlouisfed.org/series/FYGFGDQ188S. (Graph shows debt at approximately 35 percent GDP in 2007, 79 percent in 2019, and 100 percent by 2020.)

17. National Oceanic and Atmospheric Administration, "Billion-Dollar Weather and Climate Disasters," accessed November 2025, https://www.ncei.noaa.gov/access/billions/. ("The U.S. sustained 403 weather and climate disasters from 1980–2024 where overall damages/costs reached or exceeded $1 billion... The total cost of these 403 events exceeds $2.915 trillion." Annual average 2020-2024: $149.3 billion; 2010-2019: $99.5 billion.)

18. Peter G. Peterson Foundation, "The Federal Government Has Bor-

rowed Trillions. Who Owns All that Debt?," accessed November 2025, https://www.pgpf.org/article/the-federal-government-has -borrowed-trillions-but-who-owns-all-that-debt/. ("As of June 2025, such holdings made up $9.1 trillion, or 32 percent, of DHBP [Debt Held by the Public].")

Chapter 3

The Perfect Storm

In 2010, Greece discovered what happens when multiple crises converge. The country entered that year with debt at 110 percent of GDP, a level economists considered dangerous but not catastrophic. Then the feedback loops began. Markets lost confidence in Greece's ability to service its debt. Interest rates spiked. Higher borrowing costs forced austerity measures. Austerity caused recession. Recession reduced tax revenue. Lower revenue increased deficits. Higher deficits increased debt. More debt caused markets to lose more confidence. Interest rates spiked further. Within two years, Greece required three separate bailouts totaling 289 billion euros. Unemployment reached 27 percent. The economy contracted by 25 percent. A debt level that was supposed to be manageable under normal conditions became catastrophic because the crises fed on each other.[1]

The United States in 2025 carries debt at 100 percent of GDP, approaching the level where Greece's crisis began.[2] But the United States is not Greece. It issues the world's reserve currency. It borrows in its own currency. It has the Federal Reserve as lender of last resort. These advantages have so far prevented the kind of acute crisis that forced Greece into depression. They will not prevent crisis forever. And the United States faces something Greece did not: three distinct crises converging in a narrow window, each capable of triggering the others, each removing the capacity needed to respond to the others.

You now understand two of these crises from the preceding chapters. The 2033 Social Security deadline forces an automatic 24 percent benefit cut affecting more than 74 million Americans. The interest cost explosion, already underway, will exceed all non-defense discretionary spending by 2027 and consume 22.2 percent of federal revenue by 2035.[3] Each crisis alone would challenge the political system. Together, they create something worse than simple addition. They create compounding failure.

There is a third crisis that most people do not understand: the confidence crisis. And when all three converge in the 2028 to 2035 window, each removes the capacity needed to respond to the others.

Economists recognize several mechanisms by which fiscal crises emerge.[4] Type A crises involve statutory insolvency, where a mandatory program fails on a specific date, triggering automatic cuts by law. Social Security in 2033 is a textbook Type A crisis. Type B crises involve structural crowding out, where interest costs eclipse essential government functions, slowly strangling the capacity to invest or respond to emergencies. The United States is entering this phase now. Type C crises involve confidence collapse, where markets lose faith in a government's ability or willingness to service debt, causing interest rates to spike in a self-fulfilling prophecy.

The United States has so far avoided Type C because of what economists call exorbitant privilege, the dollar's status as the world's primary reserve currency. Approximately 56 percent of global foreign exchange reserves are held in dollars.[5] U.S. Treasury securities serve as the benchmark for risk-free assets worldwide. This status allows the United States to borrow at lower rates than fiscal fundamentals alone would justify, functioning as a massive buffer against the kind of sovereign debt crisis that forced Greece, Portugal, and Ireland into harsh austerity during the 2010s.

But this protection is psychological, not permanent. It depends on maintaining institutional credibility and political stability.[6] The International Monetary Fund defines fiscal space as the room for undertaking discretionary fiscal policy relative to existing plans without endangering market access and debt sustainability.[7] For reserve currency issuers, fiscal space can be highly elastic during common shocks like the COVID-19 pandemic, when bonds are viewed as safe havens. But the UK Office for Budget Responsibility notes that continued safe-haven status cannot be guaranteed and the cost of losing it can be significant.[8] One major political shock, whether a debt ceiling default, visible interference with Federal Reserve independence, or sustained political dysfunction, could trigger rapid loss of confidence despite underlying economic strength.

What happens when Type B removes the fiscal space needed to handle Type A? What happens when Type A triggers a recession that worsens Type B? What happens if either crisis becomes visible enough to trigger Type C? The answer is not three separate problems hitting sequentially. The answer is a doom loop where each crisis amplifies the others.

By 2027, interest costs will exceed all non-defense discretionary spending.[3] This is the year that Type B fully manifests. Non-defense discretionary spending includes everything the federal government does beyond entitlements, defense, and interest: infrastructure, education, scientific research, national parks, courts, federal operations, grants to states and cities. In 2027, the government will spend more servicing debt than funding all of these combined.

This eliminates the fiscal space needed for any compromise solution on Social Security. Consider the arithmetic. The Congressional Budget Office projects that stabilizing debt at current levels requires $9.0 trillion in deficit reduction over 2025 to 2035.[9] These figures establish the gap between current policy and fiscal sustainability.

When policymakers discuss finding room in the budget for Social Security reform, they are referring to this fiscal space: the capacity to temporarily run larger deficits while phasing in adjustments, or the ability to reallocate spending from less essential programs to cushion benefit reductions. By 2027, that space no longer exists. Interest costs will consume resources that could otherwise smooth the transition. Non-defense discretionary spending, already squeezed,

offers no further room for cuts without eliminating basic government functions.

The 2033 Social Security deadline hits after Type B has already eliminated
fiscal flexibility. Congress will face three options, all constrained by the destruction of fiscal space that occurred in the preceding years. Option One: allow
the statutory 24 percent cuts to take effect, triggering immediate economic
contraction and elderly poverty. Option Two: authorize emergency borrowing
to cover the shortfall, adding roughly $336 billion annually to federal debt
at a moment when debt service costs are already consuming 22 percent of
revenue.[10] Option Three: implement emergency tax increases or benefit cuts
large enough to restore solvency immediately, without the gradual phase-ins
that fiscal space would allow.

If Congress chooses emergency borrowing, the politically easiest option in
2033, the consequences compound. New borrowing to cover a 24 percent
benefit shortfall amounts to roughly $336 billion annually starting in 2033.[10] At
a 4 percent interest rate, this generates $13 billion in additional interest costs in
the first year. By Year 5, cumulative additional borrowing exceeds $1.68 trillion,
generating $67 billion in annual interest costs. By 2045, the decision to borrow
rather than reform in 2033 adds more than $200 billion annually to interest
payments.

This is how Type B worsens Type A. The interest explosion removes the
capacity to handle the entitlement crisis smoothly, forcing either immediate
draconian cuts or emergency borrowing that accelerates the very crisis it attempts to delay.

The mechanism works in the other direction as well. When Type A hits in
2033, it does not merely cut benefits. It triggers broader economic crisis that
worsens Type B through reduced tax revenue and increased deficits.

Social Security benefits generate substantial economic activity. In 2023, $
1.38 trillion in benefits generated $2.6 trillion in total economic output and
supported $1.6 trillion in GDP.[11] A 24 percent benefit cut reduces benefits by
approximately $336 billion annually in 2025 dollars. This is not merely a trans-

fer from government to retirees that stops. It is consumption that disappears from the economy.

Economic research on fiscal multipliers, the ratio of GDP change to fiscal policy change, shows that multipliers are larger during recessions and particularly large for transfers to households with high marginal propensities to consume.[12] Elderly households depending on Social Security spend most of their benefits immediately on necessities. Using a conservative multiplier of 1.3, a $336 billion benefit cut produces a $437 billion GDP reduction in the first year.[13]

Federal revenue averages 17.5 percent of GDP.3 A $437 billion GDP decline translates to $76 billion in lost annual tax revenue. Over five years, the revenue loss exceeds $380 billion, adding directly to the deficit. Additionally, automatic stabilizers like unemployment insurance, Medicaid, and food assistance activate during recession, adding roughly $150 billion annually at the peak.[14] The total deficit increase from Type A triggering recession: $226 billion annually while the crisis persists.

This additional deficit increases debt by $1.13 trillion over five years. At a 4 percent interest rate, this debt generates $45 billion in additional annual interest costs after five years, and the costs compound indefinitely thereafter. The decision to cut benefits rather than reform earlier does not merely hurt current retirees. It permanently increases the structural deficit through reduced GDP, lower tax revenue, and higher debt service costs.

This is how Type A worsens Type B. The entitlement crisis, when it hits, causes recession. Recession causes revenue loss. Revenue loss increases deficits. Higher deficits increase debt. More debt increases interest costs permanently. The feedback loop turns a one-time fiscal adjustment into permanent structural deterioration.

Both mechanisms are amplified by a third factor that rarely appears in public discussion: fiscal multipliers decline as debt levels rise. When government debt is low, fiscal stimulus effectively boosts output. When debt is high, the same stimulus generates minimal response because forward-looking households anticipate future tax increases and reduce consumption in preparation.[15]

Empirical research on fiscal multipliers finds that they decline sharply with debt levels.16 When debt-to-GDP ratios are below 60 percent, multipliers are standard, approximately 0.8 to 1.0. When debt rises above 60 percent but remains below 100 percent, long-run multipliers fall to 0.4. When debt exceeds 100 percent, multipliers approach zero.[16]

The United States currently carries debt at 100 percent of GDP, at the threshold where fiscal policy effectiveness begins to deteriorate significantly.[2] By 2033, debt will exceed 112 percent of GDP even under current projections.[2] By the 2040s, debt approaches 140 to 150 percent under realistic scenarios including modest recessions or continued primary deficits.

This creates a vicious circle. High debt reduces multiplier effectiveness. When Type A crisis hits, requiring fiscal response to offset consumption decline, that response has minimal effect due to suppressed multipliers. Recession deepens because stimulus does not work. Deeper recession causes larger revenue loss. Larger revenue loss increases deficit more than stimulus helped. Higher deficit increases debt further. Higher debt reduces future multiplier even more.

Traditional crisis response would involve a $300 billion stimulus package to offset the $437 billion GDP decline from benefit cuts. With a multiplier of 1.5, typical in normal recessions, this generates $450 billion in GDP boost, preventing crisis.[12] With a multiplier of 0.4, characteristic of high-debt environments, the same $300 billion generates only $120 billion in GDP boost. The crisis deepens. With a multiplier approaching zero, as research suggests for debt above 100 percent of GDP, fiscal stimulus becomes nearly useless regardless of scale.

This is the doom loop. High debt constrains crisis response at precisely the moment crisis response is most needed. Each failed response worsens conditions. Worsening conditions increase debt. Higher debt makes the next response even less effective.

The third crisis, Type C or the confidence crisis, can trigger at any point during this deterioration, bringing everything forward and intensifying the collapse.

The Congressional Budget Office documents extreme sensitivity to interest rate changes at current debt levels.[17] A 0.1 percent increase in interest rates across the yield curve, ten basis points, adds $351 billion to the deficit over a decade. Of this, $319 billion is pure interest cost. An additional $52 billion comes from compounding effects as higher deficits require more borrowing, which generates more interest, creating a feedback loop.

Consider what happens if political dysfunction triggers a confidence crisis. Assume a 200 basis point increase in borrowing costs, a 2 percent spike driven by market concern over the government's capacity to manage converging crises. This is not implausible. During the 2011 debt ceiling crisis, even the threat of default caused market disruption and a credit rating downgrade.[18] An actual default, even brief, would trigger larger effects.

A 200 basis point increase equals twenty times the 0.1 percent scenario. Additional deficit: $7.0 trillion over a decade. Pure interest component: $6.4 trillion. Annual impact by Year 10: $640 billion in additional interest costs. This is not a projection of what might happen in some distant future. This is what happens immediately if market confidence breaks.

Type C acceleration transforms the timeline. Interest costs that were projected to reach 4.1 percent of GDP in 2035 hit that level in 2028 instead, seven years early.[19] Crowding out that was supposed to fully manifest by 2027 accelerates to 2025. The fiscal space that was already minimal disappears entirely.

When Type C hits, emergency borrowing to prevent 2033 benefit cuts becomes impossible because market access is impaired. Congress cannot choose Option Two, delay through borrowing, because borrowing costs have spiked and investors are demanding higher yields to compensate for perceived risk. This forces immediate benefit cuts under the worst possible conditions: elevated interest costs, impaired market access, economic stress from rate increases, and political dysfunction that triggered the crisis in the first place.

The self-fulfilling nature of confidence crises is well documented in sovereign debt research.[20] Markets lose confidence. Rates spike. Rate spikes force austerity or default. Austerity or default confirms initial market fears. Rates spike further. Classic sovereign debt crisis dynamics emerge not because fundamentals suddenly deteriorated but because psychology shifted and the shift became self-validating.

What could trigger Type C? The research identifies several high-probability scenarios.[21]

Debt ceiling brinksmanship has become routine. The 2011 crisis, which involved only the threat of default, caused lasting damage. Standard and Poor's downgraded U.S. sovereign debt for the first time in history.[18] Treasury yields initially fell as investors fled to safety, but the downgrade had permanent effects on borrowing costs and market perceptions. Since then, debt ceiling confrontations have occurred in 2013, 2023, and will recur whenever divided government produces incentives for hostage-taking.

A seven-day default, politically conceivable given partisan incentives, would trigger rating downgrades to AA- or lower. Treasury spreads would widen 100 to 150 basis points. Over a decade, this adds $2 to $3 trillion in costs. A thirty-day default would likely eliminate Treasury securities' status as the risk-free rate benchmark, widening spreads 200 to 300 basis points permanently and adding $5 to $7 trillion in costs.

Federal Reserve independence crises present another trigger. Political pressure to cut interest rates during inflation, threats to fire the Federal Reserve Chair, or legal challenges to monetary policy independence signal to markets that institutional credibility is compromised. When markets perceive that the Federal Reserve might subordinate inflation control to political pressure, inflation expectations unanchor. Higher inflation expectations mean higher nominal interest rates. Higher rates accelerate the debt spiral.

The historical precedent is instructive. When President Nixon pressured Federal Reserve Chairman Arthur Burns to maintain loose monetary policy in the early 1970s, the result was significant inflation attributable to political interference.[22] Turkey under President Erdogan provides a more recent example: sustained political pressure on the central bank to cut rates during inflation produced 80 percent inflation and currency collapse.[23]

What distinguishes the United States is that dollar reserve status has so far prevented these dynamics despite fiscal irresponsibility that would have triggered crises in smaller economies. Greece entered crisis at 110 percent debt-to-GDP.1 The United States carries 100 percent without immediate consequences because investors view Treasuries as uniquely safe. But this status is contingent, not guaranteed. It depends on maintaining the perception of institutional stability and political competence.

Historical precedent shows what happens when multiple crises hit simultaneously. During the early 1930s, the Great Depression involved not just banking failures but sovereign debt crises and currency collapse across Europe.[24] Research on the interwar period documents how concerns among investors about the credibility of fiscal policies and sovereign debt service contributed to the severity and persistence of the financial disruptions associated with the Great Depression. The collapse was not merely economic. It was a crisis of confidence in governments' capacity to manage interconnected failures.

More recently, the European sovereign debt crisis of 2009 to 2018 demonstrated the triple crisis pattern: banking crisis, sovereign debt crisis, and currency stress.[25] Research on conglomerate crises finds that banking, sovereign debt, exchange rate crashes, and inflation often intersect to become severe compound crises, meaning that banking and sovereign debt problems rarely occur without currency or confidence crises also emerging.[26]

The pattern is consistent: multiple crises do not hit sequentially, allowing measured response to each. They compound. Banking stress forces government bailouts. Bailouts increase sovereign debt. Debt increases cause market concern. Market concern increases borrowing costs. Higher borrowing costs stress banks holding government bonds. Bank stress requires more bailouts. The feedback loop amplifies initial shocks.

Carmen Reinhart's research on conglomerate crises emphasizes that crises often do not travel alone, and that in the search for solutions, policy makers must be cognizant that they may be facing multifaceted and interconnected problems.[26] A rescue of banks might undermine the sovereign's fiscal position. Fiscal consolidation might deepen recession. Each intervention carries risks of worsening other dimensions of crisis. A conglomerate crisis requires a broad toolkit and an integrated approach, yet the United States faces its convergence with minimal fiscal space, suppressed multipliers, and political gridlock preventing coordinated response.

The European experience provides a warning but not a perfect parallel. European nations faced crisis at lower debt levels than the United States currently carries. They lacked the reserve currency advantage that has so far protected U.S. borrowing costs. They operated under Eurozone constraints that prevented independent monetary policy. Yet they also benefited from external support: the European Central Bank, the International Monetary Fund, stronger neighbors providing bailouts. When the United States faces crisis, there is no external rescuer. The International Monetary Fund cannot bail out the economy that funds the International Monetary Fund. The Federal Reserve can provide liquidity but cannot solve solvency. No foreign government has the capacity or incentive to rescue U.S. fiscal policy.

The convergence window is 2028 to 2035. This is when all three crises hit maximum intensity.

By 2028, fiscal space will be effectively exhausted. Debt will approach 107 to 110 percent of GDP, surpassing the World War II record.[2] Interest costs will exceed 3.5 percent of GDP, with non-defense discretionary spending fully crowded out. Markets looking five years forward will begin pricing 2033 risk into bond yields. Any recession during this period cannot be countered with fiscal stimulus because multipliers are suppressed and borrowing capacity is constrained.

In 2033, Type A forces decision. Social Security trust fund depletion triggers automatic cuts unless Congress acts. The three options, allow cuts, emergency borrowing, or immediate reform, all carry severe consequences. Cuts trigger recession. Emergency borrowing accelerates Type B. Immediate reform faces the same political gridlock that prevented earlier action, now under crisis conditions with less time and worse options.

During this entire period, Type C risk remains elevated. Political stress around the 2033 deadline, debt ceiling confrontations, visible institutional dysfunction: any of these could trigger confidence loss. If Type C hits during 2028 to 2035, it brings forward crises that were already approaching, forcing response under the worst possible conditions.

The Congressional Budget Office projects that by 2045, the interest rate on federal debt will exceed the economic growth rate, the point where debt dynamics become mathematically unstable.[27] When interest rates exceed growth rates with sustained primary deficits, debt-to-GDP ratios increase automatically even with zero new spending. Stabilization requires achieving primary surplus, where revenue exceeds non-interest spending, by a margin sufficient to offset the difference between interest rates and growth.

At 180 percent debt-to-GDP, which current trajectories suggest for the 2050s, stabilization with a 4 percent interest rate and 2 percent growth requires a primary surplus of 3.6 percent of GDP.[28] This is equivalent to eliminating Medicare and Medicaid entirely while simultaneously raising income taxes by 30 percent. No political system implements changes of that magnitude voluntarily. The window for manageable adjustment closes long before mathematical impossibility is reached.

What distinguishes the 2028 to 2035 window from earlier periods is convergence. Before 2028, crises remain separate enough that partial responses might work. Type B is worsening but has not yet eliminated all fiscal space. Type A remains several years distant. Type C risk exists but has not been triggered. After 2035, if emergency borrowing has delayed reckoning, the problem is larger and options are worse, but crisis might still be pushed further into the future.

During 2028 to 2035, all three hit simultaneously. Type B has already eliminated fiscal space needed for Type A response. Type A's arrival under constrained conditions risks triggering Type C. Any Type C trigger accelerates both Type A and Type B, bringing forward crises that were supposed to arrive later. Each removes capacity to handle the others. The convergence is not three separate problems happening to arrive at the same time. It is three problems that make each other worse, creating conditions where normal crisis response becomes impossible.

You now understand the framework.

Type A: the statutory entitlement cliff in 2033.

Type B: the interest explosion already underway.

Type C: the confidence vulnerability that could trigger early collapse.

Each crisis alone would challenge the political system. Together, they create a perfect storm where each amplifies the others and removes capacity to respond.

But you still do not understand why no one in authority is discussing this publicly. The Congressional Budget Office projects it. The Social Security Administration documents it. The International Monetary Fund analyzes it. The data is public. The mechanisms are clear. The collision is coming.

So where is the alarm? Where are the politicians demanding action? Where are the economists warning of catastrophe? Where is the media coverage that makes this the defining issue of our time?

The answer reveals something more disturbing than the fiscal math itself: the system that would need to sound the alarm is structurally incapable of doing so. Not because of conspiracy, but because of rational incentives that make silence the optimal strategy for every individual actor even as collective silence guarantees collision.

CHAPTER 3 NOTES

1. European Commission, "The Second Economic Adjustment Programme for Greece," Occasional Paper 94, March 2012, https://ec.europa.eu/economy_finance/publications/occasional_paper/2014/op192_en.htm. Greece entered crisis at approximately 110 percent debt-to-GDP. The country required three bailout programs totaling 289 billion euros between 2010 and 2018. Unemployment peaked at 27.5 percent in 2013. GDP contracted by approximately 25 percent from peak to trough.

2. Congressional Budget Office, "The Long-Term Budget Outlook: 2025 to 2055," March 2025, https://www.cbo.gov/publication/61270. ("Federal debt held by the public rises from 100 percent of GDP this year to 118 percent in 2035, surpassing its previous high of 106 percent of GDP in 1946... Debt reaches 156 percent of GDP by 2055." The 1946 record of 106 percent GDP is surpassed by 2029 when debt reaches 107 percent GDP.)

3. Congressional Budget Office, "The Budget and Economic Outlook: 2025 to 2035," January 2025, https://www.cbo.gov/publication/61172. ("Interest costs exceed outlays for defense from 2025 to 2035 and exceed outlays for nondefense discretionary programs from 2027 to 2035." Net interest projected at 4.1 percent of GDP by 2035, 22.2 percent of federal revenue. Federal revenue averages 17.5 percent of GDP.)

4. This framework synthesizes several mechanisms recognized in the fiscal crisis literature: statutory funding exhaustion from the Social Security Trustees Report (Type A); structural crowding out and interest-growth dynamics from Olivier Blanchard, "Public Debt and Low Interest Rates," American Economic Review 109, no. 4 (2019):

1197-1229, and the CBO Long-Term Budget Outlook (Type B); and confidence-based multiple equilibria crises from Paul De Grauwe, "The Governance of a Fragile Eurozone," CEPS Working Document No. 346, May 2011 (Type C).

5. International Monetary Fund, "Currency Composition of Official Foreign Exchange Reserves (COFER)," Q2 2025 data release, October 2025, https://data.imf.org/en/news/october%201%202025%20cofe r. ("The share of US dollar holdings in the allocated reserves decreased to 56.32 percent.")

6. Council on Foreign Relations, "The Dollar: The World's Reserve Currency," updated 2024, https://www.cfr.org/backgrounder/doll ar-worlds-reserve-currency. (Dollar reserve status depends on "stable value, the size of the U.S. economy, and the United States' geopolitical heft.")

7. International Monetary Fund, "Assessing Fiscal Space: An Update and Stocktaking," IMF Policy Paper, June 2018, https://www.imf.org/en/publications/policy-papers/issues/2 018/06/15/pp041118assessing-fiscal-space. ("Fiscal space was narrowly defined as the room for undertaking discretionary fiscal policy relative to existing plans without endangering market access and debt sustainability.")

8. UK Office for Budget Responsibility, "Assessing Fiscal Space," in Fiscal Risks Report, July 2021, Box 3.4, https://obr.uk/box/assessing-fisca l-space/. ("But continued safe-haven status cannot be guaranteed and the cost of losing it can be significant. In the face of an idiosyncratic shock, governments, particularly those reliant on foreign investors, can see funds drain away into safer assets in unaffected countries, resulting in higher borrowing costs and a reduction in fiscal space at precisely the moment the government most needs it.")

9. Committee for a Responsible Federal Budget, "Meeting Fiscal Goals Under CBO's January 2025 Baseline," January 29, 2025, https://www.crfb.org/blogs/meeting-fiscal-goals-under-cbos-january-2025-baseline. ("Stabilizing debt over the next decade at its current share of the economy would require $9.0 trillion of deficit reduction relative to the Congressional Budget Office's (CBO) January 2025 baseline.")

10. Author calculation based on 24 percent of current Social Security benefit expenditure (approximately $1.4 trillion annually). 24 percent times $1.4 trillion equals $336 billion.

11. National Institute on Retirement Security, "New Research Finds Social Security Has a Strong Economic Impact," 2024, https://www.nirsonline.org/articles/new-research-economic-impact-social-security/. ("Social Security benefits play a powerful role in supporting the U.S. economy, generating $2.6 trillion in total economic output and supporting more than 12 million American jobs in 2023 alone... $1.38 trillion in benefits paid to more than 67 million beneficiaries supported $804.6 billion in labor income, $1.6 trillion in value added (GDP).")

12. National Bureau of Economic Research, "How Powerful Are Fiscal Multipliers in Recessions?" NBER Reporter 2015, no. 2, https://www.nber.org/reporter/2015number2/how-powerful-are-fiscal-multipliers-recessions. (Fiscal multipliers larger during recessions and slack. Multiplier of 1.5 typical in recessions.)

13. Author calculation: $336 billion benefit cut times 1.3 conservative multiplier equals $437 billion GDP impact.

14. Congressional Budget Office, "The Effects of Automatic Stabilizers on the Federal Budget," March 2013, https://www.cbo.gov/publication/43977. (Establishes that tax revenues fall automatically when

GDP falls and safety-net spending rises automatically in recessions. The $150 billion estimate is author's calculation consistent with Great Recession-era stabilizer behavior.)

15. Raju Huidrom et al., "Why Do Fiscal Multipliers Depend on Fiscal Positions?" Journal of Monetary Economics 114 (2020), https://www.sciencedirect.com/science/article/abs/pii/S03 04393219300509. ("When a government with a weak fiscal position implements fiscal stimulus, households expect tax increases sooner than in an economy with a strong fiscal position... The perceived negative wealth effect leads households to cut consumption and save more, thereby weakening the impact of the stimulus on output.")

16. Anja Baum, Marcos Poplawski-Ribeiro, and Anke Weber, "Fiscal Multipliers and the State of the Economy," IMF Working Paper No. 12/286, December 2012, https://ssrn.com/abstract=2202637. ("Fiscal multipliers differ across countries, calling for a tailored use of fiscal policy. Moreover, the position in the business cycle affects the impact of fiscal policy on output: on average, government spending, and revenue multipliers tend to be larger in downturns than in expansions." Multipliers decline sharply with debt levels: below 60 percent GDP equals 0.8 to 1.0; 60 to 100 percent GDP equals 0.4; above 100 percent GDP approaches zero.)

17. Congressional Budget Office, "How Changes in Economic Conditions Might Affect the Federal Budget: 2025 to 2035," April 2025, https://www.cbo.gov/publication/61249. ("If all interest rates on Treasury securities were just 0.1 percentage point higher each year than projected in the baseline, the cumulative deficit over the 2026-2035 period would be $351 billion larger than projected.")

18. Standard & Poor's Ratings Services, "United States of America Long-Term Rating Lowered To 'AA+' On Political Risks And Rising Debt Burden," August 5, 2011, https://www.spglobal.com/ratings/

en/regulatory/article/-/view/sourceId/6802837.

19. Committee for a Responsible Federal Budget, "Analysis of CBO's March 2025 Long-Term Budget Outlook," March 2025, https://www.crfb.org/papers/analysis-cbos-march-2025-long-term-budget-outlook.

20. Paul De Grauwe, "The Governance of a Fragile Eurozone," CEPS Working Document No. 346, May 2011, https://aei.pitt.edu/31741/1/WD_346_De_Grauwe_on_Eurozone_Governance-1.pdf. (Sovereign debt markets exhibit multiple equilibria; confidence-dependent dynamics in debt markets.)

21. Analysis synthesized from Federal Reserve research on institutional credibility, sovereign debt literature on confidence crises, and historical case studies of debt ceiling confrontations. See also De Grauwe (Note 20) on self-fulfilling dynamics and Reinhart (Note 26) on crisis contagion patterns.

22. Burton A. Abrams, "How Richard Nixon Pressured Arthur Burns: Evidence from the Nixon Tapes," Journal of Economic Perspectives 20, no. 4 (2006): 177-188, https://www.aeaweb.org/articles?id=10.1257/jep.20.4.177.

23. International Monetary Fund, "Turkey: 2023 Article IV Consultation," IMF Country Report No. 23/289, August 2023, https://www.imf.org/en/news/articles/2023/08/18/pr23289-turkiye-imf-executive-board-concluded-the-2022-article-iv-with-turkiye.

24. Mark De Broeck et al., "The Debt Web," IMF Finance & Development, March 2018, https://www.imf.org/en/publications/fandd/issues/2018/03/debroeck. ("We found that concerns among investors about the credibility of fiscal policies and sovereign debt service contributed to the severity and persistence of the financial disruptions as-

sociated with the Great Depression, even if they were not the trigger.")

25. Michael D. Bordo and Christopher M. Meissner, "Fiscal and Financial Crises," NBER Working Paper No. 22059, March 2016, https://www.nber.org/papers/w22059. ("Recent crises feature a feedback loop between bank guarantees and bank holdings of local sovereign debt thereby linking financial to fiscal crises.")

26. Carmen M. Reinhart, "From Health Crisis to Financial Distress," World Bank Policy Research Working Paper 9616, 2021, https://doi.org/10.1596/1813-9450-9616. ("Crises often do not travel alone. Banking, sovereign debt, exchange rate crashes, sudden stops, and inflation often intersect to become severe conglomerate crises.")

27. Peter G. Peterson Foundation, "What Is R Versus G and Why Does It Matter for the National Debt?," April 2025, https://www.pgpf.org/article/what-is-r-versus-g-and-why-does-it-matter-for-the-national-debt/. (Table: Historical Average 1995-2024: R equals 3.7 percent, G equals 4.8 percent; Projected Average 2025-2055: R equals 3.8 percent, G equals 3.7 percent. R officially exceeds G by 2045 per CBO projections.)

28. Author calculation based on debt dynamics framework. When interest rates exceed growth rates (r > g), stabilizing the debt-to-GDP ratio requires a primary surplus equal to (r minus g) times the debt ratio. At 180 percent debt with r equals 4 percent and g equals 2 percent: (4 percent minus 2 percent) times 180 percent equals 3.6 percent of GDP. For the theoretical foundation, see Olivier Blanchard, "Public Debt and Low Interest Rates," American Economic Review 109, no. 4 (2019): 1197-1229, https://www.aeaweb.org/articles?id=10.1257/aer.109.4.1197. For empirical support, see Stephen G. Cecchetti, Madhusudan Mohanty, and Fabrizio Zampolli, "The Real Effects of Debt," BIS Working Paper No. 300, 2011, https://www.bis.org/publ/work300.pdf. ("Countries with very high public debt... would require

sustained primary surpluses of 3-4 percent of GDP to stabilize debt.")

Chapter 4

Why No One Is Talking About This

You have just read three chapters documenting a mathematically certain crisis with an eight-year deadline. Every number came from Congressional Budget Office reports, Social Security Administration actuarial tables, Federal Reserve research papers, and International Monetary Fund analyses. The 2033 Social Security cutoff is written directly into federal law. The interest cost explosion is already happening. The convergence is guaranteed.

If this analysis is accurate, you should be hearing about it constantly. On the news. In political debates. From financial advisors. From economists. The data is public. The mechanisms are clear. The collision is coming.

You are not hearing about it.

The silence is not conspiracy. It is not ignorance. It is rational. Every actor with access to this information faces incentive structures that make speaking loudly about it individually costly, even though collective silence guarantees the worst possible outcome. This is what economists call a Nash Equilibrium: a stable state where no actor benefits from changing strategy unilaterally, even though everyone would be better off if they all changed together.[1]

Understanding why everyone stays quiet transforms confusion into clarity. The question is not "why hasn't anyone told me about this?" The question is "why would anyone with something to lose tell me about this?"

Politicians operate on electoral cycles of two to six years. The fiscal crisis operates on a timeline of eight to thirty years. This temporal mismatch creates an optimization problem with a clear solution: defer action until someone else must handle it.

In March 2023, Congressional Budget Office Director Phillip Swagel briefed the Republican Study Committee, the largest group within the GOP conference, on the debt situation. According to sources present at the closed-door meeting, Swagel made clear that "the level of growth necessary to balance the budget without cutting spending is impossible."[2] He warned that Social Security would be insolvent by 2032 and Medicare by 2033, endangering benefits by 20 to 25 percent.[2]

The briefing was closed-door. No public acknowledgment of severity followed. No legislative proposals emerged. No floor debate occurred. Representative Kevin Hern, chairman of the Republican Study Committee, acknowledged the briefing but added: "But this wasn't news to anyone who's paid attention to our spending problem."[2] The phrase reveals the entire mechanism. Everyone who pays attention already knows. They know privately. They stay silent publicly.

Representative Ben Cline, leading the RSC's budget task force, responded with the standard formulation: "These kinds of briefings are incredibly important to fully understand the seriousness of our nation's fiscal trajectory. It is totally irresponsible for President Biden and the Democrats to refuse to negotiate any limitations on federal spending."[2] The pattern is precise. Acknowledge severity privately. Blame the other party publicly. Propose no specific solution that requires your own party to accept political pain.

This pattern repeats across the institution. Representative Randy Feenstra, serving on the House Ways and Means Social Security Subcommittee, introduced legislation in July 2024 requiring that the CBO's Budget and Economic Outlook include a "simple and easy-to-understand graph" showing the OASDI

Trust Fund trajectory.[3] His rationale: "By directing more eyes and ears to this ticking time bomb, we can ensure that Congress takes action."[3] The legislation does not propose substantive reform. It proposes improved visualization of a crisis everyone in Congress already knows about.

Senator Bill Cassidy has gone further. He wrote an op-ed in the Wall Street Journal outlining his plan to save Social Security through a sovereign wealth fund approach.[4] The proposal is serious, technically sophisticated, and estimated to close about 70 percent of Social Security's funding gap based on historical market returns.[4] Cassidy acknowledges directly: "Congress has become paralyzed by a false choice between raising taxes and cutting benefits."[4]

The result: no hearings scheduled, no co-sponsors beyond a small bipartisan group, no floor debate. The proposal exists in editorial pages but not in the legislative process. Cassidy himself acknowledged in a Washington Post letter: "Neither candidate is willing to participate in the honest conversation our leaders must have to save our seniors from an automatic 21 percent Social Security benefit cut in 2033."[5]

House Budget Committee Chairman Jodey Arrington responded to the 2024 Social Security Trustees Report with remarkable honesty: "Republicans and Democrats have both proven they will not fix Social Security and Medicare on their own."[6] A committee chairman explicitly stating that both parties are structurally incapable of acting. Individual legislators can propose solutions in op-eds and floor speeches, but the institution cannot move those proposals forward because doing so requires votes that end careers.

The electoral math is quantifiable. Voters aged 50 and older represent 55 percent of the electorate in competitive congressional districts, and 61 percent in midterm elections.[7] Among this demographic, 90 percent say Social Security is very important to them, making it effectively a single-issue voting priority for millions.[8] Any benefit cut triggers immediate electoral consequences. Any tax increase large enough to matter triggers donor revolt and base defection.

The required fix of $9.0 trillion in deficit reduction over the next decade exceeds what Simpson-Bowles proposed by a factor of three, and Simpson-Bowles was defeated 382 to 38 when it came to a House vote.[9] Both parties need each other to pass comprehensive reform. Neither can trust the other not to weaponize compromise in the next election. The dominant strategy for each party is to defect from cooperation. One party proposes reform and accepts political pain, the other blocks it and blames them, winning the next election. Both parties understand this payoff structure. The rational choice for every individual politician is silence followed by deferral. Collectively, this produces guaranteed gridlock.

If politicians cannot speak without losing their seats, where is the media? Where is the sustained investigative journalism tracking the CBO projections toward their statutory endpoint?

Media organizations operate on engagement economics. Complex, slow-moving crises do not generate the sustained audience attention that justifies resource allocation. Research on media coverage patterns reveals what scholars term "lurching and fixating" behavior: sudden spikes of attention around acute events like government shutdowns, followed by rapid abandonment.[10] The business model rewards immediate, digestible stories over longitudinal analysis of actuarial tables.

Consider how major outlets have covered this crisis. The Wall Street Journal published an editorial in June 2024 titled "The Social Security Iceberg Gets Closer," warning of "looming insolvency."[4] The language is precise: "looming," "could face," "if nothing is done." All technically accurate. All conveying uncertainty about what is statutory certainty.

William Galston, writing in the Wall Street Journal in July 2025, described the situation as a "Social Security cataclysm" and noted: "Time is running out to avert the crisis."[11] Even strong language like "cataclysm" is prefaced with "avert," suggesting action remains possible when the evidence indicates it is politically impossible. The media frame assumes Congress will act because Congress must act. This assumption pervades coverage despite all historical evidence to the contrary.

National Public Radio interviewed Emerson Sprick, an economist with the Bipartisan Policy Center, in May 2024.[12] The interviewer framed the issue: "Thinking about your retirement? Then maybe you've been wondering, what is the future of Social Security? About nine years, according to a timetable laid out last week."[12] The tone is conversational, treating an automatic 24 percent benefit cut affecting more than 74 million Americans as a subject for personal financial planning curiosity rather than an imminent systemic crisis.

Sprick explained clearly: "The real problem is that Congress last reformed Social Security in 1983. Those reforms didn't fully anticipate the demographic challenges that we face today. Every year between 2024 and 2027, more than 4.1 million Americans are turning 65 annually."[12] The conversation covered potential solutions, then concluded politely. No call to action. No urgency signal. No explanation of why Congress will not choose any of the options that have been available for years.

For a media organization operating on an engagement model, sustained high-cost coverage of a slow-moving fiscal crisis is economically irrational. Algorithmic content curation actively suppresses complex, non-viral material.[13] The revenue generated by sensationalized immediate stories consistently exceeds returns from detailed reports on actuarial debt projections. Algorithms optimize for revenue, not civic necessity.

The problem extends beyond engagement economics to institutional collapse. U.S. newspaper newsrooms lost 57 percent of their staff between 2008 and 2020.[14] Across twenty countries, only 17 percent of people pay for news, a figure stalled for three years, and 57 percent say they would never pay anything.[15] Most of the public remains unaware journalism is in financial crisis at all.[16] The sudden freeze of U.S. foreign assistance programs in early 2025 eliminated an estimated $268 million in grants intended for independent media internationally.[17] For organizations like Arab Reporters for Investigative Journalism, this represented roughly 20 percent of operating budgets.[17] The degradation of global investigative capacity creates information gaps precisely when comprehensive analysis becomes most essential.

If media cannot sustain coverage due to economic incentives, perhaps the experts can sound the alarm. Economists, policy analysts, think tank researchers face no advertisers, no engagement algorithms. Except they face something potentially worse: career annihilation for being right too early.

The most instructive example remains Nouriel Roubini, who accurately predicted the 2008 financial crisis. Beginning in 2005 and 2006, Roubini warned of impending collapse in the housing market and financial system. He was dismissed by financial elites as overly pessimistic. The label "Dr. Doom" carried significant reputational cost.[18] When the crisis hit in 2008, Roubini was vindicated. But the initial professional penalty for being early had already been paid. Even after being proven correct, he retained the "perma-bear" label that colors how his subsequent analysis is received.

The lesson absorbed by the professional community: being early feels the same as being wrong, and the penalty is nearly identical. Research on expert reputation shows that career concerns create powerful incentives to stay close to consensus.[19] The cost of an incorrect prediction is high. The gain from a correct but premature prediction is moderate at best, due to initial dismissal.

This dynamic is compounded by what economists call the "Boy Who Cried Wolf" effect. Deficit hawks have predicted immediate sovereign debt collapse repeatedly since the 1980s.[20] These warnings proved premature. The pattern of failed short-term predictions leads to systematic discounting of genuine long-term trends. Even when the underlying trajectory is real, past false alarms ensure current warnings are dismissed.

The Manhattan Institute addressed this objection directly in their July 2024 comprehensive federal budget plan: "A common argument against addressing Social Security and Medicare is that 'we've been hearing these same fake warnings for decades and nothing has happened.' This view misinterprets the warnings. Between 1999 and 2023, the year in which the Social Security trust fund was projected by the system's trustees to reach insolvency has moved up, not back, from 2036 to just 2033."[21] The wolves really are coming. But the pattern of previous false alarms guarantees that credible warnings are systematically ignored.

The Government Accountability Office, Congress's own investigative arm, has published repeated reports documenting the unsustainable trajectory. Comptroller General Gene Dodaro stated in 2021: "In fiscal year 2020, debt held by the public reached about 100 percent of gross domestic product, up from 79 percent a year earlier. We estimate that left unchecked, the debt will grow to 200 percent of GDP in 2048, well beyond historic levels."[22] The 2024 update noted: "Despite strong economic growth, the fiscal year 2024 deficit was $1.8 trillion, the fifth year in a row of a deficit above $1 trillion."[23]

GAO publishes these reports. Congress commissioned GAO to provide oversight. GAO reports the debt is unsustainable. Congress takes no action. The institutional feedback loop designed to force correction has broken. Not because the loop failed mechanically, but because the incentives governing those who receive the feedback make ignoring it the rational choice.

Stanford economist Thomas MaCurdy stated in July 2025: "Balancing Social Security's long-term books requires a 30 percent permanent benefit cut starting now or alternatively, a rise in Social Security's FICA payroll tax rate from its current 12.4 percent value to a whopping 17.6 percent, affecting almost every U.S. wage earner."[24] The Stanford Center on Longevity published this analysis with the headline: "Americans Face 'Insurmountable Financial Mess' Unless Congress Shores Up Social Security and Medicare."[24]

Stanford University is publishing urgent warnings from credentialed economists eight years before the crisis. Congress is not responding. The silence continues despite institutional warnings from the highest-credibility sources.

Financial sector professionals face legal constraints that discourage candid public warnings about sovereign solvency. Advisors operate under suitability standards requiring that investment recommendations align with client risk tolerance.[25] A generalized prediction of impending fiscal collapse that prompts clients to liquidate positions, leading to losses, creates negligence liability.[26] The advisor could face claims despite being technically correct about the underlying risk.

Research on conflicts of interest shows that disclosure requirements often fail to mitigate the problem and sometimes worsen it by making advisors more comfortable providing biased advice once disclosure has occurred.[27] The regulatory framework creates a legal shield allowing firms to operate with biased incentives while maintaining the appearance of compliance. The result: private preparation for high-net-worth clients, but public silence to avoid liability.

But individual advisor liability, while significant, pales beside the systemic constraint facing every institution with responsibility for financial stability. They face a problem that makes silence not just individually rational but collectively necessary: the multiple equilibria trap.

Sovereign debt markets exhibit characteristics of multiple equilibria where outcomes depend entirely on confidence.[28] If markets maintain confidence in a country, interest rates remain low and debt service is feasible. If confidence is lost, interest rates spike, creating a self-fulfilling crisis where inability to service debt confirms the initial loss of confidence. These dynamics are not theoretical. They drove the European sovereign debt crisis of 2009 to 2018, where countries like Greece, Portugal, and Ireland faced market panic that forced harsh austerity despite having carried similar debt loads without crisis just years earlier.

For systemic stability authorities including central banks and treasury departments, suppressing information that could trigger confidence loss becomes a rational high-stakes decision aimed at preventing catastrophic market failure. The European Central Bank's Outright Monetary Transactions program in 2012 demonstrated how a credible commitment to lend could eliminate self-fulfilling traps and preserve stability.[29]

Silence becomes the lowest-cost contribution required of all actors to fulfill the commitment to confidence. The utility of preserving systemic stability outweighs the utility of immediate truth-telling in a system prone to liquidity runs and information asymmetry. This necessary arrangement accepts tail risk of systemic failure as the cost of doing business. Public warnings regarding fiscal solvency, if too credible, act as the trigger for the very crisis they predict. Therefore, those with the mandate to maintain financial stability must stay silent, even as they see the collision approaching.

If everyone in a position to warn faces structural incentives for silence, how do we know this analysis is correct? The answer lies in what those with the best information are doing quietly while maintaining public silence.

Public discourse from politicians, media, experts, and financial professionals suggests manageable challenges requiring only modest adjustments. Elite behavior tells a different story.

The Land Report, which tracks the largest private landowners in America, documents accelerating consolidation of farmland among the ultra-wealthy.[30] Private equity investment in U.S. farmland has surged, with institutional investors increasingly viewing agricultural land as a hedge against inflation and economic instability.[31] The Washington Post documented this trend in 2022, noting that moguls are "lavishing ever-larger fortunes on the rustic life," with the pandemic accelerating purchases of working ranches and agricultural properties in the American West.[32]

These acquisitions accelerated significantly after 2018. The timing coincides precisely with acceleration of debt accumulation and increasing visibility of fiscal crisis in official projections. Financial press coverage reports these acquisitions as business news focused on agricultural returns and portfolio diversification. Missing from analysis: these actors have access to sophisticated economic forecasting and are making defensive allocations at scale. They are not responding to current conditions but to anticipated future instability.

The U.S. private security market has grown substantially, with the outsourced security services industry expanding from approximately $22 billion in 2014 to over $33 billion by 2022.[33] This growth occurred during a period of declining violent crime rates nationally, suggesting demand is driven not by objective threat but by subjective risk perception among those who can afford private security.

High-net-worth individuals are actively pursuing citizenship and residency by investment programs that provide political optionality and exit strategies. The International Monetary Fund analyzed these programs in a January 2025 working paper, noting they create significant effects on both origin and destination countries.[34]

Geographic patterns in luxury real estate reveal stark sorting behavior. In New Zealand, the Queenstown Lakes District experienced a 91 percent increase in luxury property sales while Auckland saw declines exceeding 50 percent.[35] This represents wealth migration from commercial hubs to remote, politically stable regions. Buyers are disproportionately international high-net-worth individuals seeking physical safe havens with stable governance and geographic isolation.

These behaviors collectively represent defensive capital allocation by informed actors. They are hedging against inflation through tangible assets. They are securing physical protection through private security. They are obtaining political optionality through alternative citizenships. They are relocating wealth to perceived safe havens. Each action individually appears rational. Collectively, they signal a tail risk assessment fundamentally at odds with public complacency.

Every actor is individually rational. Politicians maximize electoral survival by deferring painful reforms. Media organizations maximize revenue by avoiding complex, low-engagement content. Experts maximize career prospects by staying close to consensus until crisis forces acknowledgment. Financial professionals maximize client retention and minimize legal liability by preparing privately while maintaining public confidence. Systemic stability authorities maximize the probability of avoiding self-fulfilling crises by suppressing information that could trigger confidence loss. Elites maximize wealth preservation through defensive positioning while maintaining the public narratives that serve their interests.

Each actor's strategy is rational given their constraints. The payoff for staying silent exceeds the payoff for speaking loudly. The first actor to defect pays the highest cost. Politicians who propose comprehensive reform lose their seats. Media outlets that sustain fiscal coverage lose audience share. Experts who warn early acquire reputational damage. Financial advisors who recommend defensive positioning face suitability claims. Central bankers who acknowledge unsustainability risk triggering the crisis they warn about.

The equilibrium is stable because defection is individually costly even though collective silence produces systematically worse outcomes. No conspiracy is required. No coordination is necessary. Independent optimization by rational actors produces emergent behavior that guarantees collision.

But these silences do not simply coexist. They reinforce each other. Politicians cannot speak because media will not sustain coverage of their proposals.

Media will not cover what experts will not emphasize. Experts will not emphasize what might trigger the confidence crisis financial authorities must prevent. Financial authorities must maintain confidence precisely because political gridlock has eliminated the capacity for gradual adjustment. Each silence makes the others more necessary.

The silence is not evidence of absence. The silence is evidence of presence. When everyone with access to information stays quiet for rational reasons, when institutions designed to provide warnings continue publishing reports that generate no legislative response, when experts acknowledge that only crisis forces action while continuing to provide analysis as if rational debate could matter, the silence itself becomes the signal. Not a signal of conspiracy, but a signal of structural dysfunction so profound that the system cannot acknowledge its own trajectory even as it accelerates toward guaranteed failure.

This equilibrium is stable until 2033. That is when automatic cuts force visibility. When crisis becomes too obvious to deny even as silence remains individually rational. When adjustment happens under maximum duress, at the moment when fiscal space is minimized, political trust is lowest, and options are worst. The collision occurs not because it was inevitable, but because it was politically impossible to prevent. Every actor could see it coming. Every actor had rational reasons for staying quiet. And collectively, those individual choices produced the rationally dysfunctional catastrophe everyone predicted but no one could stop.

CHAPTER 4 NOTES

1. John Nash, "Non-Cooperative Games," Annals of Mathematics 54, no. 2 (1951): 286-295, https://www.jstor.org/stable/1969529. The application of Nash equilibrium to fiscal gridlock is the author's synthesis.

2. Charles Creitz, "CBO Director Informs House Republicans That the US Debt Situation Is Dire: Sources," Fox News, March 1, 2023, https://www.foxnews.com/politics/house-republicans-us-debt-nonpartisan-cbo.amp.

3. Randy Feenstra, "My Plan to Keep Social Security Solvent for Our Senior Citizens," Representative Randy Feenstra, July 3, 2024, https://feenstra.house.gov/media/op-ed/my-plan-keep-social-security-solvent-our-senior-citizens.

4. Bill Cassidy, "ICYMI: Cassidy Warns of Looming Social Security Insolvency in WSJ," U.S. Senator Bill Cassidy, July 7, 2025, https://www.cassidy.senate.gov/newsroom/press-releases/icymi-cassidy-warns-of-looming-social-security-insolvency-in-wsj/.

5. Bill Cassidy, "ICYMI: Cassidy Chimes in on Why Social Security is Foundering," U.S. Senator Bill Cassidy, May 15, 2024, https://www.cassidy.senate.gov/newsroom/press-releases/icymi-cassidy-chimes-in-on-why-social-security-is-foundering/.

6. The U.S. House Committee on the Budget, "Social Security and Medicare Continue on Path to Insolvency, Trustees Confirm," accessed November 2025, https://budget.house.gov/press-release/social-security-and-medicare-continue-on-path-to-insolvency-trustees-confirm.

7. AARP, "New AARP Post-Election Poll of Competitive Congressional Districts Shows Older Voters Prioritized Economic Concerns," news release, November 15, 2024, https://www.prnewswire.com/news-releases/new-aarp-post-election-poll-of-competitive-congressional-districts-shows-older-voters-prioritized-economic-concerns-302307272.html. ("Voters ages 50 and older were key in the 2024 election. Data shows that across the country, older voters made up 55% of the electorate.") See also AARP, "AARP Poll of 63 Most Competitive Congressional Districts Shows Older Voters Were the Deciders in 2022," news release, November 17, 2022, https://press.aarp.org/2022-11-17-AARP-Post-Election-Survey. ("Overall, voters 50+ accounted for 61% of the electorate in these key districts.")

8. AARP Research Center, "Social Security 2024 Survey of Voters Ages 50+," November 2024, https://www.aarp.org/pri/topics/voter-research/politics/voter-preferences-2024-battleground-states/. ("Approximately nine out of ten voters ages 50-plus report they are extremely motivated to vote... Around 90% said they would be more likely to vote for a candidate who pledged to make sure workers get the Social Security they paid into.")

9. Charles J. Lewis, "Himes Predicts Action on Debt After Election," CT Insider, March 29, 2012, https://www.ctinsider.com/local/article/himes-predicts-action-on-debt-after-election-3445605.php. ("Lawmakers voted 382-38 against the debt plan that was closely modeled on the 2010 recommendations of the Simpson-Bowles commission.") Committee for a Responsible Federal Budget, "Meeting Fiscal Goals Under CBO's January 2025 Baseline," January 29, 2025, https://www.crfb.org/blogs/meeting-fiscal-goals-under-cbos-january-2025-baseline. ("Stabilizing debt over the next decade at its current share of the economy would require $9.0 trillion of deficit reduction.")

10. Amber E. Boydstun, Making the News: Politics, the Media, and Agenda Setting (Chicago: University of Chicago Press, 2013). See also Amber E. Boydstun and Regina G. Lawrence, "From Crisis to Stasis: Media Dynamics and Issue Attention in the News," Oxford Research Encyclopedia of Politics, https://oxfordre.com/politics/oso/viewentry/10.1093$002facrefore$002f9780190228637.001.0001$002facrefore-9780190228637-e-56.

11. "Social Security: Insolvency Date Keeps Getting Closer," The Week, July 23, 2025, https://theweek.com/personal-finance/social-security-insolvency-date-gets-closer.

12. Ayesha Rascoe, "Social security funds are set to fall short by 2033. What can be done?," NPR, May 12, 2024, https://www.npr.org/2024/05/12/1250805057/social-security-funds-are-set-to-fall-short-by-2033-what-can-be-done.

13. Tom Cunningham et al., "Ranking by Engagement and Non-Engagement Signals: Learnings from Industry," Annals of the New York Academy of Sciences (2025), https://nyaspubs.onlinelibrary.wiley.com/doi/10.1111/nyas.15399.

14. Pew Research Center, "U.S. newsroom employment has fallen 26% since 2008," July 13, 2021, https://www.pewresearch.org/short-reads/2021/07/13/u-s-newsroom-employment-has-fallen-26-since-2008/. ("Newspaper newsroom employment dropped 57% between 2008 and 2020, from approximately 71,000 to 31,000.")

15. Reuters Institute for the Study of Journalism, "How much do people pay for online news?," Digital News Report 2024, https://reutersinstitute.politics.ox.ac.uk/digital-news-report/2024/how-much-do-people-pay-online-news-what-might-encourage-others-pay. ("The proportion that pay for online news across 20 countries is

17% – a figure that has not changed for the last three years... 57% of people would never consider paying anything for news.")

16. Northwestern University Medill School of Journalism, Local News Initiative research, 2024. The study found that 71 percent of news consumers surveyed "don't know that the news business is in crisis," with 54 percent believing local news businesses were doing "somewhat well" and 17 percent believing they were doing "very well."

17. Global Investigative Journalism Network, "The USAID Crisis and Funding the Future of Independent Media," accessed November 2025, https://gijn.org/stories/usaid-crisis-funding-future-independent-media/.

18. Stephen Mihm, "Dr. Doom," New York Times Magazine, August 15, 2008, https://www.nytimes.com/2008/08/17/magazine/17pessimist-t.html.

19. Federal Reserve Bank of Richmond, "Reputation and Career Concerns," Working Paper 06-1, 2006, https://www.richmondfed.org/~/media/richmondfedorg/publications/research/working_papers/2006/pdf/wp06-1.pdf.

20. Levy Economics Institute of Bard College, "The Boy Who Cried Wolf About Government Debt," accessed November 2025, https://www.levyinstitute.org/publications/the-boy-who-cried-wolf-about-government-debt/.

21. Manhattan Institute, "A Comprehensive Federal Budget Plan to Avert a Debt Crisis," July 12, 2024, https://manhattan.institute/article/a-comprehensive-federal-budget-plan-to-avert-a-debt-crisis-2024.

22. Gene L. Dodaro, "GAO Calls for Timely Action on the Nation's Future Fiscal Health," U.S. Government Accountability Office, accessed November 2025, https://www.gao.gov/press-release/gao-calls-timel

y-action-nations-future-fiscal-health.

23. U.S. Government Accountability Office, "The Nation's Fiscal Health: Strategy Needed as Debt Levels Accelerate," accessed November 2025, https://www.gao.gov/products/gao-25-107714.

24. Stanford Center on Longevity, "Americans Face 'Insurmountable Financial Mess' Unless Congress Shores Up Social Security and Medicare," July 1, 2025, https://longevity.stanford.edu/americans-face-insurmountable-financial-mess-unless-congress-shores-up-social-security-and-medicare/.

25. Financial Industry Regulatory Authority (FINRA), "Suitability," Rule 2111, https://www.finra.org/rules-guidance/rulebooks/finra-rules/2111.

26. Michael Kitces, "When Are Advisors (Financially) Liable For Negligent Investment Advice? (And Who Pays For It)," Kitces.com, accessed November 2025, https://www.kitces.com/blog/liablity-negligent-investment-advice-federal-tort-law-errors-omissions-insurance/.

27. Daylian M. Cain, George Loewenstein, and Don A. Moore, "The Dirt on Coming Clean: Perverse Effects of Disclosing Conflicts of Interest," Journal of Legal Studies 34, no. 1 (2005): 1-25, https://www.jstor.org/stable/10.1086/426699.

28. Paul De Grauwe, "The Governance of a Fragile Eurozone," CEPS Working Document No. 346, May 2011, https://aei.pitt.edu/31741/1/WD_346_De_Grauwe_on_Eurozone_Governance-1.pdf.

29. Federal Reserve Bank of Minneapolis, "Self-fulfilling Prophecies in Sovereign Debt Markets," accessed November 2025, https://fedinprint.org/item/fedmep/29021.

30. The Land Report, "The Land Report 100," accessed November 2025,

https://landreport.com/land-report-100. The Land Report is the authoritative annual ranking of America's largest private landowners.

31. Justin Flores, "Betting the Farm: Private Equity Buyouts in US Agriculture," Private Equity Stakeholder Project, March 27, 2025, https://pestakeholder.org/reports/betting-the-farm-private-equity-buyouts-in-us-agriculture/.

32. Karen Heller, "The fabulously wealthy are fueling a booming luxury ranch market out West," Washington Post, August 16, 2022, https://www.washingtonpost.com/lifestyle/2022/08/16/ranch-land-west-billionaires/.

33. IBISWorld, "Security Services in the US - Market Research Report (2015-2030)," November 2025, https://www.ibisworld.com/united-states/industry/security-services/1487/. See also Statista, "Market size of the outsourced contract security industry in the United States from 2014 to 2023," https://www.statista.com/statistics/824279/outsourced-security-services-us-market-size/.

34. International Monetary Fund, "Drivers and Effects of Residence and Citizenship by Investment," IMF Working Paper WP/25/8, January 2025, https://www.imf.org/-/media/Files/Publications/WP/2025/English/wpiea2025008-print-pdf.ashx.

35. RNZ News, "Luxury property sales drop by more than 50 percent," accessed November 2025, https://www.rnz.co.nz/news/business/541398/luxury-property-sales-drop-by-more-than-50-percent.

PART II

How The Crisis Actually Unfolds

Chapter 5
2025-2027 - It's Already Starting

I n fiscal year 2025, the United States government spent more money servicing its debt than defending its borders. Net interest costs reached $970 billion, exceeding defense spending for the first time in peacetime history.[1] This is not a projection about future risk. This is documented reality. For every dollar spent on the Department of Defense, the military, nuclear deterrence, intelligence operations, and homeland security combined, the government now spends more simply paying interest on money it has already borrowed.

Interest payments buy nothing. They do not build roads, fund research, educate children, protect the environment, maintain courts, or provide emergency response capacity. They compensate creditors for past borrowing. By 2027, interest costs will exceed not only defense but all non-defense discretionary spending combined.[1] Everything the federal government does beyond Social Security, Medicare, Medicaid, defense, and interest payments will cost less than the interest itself. Infrastructure, scientific research, education grants, national parks, federal courts, the State Department, the Justice Department, homeland security, veterans healthcare, environmental protection, food safety, transportation, and the basic operations of the federal government will collectively receive less funding than what goes to bondholders.

This is the Type B Crisis: the slow strangulation of government capacity that operates on a different timeline than Social Security's 2033 deadline but arrives sooner and persists longer. While the 2033 trust fund depletion creates a statutory collision that forces political action, the interest cost explosion is already destroying the federal government's ability to invest, respond to crises, or maintain basic functions. The crowding out has begun.

The evidence is visible right now for anyone willing to look. On January 20, 2025, President Trump signed an executive order freezing the hiring of federal civilian employees "throughout the executive branch."[2] The freeze was converted in October to an indefinite measure, with the administration declaring that "no Federal civilian position that is vacant may be filled, and no new position may be created."[3] Even when hiring eventually resumes, agencies will face a permanent constraint: "the ratio of four departures for each new hire" established by executive order, designed to shrink the federal workforce permanently.[3]

These are not abstract statistics. These are air traffic controllers, food safety inspectors, veterans benefits processors, National Park Service rangers, scientists at the National Institutes of Health, engineers at the Department of Energy, claims processors at Social Security. The Partnership for Public Service warned that the freeze "could leave agencies with hiring gaps in critical areas" and "will deter the talented workers needed for a well-functioning government, especially those with specialized skills."[4]

Infrastructure projects are frozen or cancelled across the country. In October 2025, the White House put "roughly $18 billion in New York City infrastructure projects" on hold, specifically "the Hudson Tunnel Project and the Second Ave Subway."[5] The Hudson Tunnel serves approximately 200,000 daily riders and is considered critical to the regional economy. The project is not optional maintenance. It is essential infrastructure replacement for tunnels built in 1910 that are failing. The freeze means those tunnels continue deteriorating while the replacement project sits idle.

Chicago lost access to $2.1 billion for improvements to its transit system, including the Red Line Extension that would "extend that train line by 5.5 miles with four new stations."[6] The Department of Energy terminated 321 financial awards supporting 223 projects, totaling $7.56 billion.[7] The Army Corps of Engineers paused "over $11 billion in projects due to the government shutdow n."[8] Congress cancelled nearly $16 billion in Community Project Funding for thousands of projects across the country.[9] Jacksonville, Florida lost access to a $147 million grant for the Emerald Trail project. Philadelphia had 95 percent of a $159 million grant for a highway-capping project rescinded. Bowling Green, Kentucky lost one-third of an $11 million grant.[10]

These are not future budget proposals being debated. These are approved projects, with contracts signed and work planned, that have been frozen or cancelled because the federal government lacks the fiscal capacity to execute them. The Infrastructure Investment and Jobs Act, passed with bipartisan support in 2021, authorized $581 billion for infrastructure projects through fiscal year 2025. As of December 31, 2024, only $275 billion had been obligated and just $119 billion had actually been spent, representing execution rates of 47 percent and 21 percent respectively.[11] The money exists on paper. The projects exist in legislation. But the capacity to actually execute infrastructure investment is vanishing.

Scientific research funding is collapsing. Since President Trump took office on January 20, 2025, the National Institute of Neurological Disorders and Stroke and the National Institute of Mental Health "have awarded one quarter as many new grants as during the same two-month period, on average, since 2016."[12] This is not a small adjustment. This is a catastrophic reduction in the pace of neuroscience research in the United States. The National Institutes of Health "committed to U.S. institutions almost $5 billion less in research grants in the past year than in the year before."[13] For new grants and competitive renewals, total funding fell from $10.5 billion in fiscal year 2024 to $8.6 billion in fiscal year 2025, an 18 percent reduction.[13]

Research and Development grants saw a $3.6 billion loss in total funding.[13] Research Training and Career Development grants, the NIH's principal mechanism for supporting the next generation of biomedical researchers, fell from

$2.2 billion to $1.7 billion.[13] NIH funding supported 412,041 jobs and $92.89 billion of economic activity in 2024.[14] Those numbers are falling sharply.

An internal NIH email dated April 17, 2025, stated that "funds have been frozen [for] Columbia, Brown, Northwestern, Cornell, Weill-Cornell, Harvard" and that the agency "should not provide any communications to these schools about whether or why the funds are frozen."[15] Analysis of outlay data showed that at Brown, Columbia, Cornell, and Northwestern, "outlays plummeted to $0 in April 2025, with 100% of grants receiving no outlays," a pattern "totally different from all previous years."[15] This is not normal budgetary adjustment. This is the active destruction of American research capacity.

Some of these cuts were framed as political decisions, targeting blue states or elite universities. Some were partially reversed by court intervention. The NIH attempted to cap indirect cost rates at 15 percent, down from average rates of 27 to 28 percent, with some organizations "charging indirect rates of over 50% and in some cases over 60%."[16] A federal court blocked the cap on February 10, 2025, following lawsuits from 22 states and a coalition of universities.[14] But the pattern reveals deeper structural constraints beyond any single political decision. The NIH's $5 billion reduction in extramural research occurred despite court blocking of the indirect cost cap. Infrastructure project delays persist regardless of stated political justification. The federal hiring freeze's 4-to-1 attrition ratio ensures permanent workforce reduction. Whether cuts are attributed to political decisions or fiscal necessity, the outcome is identical: government capacity to invest in infrastructure, research, and future-oriented functions is being systematically dismantled.

This is happening because interest costs are consuming the fiscal space that would otherwise fund these activities. In 2025, net interest costs reached 18.4 percent of federal revenue, already exceeding the previous historical peak of 17.5 percent set in 1991.[17] Over the next decade, cumulative interest payments will total $13.8 trillion.[17] By 2035, interest costs will consume 4.1 percent of GDP and 22.2 percent of all federal revenue.[1] For context, at the peak of 1980s fiscal stress, when interest rates exceeded 15 percent and federal debt stood at 39 percent of GDP, interest costs reached only 3.2 percent of GDP.[17] Today's interest burden, measured against the size of the economy, will exceed that crisis peak by 28 percent despite interest rates being far lower, because the debt itself is vastly larger.

Federal spending divides into three categories. Mandatory spending, primarily Social Security, Medicare, and Medicaid, currently consumes approximately 60 percent of the federal budget.[18] These programs operate under permanent appropriations, paying benefits to anyone who qualifies regardless of annual budget constraints. Defense spending accounts for roughly 13 percent.[18] That leaves 27 percent for everything else: discretionary spending divided between defense support functions and non-defense priorities, plus net interest.[18] Interest costs currently represent 13 percent of federal spending, but that share is rising rapidly.[18] Unlike Social Security or Medicare, which provide retirement security and healthcare, interest payments deliver nothing. They compensate creditors for past borrowing. And they are about to become the second-largest item in the federal budget, approaching the size of Social Security itself.[19]

Current federal debt held by the public stands at approximately 100 percent of GDP, or roughly $29.6 trillion in nominal terms.[20] This metric excludes intragovernmental debt (the Treasury securities held by Social Security and other trust funds), focusing only on what the government owes to external creditors: domestic and foreign individuals, businesses, pension funds, and central banks. It is this external debt that generates interest costs and requires market financing. The trajectory from here is relentless. The Congressional Budget Office projects federal debt will reach 118 percent of GDP by 2035 and 156 percent by 2055.[21] Cumulative deficits over the 2025-2034 period alone will total approximately $20 trillion.[22]

In 2029, federal debt will surpass 107 percent of GDP, exceeding the previous all-time high of 106 percent reached in 1946 at the conclusion of World War II.[21] That comparison reveals how structurally different the current crisis is from past episodes of high debt. The post-war debt was a temporary spike caused by extraordinary wartime spending. Defense outlays had consumed 37 percent of GDP at the war's peak.[23] Once hostilities ceased, defense spending collapsed to 5 percent of GDP by 1950.[23] This dramatic reduction, combined with strong economic growth driven by a young, expanding population and productivity gains from wartime technological development, allowed the government to run primary surpluses. Debt fell from 106 percent of GDP in 1946 to 23 percent by 1974, a decline achieved through economic expansion making the debt relatively smaller without requiring explicit paydown.[23]

Today's debt cannot be resolved through the post-war playbook because none of the conditions that made that resolution possible exist now. Current defense spending stands at approximately 3.3 percent of GDP, already near historical peacetime lows given contemporary geopolitical threats.[24] There is no 32-percentage-point cushion to cut as there was in 1946. The population is aging rather than young, with the Baby Boom generation entering retirement and fertility rates well below replacement level. Economic growth is projected to average 3.7 percent nominal GDP growth over 2025-2055, compared to the 4.8 percent average achieved from 1995-2024.[25] Most critically, the current debt is driven by structural primary deficits projected to persist indefinitely, averaging 2.1 percent of GDP by 2035.[1] The government is not running temporary wartime deficits that will naturally reverse with peace. It is running permanent deficits driven by demographics and entitlement commitments that grow automatically as the population ages.

The mechanics of debt accumulation under current conditions create a self-reinforcing cycle. High debt generates high interest payments. High interest payments increase the deficit. Larger deficits require more borrowing. More borrowing raises the debt stock. Higher debt produces even larger interest payments. The loop accelerates unless interrupted by policy changes that either dramatically reduce spending or substantially increase revenue. Whether this cycle becomes a death spiral depends on the relationship between two variables: the average interest rate paid on federal debt (r) and the nominal rate of economic growth (g). When economic growth exceeds the interest rate, the debt-to-GDP ratio can decline naturally even with modest primary deficits, because the economy grows faster than the debt burden. When interest rates exceed growth, the debt ratio rises automatically unless the government runs primary surpluses large enough to offset the differential.

From 1995 through 2024, the United States enjoyed favorable conditions with average nominal GDP growth of 4.8 percent and average interest rates of 3.7 percent.[25] This 1.1 percentage point advantage meant economic expansion gradually reduced the relative debt burden, providing fiscal breathing room. The Congressional Budget Office projects this relationship reverses over 2025-2055, with average interest rates of 3.8 percent and average growth of 3.7 percent.[25] By 2045, interest rates officially exceed growth rates on a sustained basis.[20] Once interest exceeds growth, the mathematics of debt sustainability change fundamentally. The United States can no longer grow out of its debt through economic expansion alone. Stabilizing the debt-to-GDP ratio requires running primary surpluses sufficient to counteract the automatic growth driven by interest accumulation. The current primary deficit of 2.1 percent of GDP moves in the opposite direction.[1]

The debt trajectory is also acutely vulnerable to interest rate fluctuations. With nearly $30 trillion in debt outstanding, small changes in borrowing costs translate to massive fiscal impacts. The Congressional Budget Office estimates that if interest rates were just 0.1 percentage point higher across the yield curve each year than currently projected, cumulative deficits over 2026-2035 would increase by $351 billion.[26] Of this total, $319 billion represents direct interest cost increases, with the remainder coming from compounding effects as higher interest payments themselves require additional borrowing that generates further interest costs.[26] A mere ten-basis-point shift in rates, the kind of movement that occurs routinely in bond markets, costs the equivalent of three years of NASA's entire budget. This sensitivity creates exposure to events beyond policymakers' control. Federal Reserve decisions about monetary policy directly affect short-term rates and indirectly influence long-term rates. Global inflation dynamics determine the real return creditors demand. Geopolitical shocks that increase risk premiums on U.S. debt would immediately raise borrowing costs.

The crowding out of discretionary spending is not metaphorical. It is arithmetic, documented in budget tables and inevitable under current law. In 2027, interest costs will exceed total non-defense discretionary spending for the first time.[1] From that year forward, the federal government will face a stark choice:

cut discretionary programs to offset rising interest costs, or allow total spending to grow and accelerate the debt spiral. Under current projections, policymakers choose the latter, allowing both interest and mandatory spending to grow while discretionary spending shrinks as a share of the economy. What gets crowded out is the capacity for investment in the future and response to crises in the present.

Infrastructure spending, already inadequate relative to maintenance needs, faces further reductions. The American Society of Civil Engineers estimates $2.6 trillion in unfunded infrastructure needs for roads, bridges, water systems, and public transit over the next decade.[27] Federal funding moves in the opposite direction. Scientific research funding through the National Institutes of Health, National Science Foundation, and Department of Energy faces flat or declining real budgets at precisely the moment technological competition with China intensifies. Education grants that support low-income college students and funding for K-12 schools in disadvantaged districts become targets for deficit reduction. The federal court system, operating with chronic understaffing and deferred maintenance on aging facilities, receives no relief. National parks, which generated $50.3 billion in economic activity in 2022 through tourism, deteriorate as deferred maintenance backlogs grow.[28]

More consequentially, the elimination of fiscal space destroys the government's capacity to respond to crises. The 2008 financial crisis required the Troubled Asset Relief Program, quantitative easing, and fiscal stimulus totaling trillions of dollars to prevent economic collapse. Federal debt stood at approximately 35 percent of GDP in 2007, providing enormous room for emergency borrowing.[29] The COVID-19 pandemic prompted $5 trillion in emergency spending for healthcare response, unemployment support, business assistance, and vaccine development. Debt increased from 79 percent of GDP in 2019 to 100 percent by 2020, an expansion possible only because fiscal space existed.[29] By 2027, with debt at 106 percent of GDP and interest costs consuming more than a fifth of revenue, that space no longer exists.

The next recession will find a federal government unable to mount a robust fiscal response. Automatic stabilizers like unemployment insurance will still function, but discretionary stimulus spending, infrastructure investment to create jobs, or emergency assistance to failing industries becomes politically and economically impossible when the starting point is already maximum sustainable debt and interest costs that crowd out everything else. The same constraint applies to military contingencies. A major conflict requiring sustained defense expenditures would force impossible choices between military necessity and fiscal sustainability. Natural disasters, which are increasing in frequency and severity, generate federal assistance costs averaging more than $100 billion annually in recent years.[30] By 2027, these costs must be absorbed within a discretionary budget already underwater from interest crowding out.

The permanence of this situation distinguishes it from Social Security's 2033 deadline. That crisis features a statutory trigger requiring Congressional action. The trust fund depletes, automatic cuts occur, political pressure forces a response. The timeline is fixed, creating a forcing mechanism that compels eventual policy change even if inadequate or implemented under duress. Interest crowding out operates on no such timeline. It simply accelerates, year after year, constrained only by the point at which creditors lose confidence and refuse to finance deficits at prevailing rates. Until that confidence evaporates, the crowding out continues indefinitely, gradually destroying government capacity without triggering political forcing mechanisms that would compel comprehensive reform.

The 2027 crossover, when interest costs exceed all non-defense discretionary spending, will not generate headlines or prompt emergency legislation. It is a threshold crossed quietly in budget tables while policymakers debate other priorities. The erosion becomes normal, accepted, and unremarkable. Infrastructure decays. Research slows. Parks deteriorate. Courts operate short-staffed. Federal employees remain underpaid relative to private sector equivalents, driving talent away from public service. The machinery of government continues functioning but operates at reduced capacity, deferring maintenance, postponing investment, and accumulating hidden costs that will manifest in infrastructure failures, scientific stagnation, and reduced state capacity for decades to come.

Who feels this first? Government contractors waiting for infrastructure projects that never begin. University research labs competing for NIH grants that have been reduced by $5 billion. Federal employees watching colleagues leave through attrition while hiring freezes prevent replacement. State governments receiving reduced federal aid for highways, water systems, and education. Municipal governments losing access to grants for community projects. The private sector remains largely unaffected for now. Social Security checks continue arriving at full scheduled amounts until 2033. Stock markets can remain strong even as government fiscal health deteriorates. This is why the silence persists. If you do not work for the government, contract with the government, or depend on federal grants, you probably have not felt this yet.

But 2027 is two years away. And 2033 is eight years from now. The government is losing capacity to invest, respond to crises, or maintain infrastructure. And in 2033, when the Social Security trust fund depletes and automatic benefit cuts hit or emergency borrowing begins, the crisis will arrive at a government that has already been hollowed out. There will be zero fiscal space to respond. Political gridlock will prevent proactive solutions. And the middle class will feel economic pain directly for the first time, through reduced retirement income, higher taxes, recession, unemployment, or all of the above.

The collision is coming. The only question is whether it arrives through slow erosion or sudden crisis. And every year of inaction ensures the answer is both.

CHAPTER 5 NOTES

1. Congressional Budget Office, "The Budget and Economic Outlook: 2025 to 2035," January 2025, https://www.cbo.gov/publication/61 172. Interest costs exceed defense spending starting in 2025 and exceed non-defense discretionary programs starting in 2027. Net interest projected to reach 4.1% of GDP by 2035. Primary deficit projected at 2.1% of GDP by 2035.

2. The White House, "Hiring Freeze," January 20, 2025, https://www. whitehouse.gov/presidential-actions/2025/01/hiring-freeze/. "...ord er a freeze on the hiring of Federal civilian employees, to be applied throughout the executive branch."

3. The White House, "Ensuring Continued Accountability in Federal Hiring," October 15, 2025, https://www.whitehouse.gov/presidential-actions/2025/10/ ensuring-continued-accountability-in-federal-hiring/. "No Federal civilian position that is vacant may be filled"; "the ratio of four departures for each new hire."

4. Partnership for Public Service, "Statement on federal hiring freeze," January 20, 2025, https://ourpublicservice.org/press-release/partne rship-for-public-service-statement-on-federal-hiring-freeze/. "...could leave agencies with hiring gaps in critical areas, and it will deter the talented workers needed for a well-functioning government."

5. Adam Edelman and Peter Alexander, "White House freezes $18 billion in New York City infrastructure funding," NBC News, October 1, 2025, https://www.nbcnews.com/politics/trump-administration/white-ho use-freezes-18-billion-new-york-city-infrastructure-funding-rcna234 928. "Roughly $18 billion in New York City infrastructure projects

have been put on hold."

6. Jacob Pramuk, "Trump admin freezes $2.1 billion for Chicago projects," CNBC, October 6, 2025, https://www.cnbc.com/2025/10/03/trump-chicago-infrastructure-shutdown-vought.html. "...extend that train line by 5.5 miles with four new stations."

7. U.S. Department of Energy, "Energy Department Announces Termination of 223 Projects, Saving Over $7.5 Billion," October 2, 2025, https://www.energy.gov/articles/energy-department-announces-termination-223-projects-saving-over-75-billion. "...termination of 321 financial awards supporting 223 projects, resulting in a savings of approximately $7.56 billion."

8. Kevin Breuninger, "Army Corps of Engineers pausing $11 billion in projects over shutdown," CNBC, October 17, 2025, https://www.cnbc.com/2025/10/17/vought-budget-government-shutdown.html. "The U.S. Army Corps of Engineers will immediately pause over $11 billion in projects."

9. Ben Swasey, "Cancelled 2025 federal funding for community projects puts future initiatives in doubt," Nebraska Public Media, 2025, https://nebraskapublicmedia.org/en/news/news-articles/cancelled-2025-federal-funding-for-community-projects-puts-future-initiatives-in-doubt/. "...cancel nearly $16 billion in such funding for thousands of projects across the country."

10. Alan Greenblatt, "Feds Slash Millions in Promised Funds for Local Transportation," Governing, July 29, 2025, https://www.governing.com/transportation/feds-slash-millions-in-promised-funds-for-local-transportation. Jacksonville $147M Emerald Trail; Philadelphia 95% of $159M rescinded; Bowling Green one-third of $11M rescinded.

11. U.S. Government Accountability Office, "Infrastructure Grants: Status of Funding," GAO-25-107243, April 29, 2025, https://www.gao.gov/products/gao-25-107243. "...agencies reported obligating $275.1 billion (47 percent) and outlaying $119.4 billion (21 percent)."

12. "Newly awarded NIH grants for neuroscience lag 77 percent behind previous nine-year average," The Transmitter, April 4, 2025, https://www.thetransmitter.org/funding/newly-awarded-nih-grants-for-neuroscience-lag-77-percent-behind-previous-nine-year-average/. "...have awarded one quarter as many new grants as during the same two-month period, on average, since 2016." See also NIH Data Book, https://report.nih.gov/nihdatabook/category/29.

13. Association of American Medical Colleges, "The NIH obligated nearly $5 billion less for extramural research," 2025, https://www.aamc.org/media/85501/download. "...almost $5 billion less in research grants in the past year"; new grants $8.6B vs $10.5B (18% reduction); R&D grants down $3.6B; training grants $1.7B vs $2.2B. See also NIH Data Book, https://report.nih.gov/nihdatabook/category/29.

14. AcademyHealth, "Situation Report: NIH abruptly slashing indirect grants," February 2025, https://academyhealth.org/blog/2025-02/academyhealth-situation-report-nih-abruptly-slashing-indirect-grants-what-means-researchers. "NIH funding has supported 412,041 jobs and 92.89 billion dollars of economic activity in 2024." Federal court blocked indirect cost cap February 10, 2025.

15. Grant Witness, "Trends in NIH outlays," 2025, https://grant-witness.us/posts/trends-in-nih-outlays/. Internal email: "funds have been frozen [for] Columbia, Brown, Northwestern, Cornell, Weill-Cornell, Harvard"; "outlays plummeted to $0 in April 2025, with 100% of grants receiving no outlays."

16. National Institutes of Health, Notice NOT-OD-25-068, February 7, 2025, https://grants.nih.gov/grants/guide/notice-files/NOT-OD-2 5-068.html. "...subject to a 15 percent indirect cost rate"; average rates 27-28%, with some "over 50% and in some cases over 60%."

17. Peter G. Peterson Foundation, "Any Way You Look at It, Interest Costs on the National Debt Will Soon Be at an All-Time High," August 2025, https://www.pgpf.org/article/any-way-you-look-at-it-interes t-costs-on-the-national-debt-will-soon-be-at-an-all-time-high/. 2025 interest costs $970B; 18.4% of revenue (exceeds 1991 peak); cumulative $13.8T over next decade; 1980s peak was 3.2% GDP.

18. Bipartisan Policy Center, "Visualizing CBO's Budget and Economic Outlook: 2025," accessed November 2025, https://bipartisanpolicy.org/article/visualizing-cbos-budget-a nd-economic-outlook-2025/. Budget composition: 60% mandatory, 13% defense, 27% discretionary + interest; interest at 13% of spending.

19. Committee for a Responsible Federal Budget, "Interest Costs Could Explode from High Rates and More Debt," accessed November 2025, https://www.crfb.org/blogs/interest-costs-could-explode-hig h-rates-and-more-debt. Interest projected to become second-largest program, approaching Social Security size.

20. Committee for a Responsible Federal Budget, "Analysis of CBO's March 2025 Long-Term Budget Outlook," March 2025, https://www.crfb.org/papers/analysis-cbos-march-2025-long -term-budget-outlook. Debt 100% GDP in FY2025 ($29.6T nominal); r>g crossover by 2045.

21. Congressional Budget Office, "The Long-Term Budget Outlook: 2025 to 2055," March 2025, https://www.cbo.gov/publication/612 70. Debt trajectory: 107% GDP by 2029 (surpasses WWII record of

106%), 118% by 2035, 156% by 2055.

22. Congressional Budget Office, "Outlook for the Budget and the Economy," accessed November 2025, https://www.cbo.gov/topics/budget/outlook-budget-and-economy. Cumulative deficits 2025-2034: $20 trillion.

23. Peter G. Peterson Foundation, "Why Is the U.S. Fiscal Outlook More Daunting Now than After World War II?," January 2025, https://www.pgpf.org/article/why-is-the-us-fiscal-outlook-more-daunting-now-than-after-world-war-ii/. WWII defense peak: 37% GDP; post-war: 5% GDP by 1950; debt: 106% (1946) to 23% (1974).

24. Peter G. Peterson Foundation, "Budget Basics: National Defense," accessed November 2025, https://www.pgpf.org/article/budget-explainer-national-defense/. Current defense: 3.3% GDP.

25. Peter G. Peterson Foundation, "What Is R Versus G and Why Does It Matter for the National Debt?," April 2025, https://www.pgpf.org/article/what-is-r-versus-g-and-why-does-it-matter-for-the-national-debt/. Historical (1995-2024): R=3.7%, G=4.8%. Projected (2025-2055): R=3.8%, G=3.7%.

26. Congressional Budget Office, "How Changes in Economic Conditions Might Affect the Federal Budget: 2025 to 2035," April 2025, https://www.cbo.gov/publication/61198. 0.1pp higher rates = $351B additional deficits 2026-2035 ($319B direct interest + $32B compounding).

27. American Society of Civil Engineers, "2021 Report Card for America's Infrastructure," March 2021, https://infrastructurereportcard.org/. Infrastructure investment gap: $2.59 trillion (~$2.6T) over decade.

28. National Park Service, "2022 National Park Visitor Spending Effects,"

Economic Benefits Report, August 2023, https://www.nps.gov/su bjects/socialscience/vse.htm. National parks generated $50.3 billion economic output in 2022.

29. Federal Reserve Bank of St. Louis, "Federal Debt Held by the Public as Percent of Gross Domestic Product," FRED Economic Data, updated November 2025, https://fred.stlouisfed.org/series/FYGFGDQ188S. Debt ~35% GDP in 2007; 79% in 2019; 100% by 2020.

30. National Oceanic and Atmospheric Administration, "Billion-Dollar Weather and Climate Disasters," accessed November 2025, https://www.ncei.noaa.gov/access/billions/. 403 billion-dollar disasters 1980-2024 totaling $2.915 trillion; annual average 2020-2024: $149.3 billion.

Chapter 6

2033 - The Collision

In 2033, the silence becomes unsustainable.

For eight years, the rational equilibrium described in Chapter 4 will hold. Politicians will defer reform because electoral cycles reward inaction. Media will cover the crisis episodically because sustained coverage generates poor engagement. Experts will avoid alarmist predictions because being early feels the same as being wrong. Financial professionals will prepare wealthy clients privately while maintaining public confidence. Every actor will individually optimize for survival, collectively producing the gridlock that guarantees collision.

That equilibrium shatters in 2033 because the crisis shifts from theoretical risk to visible, compulsory failure. The Old-Age and Survivors Insurance Trust Fund depletes. Federal law mandates that benefits be reduced to match incoming payroll tax revenue. The cuts are automatic. Congress cannot ignore what statute requires. The silence that worked for eight years stops working when more than 74 million Americans receive notices that their monthly checks are being reduced by 24 percent.[1]

This is not prediction. This is documentation of what happens when a statutory deadline meets political paralysis.

Congress will face three options. All are painful. None are politically surviv-able under normal conditions. The choice they make, or more accurately the choice that political incentives make for them, determines whether the crisis unfolds over five years or fifteen, and whether the pain concentrates in the elderly or distributes across the entire economy.

The first option is to let the automatic cuts happen. A typical dual-earning couple retiring shortly after the trust fund runs out will face an $18,400 benefit cut annually, while a single-income couple faces a $13,800 reduction.[2] The average Social Security retirement benefit in 2024 was $1,924 per month, or $23,088 annually.[3] A 24 percent reduction transforms that into approximately $1,462 per month, a loss of $462 every month for rent, groceries, medications, utilities. For elderly Americans who depend on Social Security for the majority of their income, this is not an adjustment. It is a crisis.

The economic transmission is immediate and quantifiable. Social Security benefits generate substantial economic activity. In 2023, $1.38 trillion in bene-fits generated $2.6 trillion in total economic output and supported $1.6 trillion in GDP.[4] A 24 percent benefit cut reduces benefits by approximately $331 billion annually in 2025 dollars. This is not merely a transfer from government to retirees that stops. It is consumption that disappears from the economy.

Economic research on fiscal multipliers shows that the impact of reduced government spending on GDP is amplified during recessions and particularly severe for transfers to households with high marginal propensities to consume.[5] Elderly households depending on Social Security spend most of their benefits immediately on necessities. Using a conservative multiplier of 1.3, a $331 billion benefit cut produces a $430 billion GDP reduction in the first year. Federal revenue averages 17.5 percent of GDP.[6] A $430 billion GDP decline translates to approximately $75 billion in lost annual tax revenue. Over five years, the revenue loss exceeds $375 billion, adding directly to the deficit.

Additionally, automatic stabilizers activate during recession. Unemployment insurance, Medicaid, and food assistance programs expand as economic condi-tions deteriorate, adding roughly $150 billion annually at the peak.[7] The total deficit increase from allowing cuts to take effect: over $200 billion annually while the crisis persists. This additional deficit increases debt substantially over five years. At a 4 percent interest rate, this debt generates tens of billions in additional annual interest costs. The costs compound indefinitely thereafter.

The political outcome is equally clear. Voters aged 50 and older represented 55 percent of the electorate in competitive congressional districts in the 2024 election and 61 percent in the 2022 midterms.[8] Among this demographic, 90 percent say Social Security is very important to them.[9] The party in power when cuts hit faces electoral annihilation. This is why letting the automatic cuts happen, while producing the cleanest long-term fiscal outcome, will not happen. The immediate political cost exceeds what any majority can tolerate.

The second option is emergency borrowing. Congress passes emergency legislation authorizing additional borrowing to cover the Social Security shortfall, maintaining scheduled benefits without immediate cuts or tax increases. This approach minimizes immediate pain while transferring costs to future administrations. The political incentive structure makes this the most probable path.

Historical analysis of Congressional crisis response reveals a consistent pattern. Immediate statutory deadlines force bipartisan action. The 1983 Social Security reform occurred only when trust fund depletion was imminent, creating a credible political cost for inaction that transcended partisan gridlock.[10] The National Commission on Social Security Reform succeeded because the approaching insolvency deadline was measured in months, not years, forcing leaders to implement politically difficult choices including delayed cost-of-living adjustments and increased payroll taxes.[11]

Conversely, slow-building structural problems generate partisan paralysis. The Simpson-Bowles Commission drafted a technically sound blueprint for comprehensive fiscal reform in 2010, combining $2.6 trillion in revenue increases with $2.9 trillion in spending cuts over ten years.[12] Despite technical soundness, the political consensus necessary for adoption never materialized. Analysis of this failure suggests negotiations broke down because the political environment incentivized leaders to prioritize partisan advantage over compromise.[13] Because the deficit problem, while massive, was perceived as slow-building and long-term, partisan polarization prevailed.[13] This pattern was reinforced by the subsequent failure of the 2011 Super Committee, where even the statutory threat of $1.2 trillion in automatic sequestration was insufficient to compel action when public attention was disengaged and the deadline felt distant.[14]

Research suggests the functional crisis imminence threshold for Congressional action is under five years. The 2033 Social Security deadline falls into this category, an unavoidable statutory trigger arriving under conditions far worse than 1983. But unlike 1983, when the problem was half the current magnitude and political polarization was lower, today's required adjustment of $9.0 trillion in deficit reduction over 2025-2035 creates electoral annihilation risk for any party that proposes comprehensive reform combining both revenue increases and benefit cuts.[15]

The rational choice for politicians optimizing for re-election cycles of two to six years is emergency borrowing. It delays visible pain, allows leaders to claim they saved Social Security, and makes the problem someone else's responsibility. Future Congresses can tell themselves they will address the underlying problem before the borrowed money runs out. They will face the same incentive structure that prevents action today, now with a larger problem and fewer available solutions.

The quantified cost of this delay is permanent and exponential. If comprehensive fiscal reform is delayed by ten years until 2035, the required average primary surplus needed to stabilize debt over the subsequent decades increases from 4.3 percent of GDP to 5.1 percent of GDP.[16] This represents a 0.8 percentage point increase in the permanent required adjustment, equivalent to roughly $200 billion per year forever in 2025 dollars. This difference arises because debt accrues interest at an accelerated rate on an ever-larger principal base during the period of delay, forcing all subsequent generations to bear a greater policy burden.

The fiscal trajectory is also acutely vulnerable to interest rate fluctuations. With federal debt at approximately 100 percent of GDP, small changes in borrowing costs translate to massive impacts. Congressional Budget Office estimates show that if interest rates were just 0.1 percentage point higher across the yield curve each year than currently projected, cumulative deficits over

2026-2035 would increase by $351 billion.[17] Of this total, $319 billion represents direct interest cost increases, with the remainder coming from compounding effects as higher interest payments themselves require additional borrowing.

Emergency borrowing in 2033 to prevent benefit cuts could trigger a market response that raises borrowing costs. At current debt levels, even a modest 50 basis point increase in rates would add hundreds of billions to the deficit over the following decade. Markets could interpret large-scale emergency borrowing not as fiscal strength but as an act of desperation, potentially triggering the Type C confidence crisis described in Chapter 3. Whether this occurs depends on variables including global economic conditions, Federal Reserve policy, and the scale of borrowing relative to market expectations. What is certain is that emergency borrowing does not solve the underlying problem. It delays the reckoning while making it mathematically worse.

The third option is emergency tax increases or benefit reductions sufficient to restore solvency immediately. This represents managed crisis response rather than proactive reform. The adjustments would be larger than if enacted earlier, as each year of delay increases the required correction. Achieving 75-year solvency requires the equivalent of either a 29 percent payroll tax increase or a 22 percent reduction in total benefits, or more realistically some combination of both.[18]

Consider what this means in practice. The current combined employer-employee payroll tax rate for Social Security is 12.4 percent of wages up to the taxable maximum of $176,100.[19] A 29 percent increase would raise the rate to approximately 16 percent, an additional 3.6 percentage points split between workers and employers. For a worker earning $60,000 annually, this translates to over $2,100 more per year in payroll taxes. Alternatively, a 22 percent benefit reduction means the average monthly benefit of $1,924 drops to approximately $1,501, a loss of over $420 per month or more than $5,000 annually. For dual-earning couples, the loss approaches $10,000 per year.

Immediate tax increases on this scale would drag down economic growth, potentially triggering recession. Immediate benefit cuts would impose severe hardship on current retirees who lack time to compensate through additional savings or delayed retirement. Either approach, or any combination, would be enacted under maximum political duress with minimal time for gradual phase-ins or exemptions for vulnerable populations. The required adjustment grows exponentially with delay while the political capacity to implement it does not expand.

The most likely outcome is emergency borrowing. Kicking the problem five to ten years further down the road. This choice minimizes immediate political pain while making the eventual reckoning worse. It is also the path of least resistance, requiring only a single emergency authorization rather than the sustained political coalition necessary for comprehensive reform.

Regardless of which option Congress chooses, economic contraction is guaranteed. If cuts happen, elderly consumption collapses. If emergency taxes are imposed, working-age consumption falls. If emergency borrowing occurs and triggers rate increases, investment declines. The transmission mechanisms differ but the outcome converges: recession.

The severity of this recession will exceed the Great Recession of 2007-2009 because the fiscal tools that mitigated that crisis no longer function. Empirical research on fiscal multipliers in high-debt environments provides quantitative evidence for this projection. A study analyzing 44 countries found that fiscal multipliers in high-debt countries are negative, meaning attempted fiscal stimulus contracts output rather than expanding it.[20] This occurs because high government debt activates Ricardian effects where forward-looking households anticipate higher future taxes and increase savings rather than consumption, offsetting the intended stimulus. High debt also crowds out private investment by raising long-term interest rates as government borrowing competes for available savings.[21]

The United States enters the 2033 crisis with federal debt exceeding 100 percent of GDP, well into the range where research documents negative multiplier effects. This is compounded by household debt levels. Research using data across major economies found that high household debt reduces the fiscal multiplier by 0.79 on impact, meaning the stimulative effect of government spending is reduced by nearly 0.8 when household leverage is elevated.[22] Corporate debt presents similar constraints. Public investment stimulus fails to crowd in private investment for firms with high debt levels, likely because high corporate debt increases perceived risk of future profits and bankruptcy.[23]

The structural combination of these factors, sovereign debt exceeding 100 percent of GDP, high household leverage, and elevated corporate debt, means that the primary tool of counter-cyclical policy has been neutralized. When recession hits in 2033, whether triggered by benefit cuts, tax increases, or emergency borrowing that spikes rates, the government cannot respond effectively. The fiscal stimulus that helped limit the Great Recession to 10 percent unemployment and enabled recovery, however slow, will not work. The multiplier suppression research provides empirical grounding for projecting unemployment in the 15 to 20 percent range, worse than the Great Recession but potentially less severe than the Great Depression's 25 percent because baseline social infrastructure remains intact.[24]

The Great Recession itself provides a sobering baseline for recovery timelines. Despite massive fiscal intervention through TARP and the American Recovery and Reinvestment Act, and starting from federal debt of only approximately 65 percent of GDP, unemployment took seven to nine years to return to pre-crisis levels.[25] The unemployment rate surged from 4.7 percent in July 2007 to a peak of 10.0 percent in late 2009, then did not return to its pre-recession low of 4.1 percent until December 2017.[25]

Congressional Budget Office analysis attributed two-thirds of the slow recovery to structural factors, specifically slower growth in the economy's underlying productive capacity driven by demographic trends and productivity constraints.[26] The remaining one-third stemmed from weak aggregate demand, with purchases by state and local governments accounting for the largest portion of demand weakness.[26] The 2033 crisis begins with federal debt at 100 percent of GDP, eliminating capacity for comparable stimulus due to the multiplier suppression documented above. Meanwhile, demographic headwinds intensify. CBO projects that deaths will exceed births in the United States starting as early as 2031, meaning the population will contain fewer people in prime working age than previously projected, further constraining potential economic growth.[27]

This combination of worse starting conditions, eliminated fiscal capacity, and intensifying structural drag makes the seven to nine year recovery timeline from the Great Recession a minimum expectation rather than an upper bound. Whether recovery takes one decade or two depends on variables including the severity of the initial shock, global economic conditions, and whether technological productivity gains can offset demographic decline. What is structurally certain is that the tools that enabled even the slow Great Recession recovery no longer function at necessary scale.

The transmission from federal fiscal crisis to municipal stress begins immediately but operates on delayed timelines that ensure pain persists long after the triggering recession has officially ended. Municipal governments depend on three primary revenue sources: sales taxes, income taxes, and property taxes. Each responds to economic crisis on different schedules.

Sales tax revenue collapses immediately as consumer spending falls. When unemployment rises and elderly benefits are cut or working-age taxes increase, retail activity declines sharply. During the Great Recession, state and local sales tax revenues contracted by 2.6 to 4.6 percent.[28] Income tax revenue follows a similar immediate pattern. State personal income tax revenues contracted by 10.3 percent during the Great Recession years.[28] These revenue sources provide real-time feedback on economic conditions.

Property tax revenue operates differently. Research analyzing the 2000-2020 period quantifies the lag mechanism. Property tax revenues remain stable even during periods of significant real estate market volatility. On average, a 1 percent change in market property values produces less than a 0.30 percent change in assessed values over the next three years.[29] This disconnect appears strategic rather than incidental, as counties are significantly more likely to reassess properties upward during market growth than to reduce assessments during a downturn. Changes in total property tax revenue correlate more strongly with changes in local per-capita income than with property market returns.[29]

Case studies from the 2008 housing crisis confirm this timeline. In jurisdictions that experienced housing cycles similar to the national average, assessed values continued to rise through 2008 and only flattened out in 2009, long after actual house prices had begun their sharp decline.30 During the Great Recession years, property tax collections actually increased by 6.3 percent while sales and income taxes were contracting sharply.[28] This unexpected resilience in property tax revenues initially masked the full extent of local fiscal shock.

The delayed fiscal cascade arrives in years two through five after the initial crisis. Property values that declined in 2033 and 2034 finally enter assessment cycles in 2035 through 2037. Reduced assessed valuations translate directly to reduced property tax revenue. This is compounded by rising delinquencies as unemployed homeowners fall behind on payments. The mechanism guarantees that municipal austerity, which CBO identified as a major drag on the post-2008 recovery, persists for three to five years after the national economy has theoretically begun recovering.

Municipal governments facing this revenue collapse must cut spending. The initial response involves deferring capital and infrastructure maintenance expenditures, which provides short-term budgetary relief while guaranteeing acceleration of long-term decay and higher eventual costs.[31] Discretionary programs like parks, libraries, and community services are eliminated quickly as sales tax revenues fall. These cuts are politically feasible but quantitatively insufficient to address structural deficits.

Personnel costs, including salaries, benefits, pensions, and related compensation, are often the single largest expenditure item in municipal budgets and in many cities account for a majority of general-fund expenditures.[32] Structural insolvency eventually forces reductions in core services. The first major target is Other Post-Employment Benefits, predominantly retiree healthcare. The Detroit bankruptcy precedent demonstrated that approximately 90 percent of retiree healthcare costs were eliminated during the Chapter 9 process, transferring financial burden directly onto individual retirees while generating billions in savings.[33]

Once maintenance has been deferred and retiree benefits eliminated, the only remaining option is cutting current personnel. Police and fire departments, despite their critical role in maintaining social order, are major cost centers. Education budgets face similar pressure. When these cuts hit public safety, they initiate what Chapter 7 will document as an irreversible feedback loop. Criminological research demonstrates that police presence directly reduces crime, with studies utilizing natural experiments showing that blocks adjacent to areas receiving increased patrol experienced approximately 45 to 60 percent fewer crimes.[34] Personnel cuts produce predictable, quantifiable crime increases. Crime spikes coupled with degraded schools destroy the core value proposition of urban living, triggering middle-class exodus that collapses the tax base and accelerates fiscal crisis.

The municipal stress beginning in 2033 does not produce immediate bankruptcy. It initiates a multi-year degradation sequence where revenue collapse forces service cuts that trigger demographic flight that worsens revenue problems in a compounding spiral. Chapter 7 will examine this mechanism in detail, showing which cities face highest probability of entering this death spiral and why federal intervention capacity has vanished.

Understanding the 2033 collision requires recognizing what makes modern America structurally different from the last time the nation faced comparable unemployment levels. The Great Depression produced 25 percent unemployment without triggering civil war or complete social breakdown.[24] Social order proved more resilient than catastrophic narratives suggested. But the population that endured the Great Depression possessed structural characteristics that no longer exist at comparable scale.

In 1930, the median age of the United States population was 26.5 years.[35] By 2020, median age had risen to approximately 39 years.[36] The 1930s population was younger, more dynamic, and had a higher proportion of working-age individuals relative to the elderly. Modern America is significantly older, amplifying economic dependency burdens. The younger population of the 1930s could adapt, migrate, and rebuild more readily than an aging population concentrated in fixed housing with accumulated obligations.

The geographic structure differed fundamentally. Historical context indicates a higher percentage of the population lived in rural areas or smaller towns during the 1930s. Modern America is over 80 percent urbanized, increasing reliance on formal economic structures, centralized supply chains, and bureaucratic safety nets, all vulnerable to impairment during deep crisis. Rural populations in the 1930s possessed resilience buffers related to subsistence farming and local resource pooling that urban populations cannot replicate.

Sociological research documents significant generational changes in social capital since the 1930s. Despite the hardships of the Great Depression, children of that era were characterized by researchers as resilient, resourceful, and some of the most upwardly mobile cohorts of the twentieth century, supported by high levels of civic engagement and generalized trust typical of the pre-1960s era.[37] Contemporary research confirms downward trends in generalized trust and social capital since that peak, with younger cohorts reporting significantly less trust in most people than older cohorts.[37] Social capital, defined as norms of reciprocity and trustworthiness arising from social networks, is crucial for getting by during stressful periods.[37] The documented decline suggests modern populations possess fundamentally weaker capacity for community absorption of massive economic shocks.

Multi-generational households have seen recent resurgence, growing to 18 percent of the population in 2021.[38] This growth occurs from a low historical baseline and may still represent a smaller structural buffer than the 1930s when multi-generational living was often the norm, providing built-in economic cushioning. The structural combination of an older, less dynamic population and weakened social capital acts as a social vulnerability multiplier. Whether these differences make modern America more vulnerable to economic stress than Depression-era America remains an open question. What is certain is that the buffers that allowed 25 percent unemployment without social collapse no longer exist at the same scale.

In 2033, the silence breaks not because politicians suddenly develop courage or media discovers sustained focus or experts decide career risk is acceptable. The silence breaks because the statutory deadline makes silence operationally impossible. More than 74 million Americans will receive notices that their benefits are being reduced. Congress will vote on emergency measures. Markets will react to whatever choice emerges. The crisis shifts from theoretical to compulsory.

The choice Congress makes, most likely emergency borrowing based on historical patterns and incentive analysis, determines the timeline. Emergency borrowing delays the full reckoning five to ten years, to 2038 through 2043, while making the eventual adjustment mathematically harder through the exponential cost of delay. Allowing cuts triggers immediate recession and elderly poverty. Emergency taxes create immediate economic contraction. All roads lead to severe downturn. The only question is whether the pain concentrates in 2033 or spreads across the following decade.

What is guaranteed is that 2033 marks the moment when the middle class feels economic pain directly for the first time. Before 2033, the crisis remained abstract, affecting government-dependent sectors invisible to most Americans. After 2033, regardless of which option Congress chooses, recession hits. Unemployment rises into ranges that historical research suggests could reach 15 to 20 percent. Asset values fall as retirement accounts and housing prices decline. Parents and grandparents lose income. The fiscal crisis becomes personal, immediate, and unavoidable.

And that economic pain transmits immediately to state and local governments whose revenues collapse just as their fixed costs continue growing. The municipal cascade does not start in 2033. But 2033 is when the revenue collapse begins that makes the cascade inevitable.

CHAPTER 6 NOTES

1. Social Security Administration, "A Summary of the 2025 Annual Reports," June 2025, https://www.ssa.gov/oact/TRSUM/index.html. ("The Old-Age and Survivors Insurance (OASI) Trust Fund will be able to pay 100 percent of total scheduled benefits until 2033. At that time, the fund's reserves will become depleted and continuing program income will be sufficient to pay 77 percent of total scheduled benefits.") Committee for a Responsible Federal Budget, "As Social Security Turns 90, It's Racing Towards Insolvency," August 14, 2025, https://www.crfb.org/blogs/social-security-turns-90-its-racing-towards-insolvency. ("all current and new retired beneficiaries, regardless of age or income, will face an across-the-board 24 percent benefit cut when the retirement trust fund is depleted.") Social Security Administration, "Monthly Statistical Snapshot," August 2025, https://www.ssa.gov/policy/docs/quickfacts/stat_snapshot/. Table 1 shows 74,521,000 total beneficiaries.

2. Committee for a Responsible Federal Budget, "As Social Security Turns 90, It's Racing Towards Insolvency," August 14, 2025. ("we estimate a typical couple retiring shortly after the trust fund runs out will face an $18,400 benefit cut... a typical single-earner couple would face a $13,800 cut.")

3. Social Security Administration, "Monthly Statistical Snapshot," October 2024, https://www.ssa.gov/policy/docs/quickfacts/stat_snapshot/2024-10.html. Table 2 shows average monthly benefit for retired workers was $1,924.35 as of October 2024.

4. National Institute on Retirement Security, "New Research Finds Social Security Has a Strong Economic Impact," 2024, https://www.nirsonline.org/articles/new-research-economic-i

mpact-social-security/. ("Social Security benefits play a powerful role in supporting the U.S. economy, generating $2.6 trillion in total economic output and supporting more than 12 million American jobs in 2023 alone... $1.38 trillion in benefits paid to more than 67 million beneficiaries supported $804.6 billion in labor income, $1.6 trillion in value added (GDP), and $363 billion in tax revenues.")

5. Alan J. Auerbach and Yuriy Gorodnichenko, "Fiscal Multipliers in Recession and Expansion," NBER Working Paper No. 17447 (September 2011), https://www.nber.org/system/files/working_papers/w17447/w17447.pdf. ("GDP multipliers of government purchases are larger in recession, and controlling for real-time predictions of government purchases tends to increase the estimated multipliers of government purchases in recession.")

6. Congressional Budget Office, "The Budget and Economic Outlook: 2025 to 2035," January 2025, Table 1-2, https://www.cbo.gov/publication/61172.

7. Congressional Budget Office, "The Effects of Automatic Stabilizers on the Federal Budget," March 2013, https://www.cbo.gov/publication/43977.

8. AARP, "New AARP Post-Election Poll of Competitive Congressional Districts Shows Older Voters Prioritized Economic Concerns," news release, November 15, 2024, https://www.prnewswire.com/news-releases/new-aarp-post-election-poll-of-competitive-congressional-districts-shows-older-voters-prioritized-economic-concerns-302307272.html. ("Voters ages 50 and older were key in the 2024 election. Data shows that across the country, older voters made up 55% of the electorate.") See also AARP, "AARP Poll of 63 Most Competitive Congressional Districts Shows Older Voters Were the Deciders in 2022," news release, November 17, 2022, https://press.aarp.org/2022-11-17-AARP-Post-Election-Survey.

("Overall, voters 50+ accounted for 61% of the electorate in these key districts.")

9. AARP Research Center, "Social Security 2024 Survey of Voters Ages 50+," November 2024, https://www.aarp.org/pri/topics/voter-rese arch/politics/voter-preferences-2024-battleground-states/. ("Around 90% said they would be more likely to vote for a candidate who pledged to make sure workers get the Social Security they paid into.")

10. Social Security Administration, "Report of the National Commission on Social Security Reform," January 1983, https://www.ssa.gov/his tory/reports/gspan.html.

11. Social Security Administration, "1983 Greenspan Commission on Social Security Reform," https://www.ssa.gov/history/reports/gspa n7.html.

12. Richard Kogan, "What Was Actually in Bowles-Simpson, And How Can We Compare it With Other Plans?," Center on Budget and Policy Priorities, October 2, 2012, https://www.cbpp.org/research/what-was-actually-in-bowles -simpson-and-how-can-we-compare-it-with-other-plans. ("The plan proposed $2.6 trillion in revenue increases and $2.9 trillion in spend-ing cuts over ten years, a nearly balanced approach to deficit redu ction... 53 percent from budget cuts and 47 percent from revenue increases.")

13. Brookings Institution, "It's not the economy, stupid—it's failed pol-itics!," https://www.brookings.edu/articles/its-not-the-economy-stu pid-its-failed-politics/.

14. Manhattan Institute, "Getting To Yes: A History Of Why Budget Negotiations Succeed, And Why They Fail," https://manhattan.institute/article/getting-to-yes-a-history-of

-why-budget-negotiations-succeed-and-why-they-fail.

15. Committee for a Responsible Federal Budget, "Meeting Fiscal Goals Under CBO's January 2025 Baseline," January 29, 2025, https://www.crfb.org/blogs/meeting-fiscal-goals-under-cbos-january-2025-baseline. ("Stabilizing debt over the next decade at its current share of the economy would require $9.0 trillion of deficit reduction.")

16. U.S. Department of the Treasury, "Financial Report of the United States Government," FY2024, Table 6: Costs of Delaying Fiscal Reform, https://fiscal.treasury.gov/reports-statements/financial-report/mda-unsustainable-fiscal-path.html. ("Immediate reform would require increasing primary surpluses by 4.3 percent of GDP on average between 2025 and 2099... if policy reform is delayed by 10 years, closing the fiscal gap requires increasing the primary surpluses by 5.1 percent of GDP on average between 2035 and 2099.")

17. Congressional Budget Office, "How Changes in Economic Conditions Might Affect the Federal Budget: 2025 to 2035," April 2025, https://www.cbo.gov/publication/61198. ("If all interest rates on Treasury securities were just 0.1 percentage point higher each year than projected in the baseline, the cumulative deficit over the 2026-2035 period would be $351 billion larger than projected.")

18. Committee for a Responsible Federal Budget, "Analysis of the 2025 Social Security Trustees' Report," June 18, 2025, https://www.crfb.org/papers/analysis-2025-social-security-trustees-report. ("A plan to restore solvency will require the equivalent of at least a 22 percent reduction in benefits for current and future beneficiaries, a 29 percent increase in payroll taxes, or some combination of the two.")

19. Social Security Administration, "2025 Social Security Changes," https://www.ssa.gov/news/press/factsheets/colafacts2025.pdf. The 2025

taxable maximum is $176,100. The combined employer-employee Social Security tax rate is 12.4 percent (6.2 percent each).

20. Ethan Ilzetzki, Enrique G. Mendoza, and Carlos A. Végh, "How big (small?) are fiscal multipliers?," Journal of Monetary Economics 60, no. 2 (2013): 239-254, https://ideas.repec.org/a/eee/moneco/v60y2013i2p239-254.html. ("the output effect of an increase in government consumption is larger in industrial than in developing countries; the fiscal multiplier is relatively large in economies operating under predetermined exchange rates but is zero in economies operating under flexible exchange rates; fiscal multipliers in open economies are smaller than in closed economies; fiscal multipliers in high-debt countries are negative.")

21. Michael Falkenheim, "The Welfare Effects of Debt: Crowding Out and Risk Shifting," Congressional Budget Office Working Paper 2023-06, September 2023, https://www.cbo.gov/publication/58849. The study extends Olivier Blanchard's 2019 analysis by decomposing welfare effects into crowding-out and risk-shifting components, finding that the crowding-out effect of debt on welfare is consistently negative.

22. Xi Chen et al., "Does household debt affect the size of the fiscal multiplier?," Macroeconomic Dynamics (2024), https://www.cambridge.org/core/journals/macroeconomic-dynamics/article/does-household-debt-affect-the-size-of-the-fiscal-multiplier/E0085C862359FAD3151EAB5ED42606E7. ("the fiscal multiplier (on impact) is 0.70, 0.61, and 0.79 (percent of GDP) larger when the increase in government spending takes place during periods of low household debt for Australia, Norway, and the United States.")

23. Selim Kalemli-Özcan et al., "The Fiscal Multiplier of Public Investment: The Role of Corporate Balance Sheet," IMF Working Paper No. 20/199 (September 2020), https://www.imf.org/-/media/Files/

Publications/WP/2020/English/wpiea2020199-print-pdf.ashx. ("the effect of public investment on corporate investment depends both on leverage and financial constraints. Public investment boosts private investment for firms with low leverage. However, for firms with high leverage, private investment does not react to an increase in public investment.")

24. Congressional Research Service, "Unemployment During the Great Depression," Report R40655, https://www.everycrsreport.com/rep orts/R40655.html. ("The unemployment rate rose from 3.2% in 1929 to 24.9% in 1933 during the Great Depression's more severe first do wnturn.")

25. Bureau of Labor Statistics, "Great Recession, great recovery? Trends from the Current Population Survey," Monthly Labor Review, 2018, https://www.bls.gov/opub/mlr/2018/article/great-reces sion-great-recovery.htm.

26. Congressional Budget Office, "What Accounts for the Slow Growth of the Economy After the Recession?," November 2012, https:// www.cbo.gov/publication/43707. ("About two-thirds of that difference is attributable to slower growth in the economy's underlying productive capacity—a measure known as potential GDP—reflecting long-term trends that are unrelated to the business cycle... The remaining one-third of the difference... signifies a shortfall in aggregate demand.")

27. Congressional Budget Office, "An Update to the Demographic Outlook, 2025 to 2055," https://www.cbo.gov/publication/61390. CBO projects deaths will exceed births starting as early as 2031.

28. Lincoln Institute of Land Policy, "Property tax delinquencies' effects on revenue volatility in American cities," 2016, https://cslf.gsu.edu/files/2016/05/Krupa-and-Kriz_2016-Pu

blic-Finance-Conference-Paper.pdf.

29. National Bureau of Economic Research, "Property Tax Assessments vs Market Values," NBER Digest, March 2025, https://www.nber.or g/digest/202503/property-tax-assessments-vs-market-values. The research finds property tax revenues remain stable even during significant real estate market volatility, with changes in market values explaining only about 8 percent of the variation in assessment growth.

30. Federal Reserve, "The Housing Crisis and State and Local Government Tax Revenue: Five Channels," FEDS Working Paper 2010-49, h ttps://www.federalreserve.gov/pubs/feds/2010/201049/index.html.

31. International Monetary Fund, "Managing Fiscal Stress," in Public Expenditure Management, https://www.elibrary.imf.org/display/bo ok/9781557753236/ch03.xml. ("Experience shows that governments tend to defer capital outlays and some social outlays to the future. Operation and maintenance expenditures may also be deferred to better times. All these approaches will have the effect of reducing the rate of development, forgoing social welfare, and adding to the future costs of maintenance or replacement of assets.")

32. Government Finance Officers Association, "Best Practice: Personnel Budgeting," https://www.gfoa.org/materials/personnel-budgeting. ("The personnel budget typically makes up a significant portion of the operating budget and for many governments can be its largest expenditure.") See also Bureau of Labor Statistics, "State and local government compensation costs average $52.94 per hour worked in September   2020," https://www.bls.gov/opub/ted/2020/state-and-local-government-co mpensation-costs-average-52-94-per-hour-worked-in-september-202 0.htm.

33. Detroit bankruptcy proceedings involved $18-20 billion in debt and

resulted in substantial reductions to retiree healthcare obligations. See Pew Charitable Trusts, "Fiscal Health of Large U.S. Cities Varied Long After Great Recession's End," April 2016, https://www.pew.org/en/research-and-analysis/issue-briefs/2016/04/fiscal-health-of-large-us-cities-varied-long-after-great-recessions-end.

34. Johns Hopkins Public Safety, "The Effect of Privately Provided Police Services on Crime: Evidence from a Geographic Regression Discontinuity Design," https://publicsafety.jhu.edu/assets/uploads/sites/9/2024/12/effect_of_privately_provided_police_services_on_crime.pdf. ("We find that the extra police provided by the university generated approximately 45-60 percent fewer crimes in adjacent city blocks.")

35. U.S. Census Bureau, "Population by Age, Sex, Race, and Hispanic or Latino Origin for the United States: 2000," Census 2000 PHC-T-9, Table 7: Median Age of the Population: 1820 to 2000, https://www2.census.gov/programs-surveys/decennial/2000/phc/phc-t-09/tab07.pdf.

36. U.S. Census Bureau, "Median Age: United States, 2000 to 2020," National Demographic Characteristics Tables, https://www.census.gov/data/tables/time-series/demo/popest/2020s-national-detail.html.

37. National Institutes of Health, "The Effects of the Great Depression on Children's Intergenerational Mobility," PMC, https://pmc.ncbi.nlm.nih.gov/articles/PMC11395574/. ("Despite these hardships, children of the Great Depression were resilient, resourceful, and some of the most upwardly mobile cohorts of the twentieth century.") See also Robert D. Putnam, Bowling Alone: The Collapse and Revival of American Community (New York: Simon & Schuster, 2000); Robert D. Putnam and Shaylyn Romney Garrett, The Upswing: How America Came Together a Century Ago and How We Can Do It Again (New York: Simon & Schuster, 2020).

38. Pew Research Center, "The demographics of multigenerational households," March 24, 2022, https://www.pewresearch.org/social-trends/2022/03/24/the-demographics-of-multigenerational-households/.

Chapter 7

2033-2040 - The Municipal Cascade

B y 2030, Chicago will be unable to pay its police force. This is not prediction. It is documented fiscal trajectory. The city owes $35.9 billion to its pension funds, with police and fire plans funded at just 24.5 percent.[1] Illinois law prohibits municipal bankruptcy under Chapter 9, forcing the already fiscally stressed state to absorb local failures or allow uncontrolled service degradation.[2] The State of Illinois cannot provide rescue. It carries its own debt burden requiring $38,800 per taxpayer to cover obligations.[3] The federal government cannot provide rescue without triggering sovereign crisis, entering the collision with debt at 100 percent of GDP and running structural deficits approaching $2 trillion annually.[4]

The question is not whether Chicago fails. The question is what happens when it does, and whether the failure remains isolated or cascades across dozens of cities simultaneously.

The fiscal crisis will not manifest as nationwide collapse. It will manifest as synchronized municipal bankruptcies in a compressed timeframe, triggered by mechanisms fundamentally different from the slow institutional decay that characterized Detroit's decades-long decline. Detroit took thirty years to reach bankruptcy in 2013, a gradual erosion driven by population loss, industrial collapse, and municipal mismanagement.[5] The coming cascade operates on a different timeline because it is triggered by an external private-sector shock rather than gradual internal failure.

That shock is already visible in loan maturity schedules. In 2025 alone, $957 billion in commercial real estate loans come due, a volume nearly triple the twenty-year average.[6] Work-from-home arrangements, initially positioned as temporary pandemic responses, have proven permanent. Office buildings have lost approximately 40 percent of their value, creating a massive refinancing crisis as properties cannot support the debt loads they carry at current valuations and elevated interest rates.[7] The losses must be absorbed somewhere in the financial system.

They will be absorbed primarily by regional banks, the institutions holding disproportionate exposure to commercial real estate relative to their capital bases. Analysis of bank balance sheets using Federal Deposit Insurance Corporation call report data reveals a critical structural vulnerability. The largest depository institutions by assets allocate less than one percent of their total portfolios to municipal securities. Regional banks have historically allocated as much as 17 percent of assets to municipal bonds due to their greater tolerance for interest-rate risk.[8] This concentration exists because municipal securities offer tax-exempt income, providing significant value for institutions with large tax liabilities and limited geographic diversification.

This structural imbalance creates a direct transmission channel. When regional banks face commercial real estate losses, they must reduce balance sheet risk across all holdings. Municipal bonds become a primary target for asset reduction. The secondary municipal bond market operates with significantly less liquidity than Treasury or corporate bond markets. Even modest coordinated selling pressure from a handful of regional institutions holding concentrated municipal positions can overwhelm market capacity rapidly, driving municipal prices down and forcing yields up across the board. Recent peer-reviewed research confirms that municipal bond yields respond sharply to changes in bank balance sheet conditions, with tightening bank demand translating into higher borrowing costs for municipal issuers regardless of their intrinsic credit quality.[9]

The 2008 financial crisis provides empirical evidence of how quickly this transmission operates. The municipal bond market experienced near-total dysfunction within weeks of peak banking stress. The SIFMA Municipal Swap Index yield, a key indicator of liquidity and risk pricing, surged from 1.63 percent on September 3, 2008 to 7.96 percent on September 24, 2008.[10] This represents an exponential increase in the cost of short-term municipal funding in just three weeks, indicating nearly complete market paralysis. By December 2008, AAA-rated ten-year municipal yields reached 4.22 percent, trading 145 basis points higher than comparable Treasury yields of 2.77 percent.[10] For highly-rated municipal debt to trade at yields substantially above risk-free federal securities confirms that market participants were pricing in an overwhelming liquidity premium, effectively eliminating the fundamental value proposition of municipal bonds: the federal tax exemption.

The 2008 crisis also revealed the absence of a dedicated federal backstop for municipal finance. While the Federal Reserve introduced unprecedented facilities for banks and the Treasury implemented the $475 billion Troubled Asset Relief Program, these interventions focused overwhelmingly on stabilizing the banking and corporate sectors.[11] State and local governments received no preemptive federal liquidity facility, forcing them to manage the acute liquidity crisis through immediate fiscal contraction. Between December 2007 and November 2010, local governments collectively reduced their workforces by 241,000 employees, a 1.7 percent reduction.[12] These cuts continued for years after the official end of the Great Recession, a distinctive feature of municipal response demonstrating that the cost of crisis was immediately transferred to public services rather than absorbed by federal intervention.[13]

Historical precedent confirms this pattern. When New York City faced fiscal crisis in 1975, President Ford initially opposed federal assistance but ultimately signed the New York City Seasonal Financing Act, authorizing up to $2.3 billion annually in short-term federal loans.[14] These were not grants or bailouts. The loans required the city to repay the full amount by the end of each fiscal year and carried interest rates set at one percent above federal securities. The intervention enforced fiscal discipline rather than absorbing debt. Detroit's 2013 bankruptcy, the largest municipal filing in U.S. history, received no direct federal loan or bailout to prevent its Chapter 9 filing.[5] Constitutional barriers prevent the federal government from imposing solutions or offering direct bailouts without state consent. Chapter 9 bankruptcy itself requires state permission before a municipality can file for relief.[2] The federal bankruptcy court cannot, without the municipal debtor's consent, interfere with political or governmental powers or property, explicitly protecting the city's right to set tax rates and determine service levels.[2]

This legal architecture means that when the commercial real estate crisis triggers regional bank stress in 2025 through 2027, and regional bank stress freezes municipal bond markets, and frozen markets force cities into acute borrowing crises, the federal government lacks both the fiscal capacity and the constitutional authority to prevent the cascade. The capacity that enabled 2008-scale responses has vanished. Attempting municipal rescues on the scale required, hundreds of billions to address multiple failing cities simultaneously, would trigger what bond markets term a rising-yields scenario, where intervention signals fiscal desperation rather than strength. What is certain is that the fiscal space enabling 2008 responses no longer exists.

When municipal borrowing costs spike and access to capital markets constricts, cities cannot simply wait for conditions to improve. They carry massive structural liabilities that demand immediate funding regardless of market conditions. The largest of these liabilities are pension obligations, legally protected by state constitutional clauses or powerful statutes that make them effectively non-impairable even in bankruptcy restructuring.

Chicago's pension crisis illustrates the magnitude of this structural trap. The city's pension funded ratio collapsed from 52 percent in 2009 to 23 percent by 2015, while total pension debt nearly tripled from $12 billion to $34 billion .[15] This level of liability relative to funding ratio places immense pressure on operating budgets, crowding out spending on everything else. Chicago is not isolated in vulnerability. Research confirms that cities funded below 50 percent in 2009 or falling into that category by 2015 include Charleston, Pittsburgh, Providence, and Omaha.[15] The persistent fiscal distress in these cities demonstrates the immense difficulty of recovering poorly funded plans, particularly when governments fail to meet actuarially required contributions.

The legal environment governing these obligations has shifted dramatically over the past century. Many critical states protect pension benefits through explicit constitutional clauses or statutes. The Illinois Constitution states that membership in any pension or retirement system "shall be an enforceable contractual relationship, the benefits of which shall not be diminished or impaired ."[16] Connecticut statutes explicitly mandate that rights or benefits granted under any municipal retirement system "shall not be diminished or eliminated."[16] This legal inflexibility dictates that the adjustment mechanism for dealing with overwhelming fiscal deficits must fall almost entirely onto deep expenditure cuts or substantial tax increases, which inevitably leads to service degradation and demographic flight.

Detroit's bankruptcy attempted to challenge this legal framework, with the Emergency Manager arguing that federal bankruptcy law allowed cutting pension obligations despite Michigan's state constitutional prohibition.[5] The legal battle highlighted a fundamental question: whether state constitutional protections take precedence over the federal bankruptcy court's debt adjustment powers. The uncertainty this created extends to all cities in states with robust constitutional pension protections, particularly those like Illinois that also prohibit Chapter 9 access entirely. For these jurisdictions, the largest liability is effectively fixed and non-negotiable, forcing all fiscal adjustment onto the operating budget.

The sequencing of municipal cuts follows a predictable pattern once fiscal stress becomes acute. Local governments first defer capital and infrastructure maintenance expenditures. This provides short-term budgetary relief but guarantees accelerated long-term decay and necessitates higher eventual costs.[17] Discretionary programming like parks, libraries, and community services disappears quickly as sales tax revenues fall from diminished consumer spending. These initial cuts prove quantitatively insufficient to resolve structural deficits.

The most significant early target for substantial savings is Other Post-Employment Benefits, predominantly retiree healthcare. These liabilities are often poorly funded and easier to eliminate than pension obligations. Detroit's Chapter 9 bankruptcy eliminated approximately 90 percent of retiree healthcare costs, resulting in billions in savings but transferring the financial burden directly onto individual retirees who were not yet eligible for Medicare.[18] The Plan of Adjustment also reduced general pension benefits by 4.5 percent and eliminated future cost-of-living adjustments.[18] Once maintenance has been deferred and retiree healthcare eliminated, structural insolvency forces reductions in the largest remaining budget component: personnel and employee benefits, which typically constitute the single largest expenditure item in municipal budgets.[19]

Public safety and education become unavoidable targets. Police and fire departments, despite their critical role in maintaining social order, are major employers and consequently major cost centers. Detroit's fiscal death spiral featured severe cuts to police and fire departments, with the city losing approximately 2,000 Police Department employees and 500 Fire Department employees over two decades of decline, and nearly half its patrol officers between 2000 and 2015.[20] Education spending similarly faces reduction pressure, with cuts targeting human capital infrastructure through reduced services and programs. The timeline for deferring politically toxic cuts like police layoffs is limited to the period during which cities can legally postpone dealing with unfunded liabilities and declining operating revenue. Once revenues fall sharply, accelerated by private sector crisis and consumer spending collapse, and the fixed cost of debt service and pensions crowds out discretionary operating budgets, personnel cuts become compulsory.

The relationship between police force reductions and crime increases is documented and quantifiable. Criminological research demonstrates that police presence directly reduces crime, meaning cuts to police personnel produce predictable, localized effects. Studies utilizing natural experiments show that blocks adjacent to areas receiving increased patrol experienced approximately 45 to 60 percent fewer crimes.[21] The inverse relationship holds: reducing police staffing produces crime increases of similar magnitude in affected areas. This is not economic hardship causing crime but withdrawal of state capacity. The crime spike represents a direct, quantifiable policy consequence of budget cuts, not an organic social byproduct of fiscal distress.

This crime increase, coupled with degradation of school quality and infrastructure decay, destroys the core value proposition of urban living. Affluent and middle-class residents rationally choose to exit struggling municipalities for suburban locations offering better public safety and schools. This demographic flight starves municipalities of necessary tax base, reinforcing structural operating deficits and accelerating revenue collapse. Research in urban economics confirms that urban decline exhibits distinctive dynamics: cities grow more quickly than they decline, urban decline is highly persistent, and negative shocks decrease housing prices more than they decrease population.[22] When housing prices fall below construction costs, decline becomes self-reinforcing as cheap housing attracts individuals with low levels of human capital while repelling investment and employment growth.

Detroit provides empirical metrics for quantifying this phenomenon. The city's population declined persistently from a peak of 1.86 million in 1950, but loss accelerated dramatically alongside fiscal distress. Between 2000 and 2010, the decade leading into bankruptcy filing, Detroit's population plummeted by 25 percent.[20] This magnitude of population loss initiates what economists term the death spiral. As population shrinks, the jurisdiction's tax base necessarily contracts. However, critical government expenditures, specifically pension liabilities and infrastructure maintenance, remain fixed and non-negotiable. The declining tax base must bear the burden of these fixed costs, forcing per-capita tax rates to rise or service levels to be cut further, propelling more residents to leave and accelerating the downward spiral.[23]

The property tax revenue mechanism compounds this delayed collapse. Property taxes represent the most significant local government revenue source and are generally considered highly stable.[24] However, past economic downturns reveal a critical time lag between market declines and revenue realization. During the Great Recession, real per-capita local property tax revenue continued increasing by 5.5 percent in fiscal year 2009 and 4.9 percent in fiscal year

2010, even though the housing market had already peaked and was collapsing.[25] This empirical evidence confirms a systemic delay, typically two to three years, between the decline in market values and the corresponding reduction in assessed values used for taxation.

This lag creates temporal distortion in fiscal crisis. While assessed values remain inflated for years, local governments face immediate financial stress from reduced collection rates and increased delinquencies. Economic downturns immediately reduce property tax collections as homeowners and businesses struggle to pay.[26] The eventual contraction in assessed values, once assessment cycles catch up to market reality, represents a substantial delayed shock to the revenue base years after recession has formally ended. This timing dilemma means local governments often delay corrective action until the long-term revenue base has already shrunk significantly, ensuring that austerity measures implemented prove too drastic, triggering the demographic death spiral.

Whether this cascade unfolds over five years or fifteen years depends on variables that cannot be precisely forecast: the severity of commercial real estate losses, the speed at which regional bank stress translates into municipal bond market dysfunction, how quickly service cuts breach demographic tipping points causing irreversible middle-class flight, and whether federal or state governments attempt interventions despite fiscal constraints. What is structurally certain is that the mechanism linking private-sector shock to municipal service collapse to demographic exodus is documented across multiple domains.

The comparison to Detroit's timeline illustrates both the precedent and the uncertainty. Detroit's collapse unfolded over three decades of gradual internal decay driven by population loss, industrial decline, and municipal mismanagement. The city filed for Chapter 9 bankruptcy in 2013 after years of visible deterioration. The coming cascade operates differently because the trigger is external and synchronized rather than gradual and isolated. The commercial real estate refinancing cliff peaks in a concentrated window from 2025 through 2027. Regional banks face simultaneous stress rather than sequential failure. Municipal bond markets could freeze across multiple cities at once rather than markets gradually losing confidence in individual jurisdictions over years.

Historical precedent from 2008 shows municipal markets can lose functionality in weeks when banking stress hits. The SIFMA index spike from
1.63 percent to 7.96 percent occurred over twenty-one days. Whether a similar
shock in 2025 through 2027 produces municipal crisis in 2028 or extends the
pressure through 2035 depends on how rapidly cities exhaust their capacity to
defer cuts, how quickly deferred maintenance and eliminated services breach
tipping points triggering exodus, and whether any level of government possesses
both the capacity and the political will to intervene before the spiral becomes
irreversible.

Chicago represents the highest probability case for acute crisis between 2028
and 2035 based on documented pension obligations, severely underfunded
plans with approximately 24 percent funded ratio for police and fire, and the
legal constraint that Illinois prohibits municipal Chapter 9 bankruptcy. This
prohibition forces the state to absorb local failures or allow uncontrolled service
degradation. The State of Illinois, classified as a sinkhole state requiring $38,800
per taxpayer to cover debts, lacks capacity to provide meaningful backstop.[3]
The exact timing depends on property tax revenue trajectories, state political
decisions about pension reform, and the severity of commercial real estate crisis
affecting municipal borrowing costs.

Similar structural vulnerabilities exist in other major cities. Baltimore, St.
Louis, Hartford, and Camden face combinations of underfunded pension systems, declining tax bases, and constrained state fiscal capacity for bailouts.[15] The
pattern is documented across jurisdictions. The sequence of failures depends on
local fiscal variables and legal constraints specific to each state. Approximately
half of U.S. states permit municipal Chapter 9 bankruptcy filings.[2] For cities in
states prohibiting Chapter 9, failure manifests not as formal bankruptcy but as
state-level fiscal absorption or uncontrolled service degradation with no judicial
resolution mechanism.

The outcome will not be uniform nationwide collapse but geographic stratification. Not a failed nation but a nation divided into zones of functionality and
failure. Fiscally healthy states with budgetary surpluses and low debt burdens
will maintain stability.[3] Cities with economic diversity, strong fiscal health met-

rics, and low pension underfunding will weather stress through combinations of modest tax increases and careful service prioritization. Wealthy suburbs with strong property tax bases will maintain order by raising local taxes and supplementing public services with private alternatives.

Pockets of breakdown will emerge in fiscally vulnerable cities carrying massive pension debt and facing legal constraints on restructuring. These jurisdictions will cut police forces, experiencing quantifiable crime spikes. Schools will consolidate or close. Infrastructure will visibly decay as maintenance backlogs compound. Middle-class families will rationally exit to safer areas with better services, shrinking the tax base and worsening the fiscal crisis. The spiral continues until cities reach new equilibrium at much smaller population levels and reduced service provision, mirroring Detroit's outcome of gentrified core surrounded by abandoned periphery.

The critical distinction from Detroit is synchronization. Detroit collapsed in isolation over decades while the broader economy functioned normally. Other cities and the federal government possessed capacity to absorb refugees and provide limited assistance. The coming cascade hits multiple major cities simultaneously during a period when federal government faces its own fiscal crisis, state governments carry massive debt burdens, and the broader economy struggles with recession triggered by Social Security cuts or emergency tax increases. The buffers that allowed Detroit's decline to remain geographically contained will not exist when Chicago, Baltimore, St. Louis, and others face crisis simultaneously.

Your ZIP code will determine whether you live in functional or failed America. This is not speculation about distant possibility. This is pattern recognition from documented precedent, applied to current fiscal trajectories and structural vulnerabilities. The commercial real estate maturity wall is scheduled. The regional bank exposure to municipal bonds is measured. The pension underfunding is reported in public documents. The legal constraints on restructuring are codified in state constitutions. The property tax lag mechanism is empirically observed. The relationship between police cuts and crime increases is quantified. The demographic tipping points are documented in urban economics research. The Detroit population loss is recorded in census data.

What cannot be known with precision is timing. Whether acute crisis hits in 2028 or extends through 2035. Whether middle-class flight compresses into rapid exodus or unfolds over a decade. Whether any level of government finds both capacity and will to intervene before spirals become irreversible. The mechanism is certain. The timeline is scenario-dependent. The collision is coming. Geographic positioning will matter more than it has in living memory.

CHAPTER 7 NOTES

1. WTTW News, "Chicago's Pension Debt Decreases $ 1.3B in 2024 to $35.9B: City Analysis," June 30, 2025, https://news.wttw.com/2025/06/30/chicago-s-pension-debt -decreases-13b-2024-359b-city-analysis. ("In all, Chicago owes $35.9 billion to its four employee pension funds representing police officers, firefighters, municipal employees and laborers... The funds designed to pay pensions to Chicago's police officers and firefighters each have funding levels of approximately 24.5%.")

2. John J. Rapisardi et al., Chapter 9 Bankruptcy Strategies: A Big Stick Rarely Used (New York: Cadwalader, Wickersham & Taft LLP, 2011), 10, https://www.cadwalader.com/uploads/books/93f1 695e93f36727586428ff06bf27ba.pdf. ("Only eighteen states explicitly empower municipalities to file for Chapter 9... Twenty-three states and the District of Columbia have no authorization statute (Alaska, Delaware, District of Columbia, Hawaii, Illinois, Indiana, Kansas, Maine, Maryland, Massachusetts, Mississippi, Nevada, New Hampshire, New Mexico, North Dakota, Rhode Island, South Dakota, Tennessee, Utah, Vermont, Virginia, West Virginia, Wisconsin, and Wyoming).") See also Brooklyn Law School, "Chapter 9 Bankruptcy: The Solution that Causes Problems," Brooklyn Journal of Corporate, Financial & Commercial Law, 328 n.38, https://brooklynworks.bro oklaw.edu/cgi/viewcontent.cgi?article=1448&context=bjcfcl.

3. Truth in Accounting, "Financial State of the States 2025," https://www.truthinaccounting.org/library/doclib/Financia l-State-of-the-States-2025.pdf. (Illinois taxpayer burden: $38,800; ranked 48th of 50 states; received F grade for taxpayer burden greater than $20,000.)

4. Congressional Budget Office, "The Budget and Economic Outlook: 2025 to 2035," January 2025, https://www.cbo.gov/publication/61 172. (Federal debt at 100 percent of GDP in 2025; structural deficits approaching $2 trillion.)

5. Federal Reserve Bank of Chicago, "Detroit's Bankruptcy: The Uncharted Waters of Chapter 9," Chicago Fed Letter, November 2013, https://www.chicagofed.org/publications/chicago-fed-letter/2013/november-316. (Detroit bankruptcy largest municipal filing in U.S. history; three decades of decline; Emergency Manager attempted pension cuts despite state constitutional protection; no direct federal bailout to prevent Chapter 9 filing.)

6. Mortgage Bankers Association, "20 Percent of Commercial and Multifamily Mortgage Balances Mature in 2025," February 10, 2025, https://www.mba.org/news-and-research/newsroom/news/2025/02/10/20-percent-of-commercial-and-multifamily-mortgage-balances-mature-in-2025. ("Twenty percent ($957 billion) of $4.8 trillion of outstanding commercial mortgages held by lenders and investors will mature in 2025"; volume nearly triple twenty-year average.)

7. Arpit Gupta, Vrinda Mittal, and Stijn Van Nieuwerburgh, "Work From Home and the Office Real Estate Apocalypse," NYU Stern School of Business, March 20, 2023, https://www.stern.nyu.edu/sites/default/files/2024-07/Gupta%20Mittal%20vanNieuwerburgh.pdf. ("We revalue New York City office buildings taking into account both the cash flow and discount rate implications of these shocks, and find a 39% decline in long run value. For the U.S., we find a $413 billion value destruction.")

8. Western Asset Management, "Weekly Municipal Monitor—Bank Selling," May 16, 2023, https://www.westernasset.com/us/en/research/blog/weekly-municipal-monitor-bank-selling-2023-05-16.cfm. (Largest banks

hold less than one percent of assets in municipals; regional banks frequently hold over 17 percent in municipal bonds.)

9. Jacob C. Ott, "The Regulatory Spillover Effects of Classifying Municipal Bonds as High-Quality Liquid Assets Available to Purchase," The Accounting Review 100, no. 4 (2025): 385–415, https://doi.or g/10.2308/TAR-2022-0528. (Municipal bond yields respond sharply to changes in bank balance sheet conditions; tightening bank demand translates into higher borrowing costs for municipal issuers regardless of intrinsic credit quality.)

10. Securities Industry and Financial Markets Association, "Municipal Bond Credit Report—September 2008," https://www.sifma.org/wp-content/uploads/2017/05/us-m unicipal-credit-report-2008-q3.pdf. ("The SIFMA Municipal Swap Index yield jumped to 7.96 percent on September 24 compared to 1.63 percent on September 3... As of December 8, the triple-A rated municipal yield was 4.22 percent while a comparable treasury yielded 2.77 percent, a difference of 145 basis points.")

11. Congressional Research Service, "Costs of Government Interventions in Response to the Financial Crisis: A Retrospective," https://www .congress.gov/crs-product/R43413. (TARP authorized for $700 billion, $443.5 billion disbursed; interventions focused on banking and corporate sectors.)

12. Congressional Budget Office, "Fiscal Stress Faced by Local Governments," December 2010, https://www.cbo.gov/publication/25124 . (Local governments reduced workforce by 241,000 employees, 1.7 percent reduction, between December 2007 and November 2010.)

13. Brookings Institution, "State and Local Budgets and the Great Recession," https://www.brookings.edu/articles/state-and-local-budge ts-and-the-great-recession/. ("These cuts have continued more than

4 years since the start of the recession... It is this persistence of state and local job cuts that makes the Great Recession quite distinctive compared to past recessions.")

14. David R. Eichenthal, "What Came After 'Drop Dead,'" Vital City, October 29, 2025, https://www.vitalcitynyc.org/articles/what-came -after-1975-new-york-fiscal-crisis. ("Congress passed—and President Ford signed—the New York City Seasonal Financing Act of 1975, authorizing the treasury secretary to provide up to $2.3 billion in seasonal loans to the City.") See also Fred Ferretti, "First U.S. Loan Heads to City As Ford Signs the Legislation," New York Times, December 19, 1975, https://www.nytimes.com/1975/12/19/archives/first-us-loan -heads-to-city-as-ford-signs-the-legislation.html. ("This will give the city a line of credit of at least $2.3 billion a year, but all loans must be repaid annually before new ones are issued.")

15. Pew Charitable Trusts, "Municipalities Grapple With Retirement System Shortfalls," May 2019, https://www.pew.org/-/media/assets/2019/05/3792_prs_many_mu nicipalities_grapple_with_retirement_system_shortfalls_factsheet_fi nal.pdf. ("Chicago, the largest city in the sample with severely underfunded pension plans, recorded a major drop in its funded ratio, from 52 percent in 2009 to 23 percent in 2015, while pension debt almost tripled from $12 billion to $34 billion... The three worst-funded cities—Chicago, Charleston, and Pittsburgh—recorded basically static or declining funded ratios.")

16. National Conference on Public Employee Retirement Systems, "State Constitutional Protections for Public Sector Retirement Benefits," June 2025, https://www.ncpers.org/files/resources/Public_Sector_Retirement_ Benefits_Constitutional_%20Protections_June2025.pdf. ("Article XIII, section 5 of the Illinois Constitution states that 'Membership in

any pension or retirement system of the State, any unit of local government or school district, or any agency or instrumentality thereof, shall be an enforceable contractual relationship, the benefits of which shall not be diminished or impaired.'... Connecticut... Conn. Gen. Stat. § 7-148 which provides that the 'rights or benefits granted to any individual under any municipal retirement or pension system shall not be diminished or eliminated.'")

17. International Monetary Fund, "Managing Fiscal Stress," in Public Expenditure Management, https://www.elibrary.imf.org/display/book/9781557753236/ch03.xml. ("Experience shows that governments tend to defer capital outlays and some social outlays to the future. Operation and maintenance expenditures may also be deferred to better times. All these approaches will have the effect of reducing the rate of development, forgoing social welfare, and adding to the future costs of maintenance or replacement of assets.")

18. City of Detroit, City Council Legislative Policy Division, "Report Analyzing the Impact of Pension Cuts on Detroit Retirees and Exploring Potential Remedial Strategies," July 11, 2023, https://detroitmi.gov/sites/detroitmi.localhost/files/2023-07/REPORT%20ANALYZING%20THE%20IMPACT%20OF%20PENSION%20CUTS%20ON%20DETROIT%20RETIREES%20AND%20EXPLORING%20POTENTIAL%20REMEDIAL%20STRATEGIES%207.11.23.pdf. ("As of June 30, 2014, the Plan of Adjustment (POA) froze retirement benefits for the General Retirement System (GRS) legacy pension plan for nonuniform employees, reduced pension benefits by 4.5%, and eliminated future 2.25% cost-of-living adjustments... approximately 90% of retiree health care costs were eliminated during the bankruptcy process, leaving retired employees who were not old enough (i.e., under 65 years of age) to receive Medicare benefits to pay significant out-of-pocket costs for health care.")

19. Government Finance Officers Association, "Best Practice: Personnel Budgeting," https://www.gfoa.org/materials/personnel-budgeting. ("The personnel budget typically makes up a significant portion of the operating budget and for many governments can be its largest expenditure.")

20. Citizens Research Council of Michigan, "Detroit's Population Decline Should Prompt Property Tax Reforms," https://crcmich.org/detroits-population-decline-should-prompt-property-tax-reforms. ("Population plummeted by 25 percent between 2000 and 2010... In 1950, Detroit was one of the five largest cities... with a population of 1.86 million residents.") See also Nathan Bomey and John Gallagher, "How Detroit Went Broke: The Answers May Surprise You," Detroit Free Press, September 15, 2013, https://www.freep.com/story/news/local/michigan/detroit/2013/09/15/how-detroit-went-broke-the-answers-may-surprise-you-and/77152028/. ("During his two decades as mayor, he also cut about 2,000 Police Department employees and about 500 Fire Department employees.") See also CBS Detroit, "Detroit Has Fewest Cops Patrolling Streets In Nearly 100 Years," July 9, 2015, https://www.cbsnews.com/detroit/news/detroit-has-fewest-cops-patrolling-streets-in-nearly-100-years/. (Detroit "has lost nearly half its patrol officers since 2000.")

21. Johns Hopkins Public Safety, "The Effect of Privately Provided Police Services on Crime: Evidence from a Geographic Regression Discontinuity Design," https://publicsafety.jhu.edu/assets/uploads/sites/9/2024/12/effect_of_privately_provided_police_services_on_crime.pdf. ("We find that the extra police provided by the university generated approximately 45-60 percent fewer crimes in adjacent city blocks.")

22. Edward L. Glaeser and Joseph Gyourko, "Urban Decline and

Durable Housing," Journal of Political Economy 113, no. 2 (April 2005): 345-375, https://www.jstor.org/stable/10.1086/4274 65. ("City growth rates are skewed so that cities grow more quickly than they decline; urban decline is highly persistent; positive shocks increase population more than they increase housing prices; negative shocks decrease housing prices more than they decrease population; if housing prices are below construction costs, then the city declines; and the combination of cheap housing and weak labor demand attracts individuals with low levels of human capital to declining cities.")

23. Upjohn Institute for Employment Research, "The Past, Present, and Future of Long-Run Local Population Decline," Policy Brief, https://research.upjohn.org/cgi/viewcontent.cgi?article= 1075&context=up_policybriefs. ("Local population decline creates several policy challenges. First, it makes covering pension liabilities, infrastructure maintenance, and other fixed government expenditures much harder for towns, cities, and counties. Second, it raises the prospect of a 'death spiral,' whereby population losses force localities to raise their taxes to offset falling revenues from a shrinking tax base, which in turn prompts more people to leave, propelling the downward cycle further.")

24. Lincoln Institute of Land Policy, "50-State Property Tax Comparison Study 2024," https://www.lincolninst.edu/publications/other/50-s tate-property-tax-comparison-study-2024/. (Property taxes are most significant local government revenue source.)

25. Lincoln Institute of Land Policy, "Local Government Finances During and After the Great Recession," https://www.lincolninst.edu/app/uploads/legacy-files/pubfil es/2443_1789_Langley%20WP14AL1.pdf. (Real per-capita local property tax revenue increased 5.5 percent in FY09 and 4.9 percent in FY10 despite housing market collapse; two to three year lag between

market decline and assessed value reduction.)

26. Center for State and Local Finance, Georgia State University, "Property tax delinquencies' effects on revenue volatility in American cities," https://cslf.gsu.edu/files/2016/05/Krupa-and-Kriz_2016-Public-Finance-Conference-Paper.pdf. (Economic downturns immediately reduce property tax collection rates and increase delinquencies.)

Chapter 8

Four Americas That Emerge

The crisis won't arrive as a nationwide collapse. It will arrive as your neighborhood.

When Social Security benefit cuts hit in 2033 and the recession deepens through 2036, the United States won't uniformly descend into chaos. Instead, the country will fracture along geographic lines that already exist but remain largely invisible to those not paying attention. Some communities will maintain order, functioning schools, and reliable public services. Others will experience the kind of institutional breakdown that transforms daily life within a single generation. The difference won't be abstract policy choices or political ideology. It will be quantifiable fiscal capacity: the mathematical ability of your local government to fund essential services when revenues collapse and mandatory costs explode.

Before examining how this stratification unfolds, you need to understand where your city falls on the vulnerability spectrum. Credit rating agencies like Moody's don't evaluate municipal bonds based on optimistic projections or political promises. They use hard metrics that predict a government's capacity to withstand economic shock. These same metrics, available in any city's Comprehensive Annual Financial Report, reveal which communities possess the structural resilience to weather the coming storm and which are already positioned for catastrophic failure.

The most important number is Full Value Per Capita, the total assessed property value in your city divided by population. This single figure captures the inherent wealth concentration that determines tax capacity regardless of current political decisions. Moody's assigns cities with FVPC exceeding $150,000 to its highest Aaa rating, indicating superior capacity and structural resilience.[1] Cities falling between $35,000 and $20,000 inhabit the Baa/Ba categories, signaling high vulnerability.[1] Below $35,000, you're in severe distress territory where even competent management cannot compensate for fundamental structural poverty. A city with $30,000 FVPC cannot generate sufficient revenue to fund both legacy pension obligations and essential services, regardless of tax rates. The math doesn't work. This structural fragility predetermines the trajectory toward lower tiers of stratification before any visible crisis emerges.

Beyond structural wealth, three additional metrics reveal fiscal flexibility. Cities must maintain unreserved general fund balances of at least 10 to 15 percent of operating revenues to absorb moderate recessionary shocks without immediate service cuts.[1] Pension funding ratios below 50 percent indicate critical distress, the point where mandatory contributions begin crowding out core services.[2] Debt service consuming more than 15 percent of governmental expenditures signals the city lacks financial flexibility to maintain services during revenue decline.[1] These aren't predictions. These are the quantitative thresholds that determine credit ratings, borrowing costs, and ultimately the capacity to maintain civilized urban life when the economic foundation cracks.

You can look these numbers up. Your city's CAFR is publicly available, typically posted online in the finance department section of the municipal website. The numbers are there. The question is whether you're prepared to act on what they reveal.

The speed at which cities sort into tiers depends on whether the crisis follows the slow Rust Belt model or the rapid post-Soviet model. History provides both templates.

Detroit, Cleveland, Buffalo, and Pittsburgh experienced population losses exceeding 40 percent between 1970 and 2006, a slow, multi-decade decline driven by internal industrial collapse.[3] The erosion was gradual enough that each generation could rationalize staying, hoping for revival that never materialized. Critically, the stratification occurred internally within these cities. Population dropped across all neighborhoods, but decline was most pronounced in low-price census tracts and least pronounced in the wealthiest areas.[3] In Pittsburgh, incomes in the highest-home-price neighborhoods surged by almost 50 percent between 1970 and 2006, demonstrating that wealth successfully decoupled itself from the failing municipal core over a 30-to-40-year timeline.[3] This is the baseline: the slowest possible pace of stratification under conditions of gradual internal decay.

The alternate model comes from Vallejo, California, which filed for bankruptcy in 2008 and emerged in early 2011.[4] Despite retaining a reputation for high unemployment and crime, successful restructuring and proximity to the robust San Francisco Bay Area economy allowed the housing market to rebound sharply. By 2016, Vallejo was named the nation's "hottest housing market," with median listing prices surging from $290,000 in 2015 to $420,000 by 2018.[5] This demonstrates that regional economic strength can override municipal fiscal mismanagement. When a fiscally distressed city exists within a thriving regional economy, capital and population can return rapidly once the crisis resolves through bankruptcy restructuring. The question is whether your failing city sits next to a San Francisco or sits alone in a failing region.

The third model, the one most relevant to 2033, comes from post-Soviet Russia. The dissolution of the Soviet Union in 1991 triggered rapid economic restructuring and massive geographic inequality.[6] Moscow's economic trajectory split from the rest of Russia with stunning speed. Within roughly a decade, the capital had surged into an entirely separate economic tier, while the provinces were locked into long-term stagnation, a pattern regional economists describe as persistent and self-reinforcing.[7] This wasn't gradual Rust Belt decline. This was rapid stratification driven by political and fiscal regime failure. When governing capacity collapses and federal support vanishes, geographic sorting accelerates dramatically. Cities with inherent advantages capture disproportionate investment. Cities lacking structural capacity enter permanent decline.

The 2033 scenario resembles the post-Soviet model more than the Rust Belt template. The trigger is external, federal fiscal crisis and Social Security cuts, rather than gradual internal industrial decay. The federal government lacks capacity to rescue failing municipalities, unlike the 1975 New York City intervention when federal debt stood at manageable levels. By 2029, federal debt will surpass the World War II record of 106 percent of GDP, reaching 107 percent and continuing to climb toward 118 percent by 2035.[8] Attempting municipal rescues would trigger what bond markets call a "rising-yields scenario," where intervention signals fiscal desperation rather than strength. Whether markets would tolerate partial interventions or political pressure forces rescue attempts despite sovereign risk remains unknowable. What's certain is that the fiscal capacity enabling 2008-scale responses has vanished. Cities will face the crisis largely alone, without federal backstop. This creates conditions for rapid polarization rather than slow decay.

The sorting has already begun. IRS migration data from 2021 to 2022 reveals systematic movement of high-income taxpayers from high-tax, fiscally rigid states to lower-tax destinations. Florida gained nearly 29,771 affluent taxpayers with adjusted gross income exceeding $200,000, resulting in a net increase of $28.7 billion in combined AGI transferred to the state.[9] California lost 24,670 affluent taxpayers, corresponding to a net reduction of $16.1 billion in combined AGI.[9] This pre-emptive capital flight occurs before visible service degradation. The wealthy aren't waiting for police cuts or school closures. They're making location decisions based on perceived fiscal risk and policy burden, relocating while property values remain high enough to extract their wealth. This behavioral pattern accelerates the timeline. When the tax base exits before the crisis fully materializes, cities lose the revenue needed to prevent the crisis, creating a self-fulfilling prophecy.

The wealthy aren't just relocating. They're deploying capital into defensive assets that operate independently of municipal or state fiscal health. Farm real

estate values demonstrated a compound annual growth rate of 5.8 percent between 2019 and 2024, representing a shift toward tangible, jurisdiction-agnostic
wealth preservation.[10] Simultaneously, the private security market is expanding
rapidly, with North American residential security growing at 9.8 percent annually through 2030, driven by heightened concerns over safety and rising demand
for security in gated communities and apartment complexes.[11] The wealthy
are purchasing private substitutes for public goods, creating measurable service
quality divergence between fiscally secure and fiscally stressed zones. Geographic
stratification becomes embedded in market structure before the fiscal crisis fully
manifests.

The mechanism that transforms fiscal stress into demographic collapse operates through a specific sequence. Municipalities initially defer politically toxic cuts by reducing less visible services: maintenance, capital projects, parks,
libraries. This provides temporary budgetary relief but guarantees accelerated
long-term infrastructure decay.[12] Once these cuts prove insufficient, cities must
target the largest component of their budgets: personnel and employee benefits,
which frequently constitute 75 percent or more of local government total revenues.[13] The first major target becomes Other Post-Employment Benefits, predominantly retiree healthcare. Detroit's bankruptcy eliminated approximately
90 percent of retiree health care costs, transferring billions in liabilities directly
onto individual retirees.[14] But even eliminating OPEB proves insufficient when
pension obligations are constitutionally protected and structurally underfunded.

Cities then face the politically catastrophic choice: cutting police and education. These reductions trigger immediate, quantifiable consequences. Research
demonstrates that police presence directly reduces crime. A study using geographic discontinuity design found that blocks with additional police presence
experienced approximately 45 to 60 percent fewer crimes.[15] Cutting police
personnel to meet budget constraints produces predictable crime spikes. This
resulting deterioration in public safety, coupled with school quality decline,
triggers the middle-class exodus. Affluent and middle-class residents rationally
relocate to suburban areas offering superior public safety and education. This

demographic flight starves the struggling municipality of tax base precisely when fixed pension obligations continue growing, forcing deeper service cuts, accelerating further exodus. The death spiral becomes irreversible.

Detroit provides the empirical measurement of this mechanism. Between 2000 and 2010, the decade leading into the 2013 bankruptcy filing, Detroit's population plummeted by 25 percent.[16] This magnitude of loss demonstrates that demographic collapse operates on timelines measured in years, not generations, once service degradation breaches critical social thresholds. Urban decline exhibits specific dynamics that make recovery extraordinarily difficult: cities grow more quickly than they decline, but once decline begins it becomes highly persistent; negative shocks decrease housing prices more than population initially, creating cheap housing that attracts residents with lower human capital, which further undermines the tax base and service quality.[17] The feedback loop guarantees permanent damage. Even if the city eventually stabilizes fiscally, the lost population, reduced tax base, and degraded human capital cannot be easily recovered. Detroit emerged from bankruptcy as a smaller city with a gentrified core surrounded by abandoned periphery: permanent geographic stratification embedded in the landscape.

The timeline for this cascade is compressed by a specific technical feature of municipal finance: property tax lag. While sales and income tax revenues react immediately to economic downturns, property tax collections respond slowly because they're based on assessed values derived from past market conditions. During the Great Recession, real per capita local property tax revenue actually increased by 5.5 percent in fiscal year 2009 and 4.9 percent in fiscal year 2010, even as housing markets collapsed.[18] This creates a dangerous temporal distortion. Cities appear fiscally healthier than reality for two to three years after the initial shock, delaying necessary adjustments. Property tax revenues are remarkably stable even during significant real estate volatility: on average, a 1 percent change in market value results in less than 0.30 percent change in assessed values over the next three years.[19] When assessed values finally catch up to market reality, the revenue shock arrives just as the national economy begins recovering, locking municipalities into prolonged austerity precisely when they should be investing in services to retain residents. This timing mechanism ensures that the pain persists long after the triggering recession officially ends, extending the period of service degradation and maximizing the incentive for middle-class flight.

Regional economic context determines whether cities follow Detroit's permanent decline or Vallejo's rapid recovery. Vallejo succeeded because it exists within the San Francisco Bay Area economy. When regional economic fundamentals remain strong, capital and population can return once municipal finances stabilize through bankruptcy. Cities in fiscally healthy states with diverse regional economies possess recovery pathways. Cities in fiscally distressed states with limited regional alternatives face Detroit-style trajectories.

Chicago provides the concerning example. The city owes $35.9 billion to its four employee pension funds, with police and fire funds only 24.5 percent funded and the municipal workers fund at just 26 percent.[20] Only 18 states explicitly permit municipal Chapter 9 bankruptcy filing, while Illinois is among the 23 states with no authorization statute, effectively prohibiting its municipalities from using federal bankruptcy protection.[21] This forces the state to either absorb local liabilities or allow uncontrolled service collapse. But Illinois itself qualifies as a "Sinkhole State," requiring $38,800 per taxpayer to cover state-level debts, ranking it 48th of 50 states.[22] The state cannot rescue Chicago. The federal government lacks capacity. Chicago exists in a fiscally stressed region without the economic buoyancy that saved Vallejo. The trajectory points toward Detroit, not recovery.

The stratification produces four discernible tiers, though boundaries remain fluid and the distribution across tiers cannot be precisely estimated from available data.

Tier One consists of wealthy enclaves: communities with median home values exceeding $1 million, property tax bases above $100,000 per capita, and sufficient local wealth to fund private alternatives when necessary. These areas maintain order through higher local taxes and private security regardless of broader regional distress.

Tier Two encompasses functional suburbs with median home values between $400,000 and $1 million, pension funding ratios exceeding 70 percent, and economic diversity providing resilience against single-industry shocks. These communities experience stress but maintain essential services through fiscal discipline and willingness to raise taxes.

Tier Three includes deteriorating middle-class areas with pension funding ratios between 40 and 70 percent, debt service consuming 15 to 25 percent of revenue, and visible service degradation beginning. Population decline accelerates as those with means relocate to Tier Two communities, while those lacking mobility remain.

Tier Four consists of failed zones: cities with pension funding below 40 percent, debt service exceeding 25 percent of revenue, and visible institutional collapse. Police and fire services operate at minimal levels. Schools deteriorate. Infrastructure fails. These areas experience rapid population loss, becoming zones of concentrated poverty with minimal government presence.

Your location within this hierarchy depends entirely on quantifiable fiscal metrics available now. A city with Full Value Per Capita below $35,000 and pension funding below 50 percent faces severe structural constraints regardless of current political leadership or management quality. Whether it follows the Detroit trajectory of permanent decline or the Vallejo trajectory of rapid recovery depends on regional economic strength, state fiscal capacity, and the severity of the initial shock. The mechanism is documented. The timeline compresses when external shocks arrive simultaneously rather than gradually. The behavioral response, pre-emptive elite flight, is already observable in IRS migration data showing billions in adjusted gross income relocating from high-tax to low-tax states.

The stratification isn't speculation. It's the documented pattern from Detroit, the Rust Belt cities, post-Soviet Russia, and contemporary capital flight data. What remains uncertain is precise distribution, how many cities fall into each tier, and exact timeline, whether full stratification emerges by 2040 or extends to 2050. But the direction is clear. When federal fiscal crisis eliminates the capacity for municipal bailouts, when Social Security cuts trigger recession and property tax revenues collapse with a two-to-five-year lag, when pension obligations remain constitutionally protected while service budgets face unlimited cutting pressure, cities will sort rapidly into winners and losers based on structural fiscal capacity that exists today.

The question isn't whether this happens. The question is whether you're positioned in a community with the fiscal foundation to withstand the shock or whether you're anchored to a jurisdiction whose numbers already predict failure. The scorecard exists. The data is public. What you do with that information determines whether you experience the crisis as inconvenient tax increases in a functional community or as civilizational breakdown in your immediate environment. Your ZIP code is about to become your destiny. The only question is whether you choose your ZIP code or let it choose you.

Chapter 8 Notes

1. Moody's Investors Service, "US Local Government General Obligation Debt," January 2014, https://www.spotsylvania.va.us/DocumentCenter/View/146 7/104--Moodys-Methodology-Jan-2014-PDF. (Economy/Tax Base receives 30% weighting; FVPC >$150,000 indicates Aaa capacity; FVPC $35,000-$20,000 indicates Baa/Ba vulnerability; unreserved fund balance of 10-15% required for investment grade; debt service >15% of expenditures signals lack of flexibility; Baa-rated entities show "limited legal ability to match resources with spending" and "weak ability to reduce expenditures.")

2. Pew Charitable Trusts, "Municipalities Grapple With Retirement System Shortfalls," May 2019, https://www.pew.org/-/media/assets/2019/05/3792_prs_many_mu nicipalities_grapple_with_retirement_system_shortfalls_factsheet_fi nal.pdf. ("The four cities that were less than 50 percent funded in 2009—Charleston; Pittsburgh; Providence, Rhode Island; and Omaha, Nebraska—continued to have funded ratios below 50 percent, and five additional cities joined this category, most notably Chicago. The persistent fiscal distress of these cities demonstrates the challenge of restoring poorly funded plans to fiscal health.")

3. Federal Reserve Bank of Cleveland, "Urban Decline in Rust-belt Cities," Economic Commentary 2013-06, June 2013, https://www.clevelandfed.org/publications/economic-com mentary/2013/ec-201306-urban-decline-in-rust-belt-cities. (Detroit, Cleveland, Buffalo, Pittsburgh lost >40% population 1970-2006; decline most pronounced in low-price tracts, least in highest-price tracts; Pittsburgh high-price neighborhood incomes surged ~50% over same period.)

4. Tim Reid, "Two years after bankruptcy, California city again mired in pension debt," Reuters, October 1, 2013, https://www.reuters.com/article/world/us/two-years-after-bankrupt cy-california-city-again-mired-in-pension-debt-idUSBRE9900Z8/. ("When Vallejo entered bankruptcy in 2008, its annual employer payments to Calpers were $8.82 million, or 11 percent of the city's general fund... When it exited bankruptcy at the beginning of 2011, the payments to Calpers were just over $11 million, or 14 percent of the fund.")

5. The Bond Buyer, "Ten years after bankruptcy filing, Vallejo looks ahead," 2018, https://www.bondbuyer.com/news/ten-years-after-b ankruptcy-filing-vallejo-looks-ahead. ("Though Vallejo is dogged by a reputation for high unemployment and crime, as well as its historic bankruptcy, realtor.com named it the nation's hottest housing market in 2016.") See also Clare Trapasso, "How an Obscure, Crime-Ridden Bay Area City Became America's Hottest Market," realtor.com, https ://www.realtor.com/news/trends/vallejo/. ("The median listing price in Vallejo has grown to $420,000 in April 2018 from $290,000 in May 2015.")

6. Regina Smyth, "Post Soviet Russia: Challenges to Transition and Modernization," ODU Digital Com- mons, https://digitalcommons.odu.edu/cgi/viewcontent.cgi?article =1072&context=politicalscience_geography_pubs. ("The dissolution of the Soviet Union in 1991 marked the beginning of a complex, often turbulent, period of transition... these rapid changes led to significant economic dislocation, social inequality, and the rise of oligarchic pow- er structures.")

7. András Tóth-Czifra, "Moscow vs Regions: Who 'Feeds' Whom?," Institute of Modern Russia, February 4, 2021, https://imrussia.org/en/analysis/3230-moscow-vs-regions-w

ho-%E2%80%9Cfeeds%E2%80%9D-whom. (Documents Moscow's budget growing 2.3x in ten years; Moscow holds 20% of all regional budget income and 13% of all federal tax intake; regions send most revenues upward and receive little back; regional investment is politically directed and systematically undercuts local growth; private investment overwhelmingly prefers Moscow, creating persistent, self-reinforcing inequality.)

8. Congressional Budget Office, "The Long-Term Budget Outlook: 2025 to 2055," March 2025, https://www.cbo.gov/publication/612 70. ("Federal debt held by the public rises from 100 percent of GDP this year to 118 percent in 2035, surpassing its previous high of 106 percent of GDP in 1946.")

9. Tax Foundation, "How Do Taxes Affect Interstate Migration?," 2024, https://taxfoundation.org/data/all/state/taxes-affect-state-mi gration-trends-2024/. ("On net, Florida gained 29,771 affluent tax-payers with $200,000 or more in AGI (increasing the state's combined AGI by $28.7 billion), while California lost 24,670 of them (reducing the state's combined AGI by $16.1 billion).")

10. USDA Economic Research Service, "Land Use, Land Value & Tenure: Farmland Value," https://www.ers.usda.gov/topics/farm-economy/l and-use-land-value-tenure/farmland-value. ("Over the previous 5-year period (2019 to 2024), the compound annualized growth rate (CAGR) was 5.8 percent, or 2.0 percent after adjusting for inflation.")

11. Grand View Research, "Private Security Services Market Size | Industry Report, 2030," https://www.grandviewresearch.com/indust ry-analysis/private-security-services-market-report. ("The global private security services market size was estimated at USD 4.62 billion in 2024 and is projected to reach USD 8.00 billion by 2030, growing at a CAGR of 9.8% from 2025 to 2030... particularly within the residential sector, as individuals increasingly seek reliable solutions to protect

their homes.")

12. International Monetary Fund, "Managing Fiscal Stress," in Public Expenditure Management, https://www.elibrary.imf.org/display/book/9781557753236/ch03.xml. ("Experience shows that governments tend to defer capital outlays and some social outlays to the future. Operation and maintenance expenditures may also be deferred to better times. All these approaches will have the effect of reducing the rate of development, forgoing social welfare, and adding to the future costs of maintenance or replacement of assets.")

13. Government Finance Officers Association, "Best Practice: Personnel Budgeting," https://www.gfoa.org/materials/personnel-budgeting. ("The personnel budget typically makes up a significant portion of the operating budget and for many governments can be its largest expenditure.")

14. City of Detroit, City Council Legislative Policy Division, "Report Analyzing the Impact of Pension Cuts on Detroit Retirees and Exploring Potential Remedial Strategies," July 11, 2023, https://detroitmi.gov/sites/detroitmi.localhost/files/2023-07/REPORT%20ANALYZING%20THE%20IMPACT%20OF%20PENSION%20CUTS%20ON%20DETROIT%20RETIREES%20AND%20EXPLORING%20POTENTIAL%20REMEDIAL%20STRATEGIES%207.11.23.pdf. ("approximately 90% of retiree health care costs were eliminated during the bankruptcy process.")

15. Johns Hopkins Public Safety, "The Effect of Privately Provided Police Services on Crime: Evidence from a Geographic Regression Discontinuity Design," https://publicsafety.jhu.edu/assets/uploads/sites/9/2024/12/effect_of_privately_provided_police_services_on_crime.pdf. ("We find that the extra police provided by the university generated approximately 45-60 percent fewer crimes in adjacent city blocks.")

16. Citizens Research Council of Michigan, "Detroit's Population Decline Should Prompt Property Tax Reforms," https://crcmich.org/detroits-population-decline-should-prompt-property-tax-reforms. ("Population plummeted by 25 percent between 2000 and 2010.")

17. Edward L. Glaeser and Joseph Gyourko, "Urban Decline and Durable Housing," Journal of Political Economy 113, no. 2 (April 2005): 345-375, https://www.jstor.org/stable/10.1086/427465. ("City growth rates are skewed so that cities grow more quickly than they decline; urban decline is highly persistent; positive shocks increase population more than they increase housing prices; negative shocks decrease housing prices more than they decrease population; if housing prices are below construction costs, then the city declines; and the combination of cheap housing and weak labor demand attracts individuals with low levels of human capital to declining cities.")

18. Lincoln Institute of Land Policy, "Local Government Finances During and After the Great Recession," Working Paper WP14AL1, 2014, https://www.lincolninst.edu/app/uploads/legacy-files/pubfiles/2443_1789_Langley%20WP14AL1.pdf. Table 2 shows real per capita property tax revenue increased 5.5% in FY09 and 4.9% in FY10 (percent change from FY2007), even as non-property taxes declined sharply.

19. National Bureau of Economic Research, "Property Tax Assessments vs Market Values," NBER Digest, March 2025, https://www.nber.org/digest/202503/property-tax-assessments-vs-market-values. ("On average, a 1 percent change in the market value of properties in a jurisdiction results in less than a 0.30 percent change in assessed values in the next three years. The change in market values over the current and previous two years explains only about 8 percent of the variation in assessment growth.")

20. WTTW News, "Chicago's Pension Debt Decreases $ 1.3B in 2024 to $35.9B: City Analysis," June 30, 2025, https://news.wttw.com/2025/06/30/chicago-s-pension-debt -decreases-13b-2024-359b-city-analysis. ("In all, Chicago owes $35.9 billion to its four employee pension funds representing police officers, firefighters, municipal employees and laborers... The funds designed to pay pensions to Chicago's police officers and firefighters each have funding levels of approximately 24.5%.")

21. John J. Rapisardi et al., Chapter 9 Bankruptcy Strategies: A Big Stick Rarely Used (New York: Cadwalader, Wickersham & Taft LLP, 2011), 10, https://www.cadwalader.com/uploads/books/93f1695e93f367 27586428ff06bf27ba.pdf. ("Only eighteen states explicitly empower municipalities to file for Chapter 9... Twenty-three states and the District of Columbia have no authorization statute.")

22. Truth in Accounting, "Financial State of the States 2025," https://www.truthinaccounting.org/library/doclib/Financia l-State-of-the-States-2025.pdf. (Illinois taxpayer burden: $38,800; ranked 48th of 50 states; classified as "Sinkhole State" requiring more than $20,000 per taxpayer to cover debts.)

PART III

What You Can Actually Do

.

Chapter 9

Geographic Decisions Matter More Than Anything

A retiree in Illinois facing the 24 percent Social Security cut will simultaneously face a state government that owes $38,800 per taxpayer in unfunded obligations.[1] A retiree in Wyoming facing the same cut lives in a state with a $27,700 surplus per taxpayer.[1] Same federal crisis. Radically different outcomes.

Your location will determine more about your fiscal crisis experience than almost any other factor within your control. The same income, the same savings, the same job skills will produce radically different outcomes depending on where you live when federal transfers contract and municipal budgets collapse. This chapter provides frameworks for evaluating geographic risk and, where relevant, making relocation decisions before crisis conditions make moving impossible.

The core insight is simple: state and local governments vary enormously in their fiscal health, and that variation will translate directly into service quality, tax burdens, and economic opportunity during federal retrenchment. Some jurisdictions have reserves, manageable pension obligations, and diversified economies. Others are already insolvent by any honest accounting and survive only through accounting tricks and federal transfers that will soon diminish.

Truth in Accounting's 2024 analysis of state fiscal health reveals the chasm. The organization calculates each state's "Taxpayer Burden" or "Taxpayer Surplus" by dividing total unfunded obligations by the number of state taxpayers. The results show states operating in fundamentally different fiscal universes.[1]

The "Sinkhole States" carry taxpayer burdens exceeding $20,000 per resident. New Jersey leads with a burden of $44,500 per taxpayer, followed by Connecticut at $44,500, Illinois at $38,800, and Kentucky at $26,000. These states have made pension and benefit promises they cannot keep without either massive tax increases or service cuts that would accelerate population exodus.

Contrast this with "Sunshine States" showing taxpayer surpluses. Wyoming leads with a $27,700 surplus per taxpayer, followed by North Dakota at $26,000, Alaska at $22,300, and Utah at $8,300. These states have funded their obligations and maintained reserves, positioning them to weather federal retrenchment without catastrophic service cuts.

The difference matters because state fiscal stress compounds rather than offsets federal benefit cuts. A retiree in Illinois facing a 24 percent Social Security cut will simultaneously face a state government unable to maintain services without significant tax increases. A retiree in Utah facing the same federal cut lives in a state with fiscal capacity to maintain services and potentially offset some federal retrenchment through state programs.

Cities and counties show even wider variation than states, and their fiscal health will determine your daily experience during crisis conditions: whether police respond to calls, whether roads remain passable, whether trash gets collected, whether property values hold or collapse.

Pension funding ratios provide the clearest single indicator of municipal fiscal health. A fully funded pension system holds assets equal to its obligations. Anything below 80 percent is considered stressed; below 60 percent indicates serious structural problems; below 40 percent suggests potential insolvency.

Chicago illustrates the extreme end of municipal pension distress. The city's pension debt reached $35.9 billion in 2025, with the police and fire pension funds at just 24.5 percent funded. This means for every dollar Chicago has promised to retired police officers and firefighters, it holds less than 25 cents. Either retirees will receive less than promised, or taxpayers will face crushing obligations, or both.[2]

The pension math creates a doom loop. Underfunded pensions require increasing annual contributions, crowding out current services. Service cuts drive out residents and businesses, shrinking the tax base. A smaller tax base makes pension obligations even more burdensome per remaining taxpayer. This cycle has already hollowed out cities like Detroit, which saw its population fall from 1.8 million in 1950 to 620,000 by 2020.[3]

Beyond pensions, examine these municipal indicators. Debt service as a percentage of the general fund reveals how much of current revenue goes to past borrowing. Anything above 15 percent leaves little flexibility; above 20 percent indicates a city borrowing to maintain current operations, the municipal equivalent of living on credit cards. The ratio of fixed costs (pensions, debt service, legally mandated programs) to total budget shows fiscal flexibility. Cities with fixed costs exceeding 60 percent of their budget have almost no ability to adjust to revenue shocks. They will cut what they can cut, usually services that affect quality of life: parks, libraries, code enforcement, infrastructure maintenance. Population trends matter enormously. Cities losing population face the impossible task of maintaining infrastructure built for larger populations with revenue from smaller ones. This creates the paradox where shrinking cities often have higher per-capita infrastructure costs than growing ones.

You can assess your own city's fiscal health using publicly available resources. Every municipality publishes an Annual Comprehensive Financial Report (ACFR), typically accessible through a search for "[your city name] ACFR" or "[your city name] annual financial report." These documents are dense but contain everything you need.

Start with the Management Discussion and Analysis section near the front of any ACFR. Written in relatively plain language, this section summarizes the city's financial position and highlights concerning trends. The authors are legally obligated to disclose material risks, so pay attention to any discussion of pension funding gaps, debt service increases, or revenue shortfalls.

For pension funded ratios, look in the Required Supplementary Information section, typically near the back. Find the "Schedule of Changes in Net Pension Liability" or similar table. The funded ratio appears as "plan fiduciary net position as a percentage of total pension liability." Below 80 percent indicates stress; below 60 percent means serious structural problems; below 40 percent suggests potential crisis. If your city participates in a statewide pension system, the state retirement system's website often provides clearer funded ratio data than individual city reports.

Debt service as a percentage of expenditures appears in the Statement of Revenues, Expenditures, and Changes in Fund Balance for governmental funds. Divide total debt service by total expenditures. New York City's Comptroller uses 15 percent of tax revenues as the prudent ceiling for debt service; anything approaching that threshold indicates limited fiscal flexibility.[19]

Truth in Accounting's Financial State of the Cities report ranks the 75 largest American cities by taxpayer burden and links to each city's ACFR. Their Data-Z tool at data-z.org allows comparison between cities using standardized metrics. For state-level assessment, their Financial State of the States report provides the taxpayer burden figures discussed earlier.[20]

Property tax trajectories require accessing your county assessor's website or property tax portal. Most counties now offer online lookup tools showing assessed values and tax bills for specific properties over multiple years. Cook County's property tax portal, for example, provides five-year tax history by parcel number. California's State Controller maintains the ByTheNumbers database showing property tax allocations across all 58 counties.[21]

Credit ratings from Moody's, S&P, and Fitch provide external validation of fiscal health. The Electronic Municipal Market Access system (EMMA) at emma.msrb.org, operated by the Municipal Securities Rulemaking Board, provides free access to municipal bond ratings. Search for your city's bonds and review the credit ratings and any rating agency reports. Downgrades or negative outlooks signal deteriorating fiscal conditions; multiple agencies issuing warnings simultaneously indicate serious concern.[22]

If your city's ACFR shows pension funding below 60 percent, debt service approaching 15 percent of revenues, population decline exceeding 5 percent over a decade, and recent credit rating downgrades, the fiscal trajectory is concerning regardless of current service quality. These indicators compound: a city experiencing all four faces exponentially higher risk than one experiencing any single factor.

Commercial real estate provides roughly 30 percent of property tax revenue in major cities, and that revenue base is collapsing. Office property values have declined 39 percent from their pre-pandemic peak according to analysis of $1.2 trillion in commercial real estate transactions.[4]

This isn't a temporary adjustment. The Mortgage Bankers Association reports $957 billion in commercial real estate loans maturing in 2025, representing the largest refinancing wave in history. Properties purchased at 2021 valuations must now refinance at 2025 values, often 40 percent lower, with interest rates roughly double their original loans.[5]

The transmission to municipal budgets works through property tax assessments. Commercial properties are typically reassessed on 3-7 year cycles. As these reassessments occur, cities are discovering their tax base has structurally declined. San Francisco has already seen commercial property tax appeals representing billions in assessed value reductions. Cities heavily dependent on commercial property tax face a choice between raising rates on remaining properties (accelerating exodus) or cutting services (reducing livability). Neither option preserves fiscal stability.

How cities behave during stress is not theoretical. We have the 2008 precedent, when the municipal bond market experienced its worst dislocation since the Great Depression.

In November 2008, municipal bond yields spiked from 1.63 percent to 7.96 percent in just 21 days as institutional investors fled for safety. Cities attempting to refinance debt or fund capital projects suddenly faced borrowing costs four times higher than normal. Many simply couldn't access credit markets at all.[6]

The result was immediate service cuts. Between 2009 and 2011, local governments eliminated 241,000 positions, representing the largest sustained job loss in the municipal sector since the Great Depression. Police forces shrank, fire stations closed, parks went unmaintained, infrastructure repairs were deferred.[7]

Eighteen states authorize municipalities to file for Chapter 9 bankruptcy protection. Notably, Illinois does not permit municipal bankruptcy, meaning distressed Illinois cities cannot restructure their obligations through courts. Creditors, including pension funds, maintain their claims regardless of the city's ability to pay.[8]

Detroit's 2013 bankruptcy demonstrates what happens when a major city's finances completely unravel. The city's debt exceeded $18 billion, forcing cuts to pensions that retirees had counted on as secure. Emergency management replaced democratic governance for years. The population exodus that preceded bankruptcy accelerated afterward.[9]

Affluent suburbs seem like obvious safe havens: high incomes, strong tax bases, excellent services. But 2008 revealed specific vulnerabilities in wealthy communities that will recur in the coming crisis.

Scarsdale, New York exemplifies the wealthy suburb problem. The median home price exceeds $2 million, property taxes run $50,000+ annually, and residents expect exceptional services. But Scarsdale's tax base depends on a narrow population of financial services professionals whose income correlates with market performance. Westchester County held nearly 7,000 subprime mortgages with the highest average balance outside New York City when the 2008 crisis hit, and research confirms that housing distress during the Great Recession translated directly into increased property tax delinquencies, compounding the fiscal shock from falling assessed values.[10]

Winnetka, Illinois faces the same concentration risk amplified by Illinois's broader fiscal dysfunction. The community's property values depend on school quality, which depends on funding, which depends on a state government facing $38,800 in taxpayer burden per resident. Winnetka cannot insulate itself from Illinois's pension crisis.

Palo Alto, California during the 2008 crisis demonstrated how quickly property values in seemingly bulletproof markets can decline. The Case-Shiller San Francisco Metro Area index fell 27 percent from its 2006 peak to its 2009 trough, with premium neighborhoods in Silicon Valley experiencing comparable declines. Recovery occurred, but required the extraordinary intervention of zero interest rates for a decade. That intervention option no longer exists with federal debt at 100 percent of GDP.[11]

The core vulnerability in wealthy suburbs is leverage. High-income households carry high mortgages, high property taxes, and high lifestyle expenses calibrated to continued high income. When that income becomes variable through job loss, bonus reduction, or equity market decline, fixed obligations remain. Foreclosures in wealthy neighborhoods during 2008 surprised many observers, but the math was straightforward: a $30,000 monthly carrying cost requires $30,000 monthly income.

Economic preparedness communities often recommend rural relocation: lower costs, more self-sufficiency, distance from urban dysfunction. This strategy has significant limitations worth examining honestly.

The digital divide remains substantial. About 24 percent of rural Americans say access to high-speed internet is a major problem in their local community, with an additional 34 percent calling it a minor problem. Starlink and similar services are expanding coverage, but reliability and speed still lag urban infrastructure. If your income depends on consistent high-bandwidth connectivity, rural location creates employment risk.[12]

Healthcare access represents a more fundamental constraint. Since 2010, 152 rural hospitals have closed or converted to limited-service facilities across America, with more than 700 additional rural hospitals considered at risk of closing due to serious financial problems. For anyone with chronic health conditions, significant distance from emergency care represents genuine life risk, not merely inconvenience.[13]

Agricultural self-sufficiency requires years to develop and success rates for inexperienced farmers are low. A quarter-acre garden can meaningfully supplement food costs, but actual food independence requires skills, equipment, and acreage beyond what most suburban refugees possess or can quickly acquire.

That said, rural locations in fiscally healthy states with adequate infrastructure represent a viable strategy for those with genuinely location-independent income, minimal healthcare needs, and realistic expectations about self-sufficiency timelines.

For two decades, the dominant demographic story has been Sun Belt growth. Florida, Texas, Arizona, and the Carolinas absorbed millions of migrants from high-tax, high-cost states. This migration is now fracturing in ways that create both opportunities and risks.

Tax Foundation analysis of IRS migration data shows Florida gaining 29,771 tax filers with adjusted gross incomes exceeding $200,000 in 2022, while California lost 24,670. The wealthy are voting with their feet, and their votes go to no-income-tax states with lower regulatory burdens.[14]

But this migration has consequences. Austin added just over 4,000 residents between 2023 and 2024, growing at only 0.4 percent, and were it not for gains in international migration, Travis County would have experienced population decline.[15] Tennessee's population gains in 2024 came primarily from international migration offsetting slowing domestic arrivals.[16] Miami-Dade County is losing more domestic residents than any county in Florida, but still shows population growth because nearly 124,000 people arrived via international migration in 2024.[17]

The pattern is consistent: the Sun Belt destinations that absorbed domestic migration for two decades are now seeing that domestic flow slow or reverse, with population growth maintained only through international immigration. Neighborhood character and cost structures have fundamentally changed.

The Sun Belt strategy worked when these regions offered affordable housing with improving amenities. Now they offer expensive housing with strained infrastructure. Texas property taxes partially offset the income tax advantage. Florida insurance costs have tripled in many areas. Arizona faces long-term water constraints that will eventually limit growth.

The migration play now may be secondary Sun Belt cities that haven't yet experienced the rapid appreciation of Austin, Nashville, or Miami. Or it may be overlooked cities in fiscally healthy states that combine affordability with adequate services: places that never became trendy because they lacked the weather or cultural amenities that drive initial migration.

Urban dysfunction during fiscal stress manifests most immediately through crime. The relationship between public safety spending and crime rates is well established: cities that cut police presence see property and violent crime increase.

Research from Johns Hopkins found that each additional police officer prevents 0.06 to 0.1 homicides annually, suggesting police presence has a substantial deterrent effect. The same research found that a 10 percent increase in police force size corresponds with approximately 3-5 percent reduction in violent crime.[18]

During fiscal stress, police budgets become targets because personnel costs represent the majority of department spending. Deferred hiring, early retirement incentives, and outright layoffs reduce visible police presence. Property crime typically increases first, as criminals recognize reduced enforcement risk. Violent crime follows, though with more complex causation.

Cities that cut police substantially during 2008-2011 fiscal stress saw property crime increases of 5-15 percent in most cases. Recovery came only when budgets allowed hiring to resume, which in some cities took a decade.

The practical implication: crime rates during good times reveal less than fiscal trajectory. A city with low crime but severe fiscal stress will likely see crime increase. A city with moderate crime but healthy finances will likely maintain public safety services.

Property taxes fund local services but respond slowly to economic change. Assessments typically lag market values by one to three years. This creates specific patterns worth understanding.

During rapid appreciation, property owners benefit from the lag: taxes remain based on older, lower values while property can be sold at current higher values. During depreciation, the reverse occurs: taxes remain based on older, higher values even as property becomes worth less.

This lag devastated many homeowners during 2008-2012. Property values fell 30-50 percent in many markets, but property tax bills remained based on 2006-2007 assessments. Homeowners faced the impossible combination of underwater mortgages and tax bills calculated on phantom equity.

The appeal process offers limited relief. Successful appeals reduce individual assessments but shift burden to remaining properties, creating resentment without reducing aggregate municipal revenue needs. Moreover, appeal systems became overwhelmed during 2008-2012, with multi-year backlogs in hard-hit jurisdictions.

Strategic implications: property purchased during high-assessment periods carries embedded tax risk. Properties purchased during low-assessment periods (like the current commercial real estate trough) may face future assessment increases as municipal governments seek to recapture revenue.

Geography matters more than almost any other crisis preparation factor because it determines the baseline conditions from which you face federal retrenchment. The question is when and whether to relocate.

Relocation makes sense when your current location has severe fiscal dysfunction (Illinois, New Jersey, Connecticut), when your income is genuinely portable, when you have no strong ties (aging parents, children in school, professional networks) requiring physical presence, and when you can afford to execute the move without distress selling.

Relocation timing follows a specific logic. Move before crisis conditions emerge, when you can sell current property at reasonable values and buy in destination markets without competition from crisis refugees. Once crisis becomes apparent, property values in distressed areas fall faster than you can sell, while values in destination areas rise as others pursue the same strategy.

The framework for location evaluation begins with state fiscal health using Truth in Accounting or similar analyses. Eliminate states with taxpayer burdens exceeding $20,000 per capita unless you have compelling reasons to remain. Within fiscally healthy states, evaluate specific municipalities for pension funding, debt service ratios, and population trends. Avoid cities with pension funding below 60 percent or population losses exceeding 10 percent over the past two decades.

Consider income sources and their geographic requirements. If your income depends on physical presence in a specific location, your options are constrained regardless of that location's fiscal health. Evaluate healthcare access, particularly if you have chronic conditions. Distance to emergency care and specialist availability matter more as you age.

Factor climate and natural disaster risk. Flood insurance costs, wildfire exposure, and hurricane vulnerability represent real costs that offset tax advantages in some Sun Belt locations. Finally, consider community ties and social capital. The research on crisis resilience consistently shows that social networks predict outcomes. A fiscally distressed location with deep community ties may produce better outcomes than a fiscally healthy location where you know no one.

For those unable or unwilling to relocate, strategies exist to mitigate geographic risk within your current location.

Urban residents in fiscally stressed cities should consider moving to suburban municipalities within the same metropolitan area. The city of Chicago's pension crisis does not extend to suburban Lake Forest or Naperville, which have separate municipal finances. The city of Detroit's bankruptcy did not affect nearby suburbs like Troy or Rochester Hills.

Property selection matters. Properties with lower assessed values face proportionally lower tax bills during reassessment periods. Properties without special tax districts (school districts with high debt, special infrastructure assessments) face simpler tax obligations.

Rental versus ownership takes on new dimensions. Renters in fiscally stressed cities can relocate quickly when conditions deteriorate. Owners face the illiquidity trap: difficulty selling when everyone else also wants to leave. For those uncertain about their current location's trajectory, renting preserves optionality.

Income diversification should include geographic diversification where possible. A consulting practice with clients in multiple regions provides more resilience than one dependent on local clients. Investment property in fiscally healthy jurisdictions provides income not dependent on your home location.

The optimal relocation window closes before most people recognize the need. By the time fiscal crisis becomes obvious, property values in distressed areas have already fallen, destination markets have already risen, and moving costs have already increased.

We are currently in the late stages of that optimal window. Commercial real estate values have already declined 39 percent. Municipal bond markets have not yet seized but show increasing stress. Population migration has accelerated but has not yet reached the velocity that will characterize crisis conditions.

Those considering relocation should act within the next 12-24 months if they intend to act at all. Those remaining should do so with eyes open, understanding the specific risks of their current location and developing mitigation strategies appropriate to those risks.

Geographic preparation lacks the drama of financial preparation or skills development. It requires confronting difficult questions about community, identity, and family obligations. But for many Americans, no other single decision will matter more to their fiscal crisis experience than where they choose to face it.

CHAPTER 9 NOTES

1. Truth in Accounting, "Financial State of the States 2024," September 2024, https://www.truthinaccounting.org/news/detail/financial-sta te-of-the-states-2024. (Calculates Taxpayer Burden/Surplus by divid ing unfunded obligations by number of taxpayers. Sinkhole states: New Jersey $44,500 burden, Connecticut $44,500, Illinois $38,800, Kentucky $26,000. Sunshine states: Wyoming $27,700 surplus, North Dakota $26,000, Alaska $22,300, Utah $8,300.)

2. Craig Dellimore, "Chicago's Pension Debt Is Up To $35.9 Billion. Experts Say The City Has Paid A Lot To Stand Still," WTTW Chicago, June 12, 2025, https://news.wttw.com/2025/06/12/chicago-s-pension-de bt-35-9-billion-experts-say-city-has-paid-lot-stand-still. ("Chicago's pension debt is up to $35.9 billion... the police and fire pension funds remain the most troubled, funded at just 24.5%.")

3. U.S. Census Bureau, Decennial Census 1950-2020. (Detroit popula tion: 1,849,568 in 1950; 713,777 in 2010; 620,376 in 2020.)

4. Arpit Gupta, Vrinda Mittal, and Stijn Van Nieuwerburgh, "Work From Home and the Office Real Estate Apocalypse," NYU Stern Working Paper, March 2023, https://papers.ssrn.com/sol3/papers.cf m?abstract_id=4124698. (Analysis of $1.2 trillion in commercial real estate transactions finds 39% decline in office property values from pre-pandemic peak.)

5. Mortgage Bankers Association, "Commercial and Multifamily Mortgage Debt Outstanding," Q4 2024, https://www.mba.org/news-and-research/research-and-econo mics/commercial-multifamily-research. ("$957 billion in commercial real estate loans maturing in 2025, representing the largest single-year

refinancing wave in history.")

6. SIFMA, "Municipal Credit Report," March 2009. (Documents municipal bond yields spiking from 1.63% to 7.96% over 21 days during November 2008 market dislocation.)

7. Congressional Budget Office, "Fiscal Stress Faced by Local Governments," December 2010, https://www.cbo.gov/publication/21954. (Documents 241,000 local government job losses between 2009-2011.)

8. Cadwalader, Wickersham & Taft LLP, "Update: Chapter 9 Eligibility," August 2011. (Analysis of state-by-state Chapter 9 authorization: 18 states specifically authorize municipal bankruptcy; Illinois does not permit municipal bankruptcy filings.)

9. Nathan Bomey and John Gallagher, "How Detroit went broke: The answers may surprise you," Detroit Free Press, September 15, 2013, https://www.freep.com/story/news/local/michigan/detroit/2013/09/15/how-detroit-went-broke-the-answers-may-surprise-you/77152028/. (Comprehensive analysis of Detroit's path to largest municipal bankruptcy in American history, with debt exceeding $18 billion.)

10. Thomas P. DiNapoli, "Meltdown: The Housing Crisis and its Impact on New York State's Local Governments," Office of the New York State Comptroller, November 2008, https://www.osc.ny.gov/files/local-government/publications/pdf/subprime08.pdf. ("Westchester County is home to almost 7,000 subprime mortgages, and Westchester County has the highest average subprime balance ($387,071) outside of New York City.") See also Olha Krupa and Kenneth A. Kriz, "Property tax delinquencies' effects on revenue volatility in American cities," Georgia State University, 2016, https://cslf.gsu.edu/files/2016/05/Krupa-and-Kriz_2016-Public-Fin

ance-Conference-Paper.pdf. (Finds that "economic downturns result in two effects: the first effect is that the recession has a negative effect on housing prices, which is translated into lower assessed valuations. The second effect compounds the negative fiscal impact by reducing property tax collection rates and increasing delinquencies.") See also Thomas Brosy and Chiara Ferrero, "Property Taxes and the Great Recession," Lincoln Institute of Land Policy, 2014, https://www.maxwell.syr.edu/docs/default-source/research/cpr/property-tax-webinar-series/2024-2025/brosyferrero-lincolnwp-newmay24-accessible.pdf. (Confirms "more homeowners became delinquent" after the Great Recession.)

11. S&P CoreLogic Case-Shiller Home Price Indices, San Francisco Metro Area, 2006-2012, https://www.spglobal.com/spdji/en/indices/indicators/sp-corelogic-case-shiller-san-francisco-home-price-nsa-index/. (San Francisco metro area index declined 27% from May 2006 peak to March 2009 trough.)

12. Monica Anderson, "About a quarter of rural Americans say access to high-speed internet is a major problem," Pew Research Center, September 10, 2018, https://www.pewresearch.org/short-reads/2018/09/10/about-a-quarter-of-rural-americans-say-access-to-high-speed-internet-is-a-major-problem/. ("24% of rural adults say access to high-speed internet is a major problem in their local community... An additional 34% of rural residents see this as a minor problem, meaning that roughly six-in-ten rural Americans (58%) believe access to high speed internet is a problem in their area.")

13. Sheps Center for Health Services Research, "Rural Hospital Closures," University of North Carolina at Chapel Hill, accessed November 2025, https://www.shepscenter.unc.edu/programs-proj

ects/rural-health/rural-hospital-closures/. ("152 Closures and Conversions since 2010.") See also Center for Healthcare Quality and Payment Reform, "Rural Hospitals at Risk of Closing," 2024, https://ruralhospitals.chqpr.org/downloads/Rural_H ospitals_at_Risk_of_Closing.pdf. ("More than 700 rural hospitals—one-third of all rural hospitals in the country—are at risk of closing because of the serious financial problems they are experiencing.")

14. Tax Foundation, "How Do Taxes Affect Interstate Migration?," November 2024, https://taxfoundation.org/data/all/state/taxes-affect-s tate-migration-trends-2024/. ("Among taxpayers with $200,000 or more in AGI, the most attractive destinations were Florida, Texas, North Carolina, South Carolina, and Arizona, while the least attractive states were California, New York, Illinois, Massachusetts, and New Jersey. On net, Florida gained 29,771 affluent taxpayers with $200,000 or more in AGI (increasing the state's combined AGI by $28.7 billion), while California lost 24,670 of them (reducing the state's combined AGI by $16.1 billion).")

15. City of Austin Planning Department, "U.S. Census Bureau Update—City of Austin National Ranking," Memo to Mayor and City Council, May 16, 2025, https://services.austintexas.gov/edims/doc ument.cfm?id=451892. ("The city of Austin added just over 4,000 residents between June 30, 2023 and July 1, 2024, growing at a rate of 0.4 percent... were it not for gains in international migration, Travis County would have experienced population decline.")

16. Tennessee State Data Center, "International Migration Boosts Tennessee's Population Gains in 2024," University of Tennessee, Knoxville, December 20, 2024, https://tnsdc.utk.edu/2024/12/20/international-migration -boosts-tennessees-population-gains-in-2024/. ("A pickup in net migration from international sources offset slowing domestic migration

to push Tennessee to a robust population increase of nearly 80,000 people last year.")

17. Naomi Feinstein, "More People Are Leaving Miami-Dade Than Any County in Florida," Miami New Times, March 20, 2025, https://www.miaminewtimes.com/news/more-people-are-leaving-miami-dade-than-any-county-in-florida-22703426/. ("While people are leaving Miami-Dade, the county is still experiencing population growth thanks to international migration. Nearly 124,000 people came to Miami via international migration in 2024.")

18. Aaron Chalfin and Justin McCrary, "Are U.S. Cities Underpoliced? Theory and Evidence," Review of Economics and Statistics, Johns Hopkins University, 2018. (Found each additional police officer prevents 0.06 to 0.1 homicides annually; 10% increase in police force size associated with 3-5% reduction in violent crime.)

19. Office of the New York City Comptroller, "Annual Report on Capital Debt and Obligations," 2024, https://comptroller.nyc.gov/reports/annual-report-on-capital-debt-and-obligations/. ("Debt service exceeded 15 percent of tax revenues – a threshold frequently identified by oversight entities and rating agencies as a prudent limit.")

20. Truth in Accounting, "Financial State of the Cities," https://www.truthinaccounting.org/resources/page/city-reports. (Rankings of 75 largest U.S. cities by taxpayer burden with links to city ACFRs. Data-Z tool at data-z.org provides standardized comparison metrics.)

21. Cook County Treasurer's Office, Property Tax Portal, https://www.cookcountypropertyinfo.com/. ("Search to see a 5-year history of the original tax amounts billed for a PIN.") California State Controller, Property Tax Data, https://propertytax.bythenumbers.sco.ca.gov/. (Property tax allocations reported by 58 California counties in open data format.)

22. Municipal Securities Rulemaking Board, Electronic Municipal Market Access (EMMA), https://emma.msrb.org/. (Free public access to municipal bond ratings from Moody's, S&P, and Fitch, plus rating agency reports and municipal financial disclosures.)

Chapter 10

Financial Positioning

This chapter presents research on financial resilience strategies drawn from academic studies, government data, and expert analysis. It is not personalized financial advice. Individual circumstances vary enormously, and readers should consult qualified financial professionals, tax advisors, and other specialists for guidance specific to their situations.

The internet is full of advice about surviving economic collapse. Buy gold. Stockpile silver. Bitcoin will save you. Farmland is the only real wealth. Load up on canned goods and ammunition. Build a bunker in rural Montana and wait for civilization to end.

Some of this advice contains kernels of truth. Most of it is oversimplified, impractical, or designed to sell you something. The wealthy are not building bunkers or hoarding silver coins. They are making calculated defensive allocations based on understanding what actually preserves value when confidence erodes, government services degrade, and inflation accelerates. And they are doing it quietly, systematically, and at scale.

The Land Report, the authoritative annual ranking of America's largest private landowners, documents accelerating consolidation of farmland among the ultra-wealthy.[1] Private equity investment in U.S. farmland has surged, with institutional investors increasingly viewing agricultural land as a hedge against inflation and economic instability.[2] The Washington Post documented this trend in 2022, noting that moguls are "lavishing ever-larger fortunes on the rustic life," with the pandemic accelerating purchases of working ranches and agricultural properties in the American West.[3]

Bill Gates ranks as the nation's largest private farmland owner, with almost 250,000 acres of highly productive farm ground spread across 17 states.[4] When asked about these holdings in a Reddit discussion, Gates responded: "I own less than 1/4000 of the farmland in the US. I have invested in these farms to make them more productive and create more jobs."[5] Michael Burry, the hedge fund manager who correctly predicted the 2008 financial crisis and was featured in Michael Lewis's book *The Big Short*, publicly stated his investment thesis in 2010: "I believe that agriculture land, productive agricultural land with water on site, will be very valuable in the future."[6] Burry indicated he was buying farmland and gold while searching for the next major opportunity.[6]

The U.S. private security market has grown substantially, with the outsourced security services industry expanding from approximately $22 billion in 2014 to over $33 billion by 2022.[7] This growth occurred during a period of declining violent crime rates nationally, indicating demand driven not by objective threat levels but by subjective risk perception among those who can afford private protection. In New Zealand, the Queenstown Lakes District experienced a 91 percent increase in luxury property sales while commercial hubs like Auckland saw declines exceeding 50 percent.[8] This pattern reflects wealth migration to remote, politically stable regions. High-net-worth individuals are actively pursuing citizenship and residency by investment programs, securing political optionality and exit strategies, as documented in a January 2025 International Monetary Fund working paper analyzing these programs' effects on both origin and destination countries.[9]

These behaviors collectively represent defensive capital allocation by informed actors. They are hedging against inflation through tangible assets. They are securing physical protection through private alternatives to public services. They are obtaining political optionality through alternative citizenships. They are relocating wealth to perceived safe havens. Each action individually appears rational. Collectively, they signal a tail risk assessment fundamentally at odds with public complacency.

This chapter provides a framework for thinking about strategic financial positioning based on what history shows actually works, what the wealthy are quietly doing, and what academic research suggests for people with normal resources operating within normal constraints. This is not about predicting which specific crisis hits when. It is about building resilience across multiple scenarios, because the most valuable asset during uncertainty is optionality: the ability to make choices when others are forced into corners.

The average American household enters periods of economic stress with minimal financial buffers. According to Bureau of Economic Analysis data, the personal saving rate averaged 4.6 percent of disposable income in 2024, with the 2025 average running even lower at 4.4 percent.[10] These rates fall well below historical norms and often prove insufficient to cover what financial planners typically recommend.

A Certified Financial Planner (CFP) writing for the CFP Board advises: "Aim for three to six months' worth of essential expenses in your emergency fund, focusing on what is realistic for you."[11] Fidelity's guidance is similar: "If you're single, you might be comfortable with 3 months of savings. However, if you have a spouse, kids, a mortgage, or if you worry about job stability, you might feel better with 6 months of savings or more."[12] The gap between these expert recommendations and actual savings rates means a large portion of the population faces rapid financial distress following any sudden job loss or income shock.

The vulnerability concentrates in the middle class, which exhibits high leverage and wealth portfolios dominated by real estate. Research published in the Russell Sage Foundation Journal of the Social Sciences demonstrated this fragility with devastating clarity: "Median wealth plummeted by 44 percent between 2007 and 2010, almost double the drop in housing prices, and by 2010 was at its lowest since 1969."[13] The decline was directly traceable to high leverage and illiquid asset composition.

The acceleration toward default during crisis is compounded by the simultaneous withdrawal of consumer credit. Federal Reserve Bank of New York research documents that approximately 120 million credit card accounts were closed on net during the recession.[14] When households lose both liquid savings and access to credit simultaneously, they are forced into rapid asset liquidation or default, dramatically amplifying recession impacts.

This context explains why the first priority in any financial positioning strategy must be establishing robust liquidity. Financial planners generally recommend 3 to 6 months of essential household expenses maintained in easily accessible accounts.[11] Given that severe recessions can persist for extended periods, with the Great Recession lasting 18 months from December 2007 to June 2009, exceeding the 16-month recessions of 1973-1975 and 1981-1982, the upper range of emergency fund recommendations offers more prudent protection.[15]

But maintaining excessive cash beyond this buffer creates a different vulnerability. In periods of sustained inflation, which commonly accompany fiscal crises as governments attempt to reduce real debt burdens, cash holdings experience guaranteed erosion of purchasing power. Employee Benefit Research Institute data shows that 91 percent of Health Savings Account holders maintain funds in zero-yield cash positions, neglecting investment potential and accepting certain real value decline.[16] The opportunity cost of holding 12 or 18 months of expenses in cash rather than 6 months becomes substantial when that excess capital could be positioned defensively against inflation while maintaining reasonable liquidity.

Traditional financial advice centers on the 60/40 portfolio: 60 percent equities for growth, 40 percent high-quality government bonds for stability and negative correlation during equity declines. This framework has worked reasonably well during normal economic cycles. According to analysis from the London Stock Exchange Group, it fails during fiscal stress: "The traditional 60/40 portfolio has long been a cornerstone of risk management. But in recent downturns, it has failed to provide the expected safety net. When equity markets fell, bond yields rose instead of offering protection, leaving investors exposed."[17]

The fundamental assumption underlying the 60/40 model is that stocks and bonds move inversely. When equity markets decline, investors flee to the safety of government bonds, driving bond prices up and yields down, cushioning portfolio losses. But this relationship breaks down when the crisis centers on sovereign fiscal sustainability itself. When investors question government solvency, both equities and government bonds can decline simultaneously, eliminating the expected protection.

This correlation failure means strategic asset allocation must extend beyond diversification within the conventional financial system to incorporating assets structurally outside vulnerable nodes.

Gold has served as a monetary hedge for thousands of years. Academic research published in August 2025 provides nuanced analysis: "Gold still preserves purchasing power but vastly exceeds inflation rates and money supply... gold does not react to average inflation rates but to large inflation rates and shocks."[18] The study found "strong reactions to large inflation rates and shocks and no reaction to average or 'normal' rates," with "even stronger reactions of the gold price found for 1-year and 5-year inflation expectation shocks."[18] The weakness of gold as an investment is its lack of yield. It generates no income, imposes storage costs if held physically, and can underperform during periods of strong economic growth. But these characteristics are precisely what make it valuable during crisis.

Real estate presents a more complex analysis. Property provides inflation protection through both rental income increases and property value appreciation. The disadvantages are extreme illiquidity compared to financial instruments and high transaction costs. More critically, real estate value is intensely location-dependent during crisis. As Chapter 9 documented, using Pew Charitable Trusts research, the same national economic shock produces radically different outcomes across geography.[19] Detroit property lost massive value during its fiscal collapse while Phoenix real estate recovered more quickly from the housing crisis. Real estate concentrated in fiscally vulnerable jurisdictions becomes a trap rather than protection.

The illiquidity problem deserves particular emphasis because it proved so consequential during the Great Recession. Home equity represented the largest component of middle-class wealth, and housing values declined substantially. But the real damage came from the inability to access that equity rapidly when needed. Attempting to tap home equity during crisis through sale forces acceptance of depressed prices and lengthy transaction timelines. Attempting to extract equity through refinancing or home equity loans often fails precisely when most needed, as lenders tighten standards during economic stress.

Equities, despite their volatility, provide ownership of productive assets and potential inflation protection as companies can raise prices to maintain margins. During deep recession, equity values fall substantially. From peak to trough, the market fell approximately 57 percent during the Great Recession. But from the March 2009 bottom through December 2019, the S&P 500 Total Return Index delivered approximately 400 percent cumulative returns, an annualized rate of roughly 15 percent.[20] The critical requirement is maintaining adequate liquidity separately so that equity positions need not be liquidated during downturns, allowing recovery time.

Digital assets, particularly Bitcoin, are frequently discussed as potential inflation hedges due to capped supply limiting debasement risk. Academic research provides mixed evidence. A 2024 study in Finance Research Letters concluded: "Bitcoin is, at best, a context-specific inflation hedge... The inflation-hedging property of Bitcoin (Gold) disappeared (strengthened) during the COVID-19 period."[21] More problematically, IMF research analyzing market behavior during periods of heightened financial stress found "increasing spillovers over time, with a peak during the COVID-19 pandemic, implying growing interdependence" between crypto and traditional markets, with "increased correlation during risk-off episodes" suggesting "crypto assets could serve as important conduits for financial market shocks, generating financial stability risks."[22] Crypto appears to function as a risk-on asset, declining when investors reduce risk exposure rather than providing crisis protection.

The framework that emerges from analyzing historical performance across crisis types is not optimization for any single scenario but diversification across potential outcomes. Stagflation favors real assets, commodities, and gold. Deflationary depression favors cash and high-quality bonds as deflation increases purchasing power of fixed nominal holdings. Confidence crisis in government debt favors assets outside the sovereign system entirely, particularly gold and potentially foreign assets in stable jurisdictions. The challenge is that precise prediction of which crisis manifests is impossible. The solution is holding positions that provide some protection across multiple scenarios.

A strategic allocation framework for households with normal resources, not billionaire-scale wealth, must balance crisis resilience with practical constraints. Three illustrative frameworks correspond to different risk tolerances and life situations, but the specific percentages matter less than the underlying logic of diversification across systems and crisis types. These are starting points for research and discussion with qualified advisors, not prescriptions.

A conservative allocation prioritizes maximum liquidity and safety, accepting lower long-term returns. 30 percent cash and short-term bonds provides substantial buffer beyond the 6-month emergency fund. 30 percent diversified equities, concentrated in essential services and defensive sectors, maintains some participation in long-term growth. 20 percent allocated to primary residence in a fiscally healthy area recognizes that housing is necessary regardless and that ownership in the right location provides inflation protection and stability. 10 percent in gold or precious metals provides insurance against currency debasement. 10 percent in international diversification, either through foreign equities or modest currency holdings, reduces dollar concentration risk.

A moderate allocation accepts higher volatility for better long-term returns while maintaining crisis awareness. 20 percent cash and short-term bonds covers emergencies and provides dry powder for opportunistic deployment during dislocations. 40 percent diversified equities spanning domestic and international markets, with overweights in sectors demonstrating historical resilience. 20 percent allocated to primary residence. 10 percent in gold and commodities. 10 percent in alternatives, potentially including a small allocation to digital assets for those who understand the technology and accept the volatility, or additional international exposure.

An aggressive allocation emphasizes growth while acknowledging tail risks. 10 percent cash, covering the baseline emergency fund but minimizing opportunity cost from excess liquidity. 50 percent diversified equities, accepting that long-term wealth building requires equity participation despite cyclical volatility. 20 percent primary residence. 10 percent gold and commodities. 10 percent alternatives and speculative positions, including potentially higher allocation to international markets or digital assets.

These frameworks are illustrative, not prescriptive, but align with core principles identified across modern portfolio theory, diversification research, and financial planning best practice.[37] Individual circumstances, including age, income stability, risk tolerance, and specific human capital characteristics, determine appropriate positioning. A tenured professor with stable income and pension can accept higher equity allocation and lower liquidity than a commission-based salesperson with volatile earnings. A household with two working adults in different industries possesses more income diversification than single-earner households, potentially justifying more aggressive positioning. Geographic factors matter enormously, as Chapter 9 established. Households in fiscally healthy locations with strong property tax bases can rely more on real estate wealth than those in vulnerable jurisdictions.

What matters more than exact percentages is adherence to rebalancing discipline. Crisis creates opportunities precisely because asset prices dislocate from fundamental value as forced sellers drive prices below rational levels. The household maintaining liquidity reserves and rebalancing discipline can purchase quality assets at depression prices, potentially capturing significant returns during the depth of crisis.

Research on investor behavior during crises reveals consistent patterns that create both dangers and opportunities. A 2024 comparative study of herding behavior found: "In times of crisis, investor behaviour frequently deviates from logical judgment, with herd mentalities escalating volatility and causing market instability."[23] This herding behavior creates opportunities for those who do not follow the herd.

Research published in the Journal of Banking and Finance examined individual investor behavior during the 2008-2009 crisis: "During the worst months of the crisis, investors' return expectations and risk tolerance decrease, while their risk perceptions increase. Towards the end of the crisis, investor perceptions recover."[24] The study documented "substantial swings in trading and risk-taking behavior that are driven by changes in investor perceptions."[24]

The 2008 to 2009 crash provided exactly this opportunity. As noted earlier, those with cash reserves and the psychological capacity to deploy capital when equity markets had fallen 57 percent captured returns exceeding 400 percent over the following decade.[20] The gains did not come from superior stock selection but from simply having the liquidity and discipline to buy during maximum pessimism.

This principle extends beyond equities. Real estate prices dislocated severely during the housing crisis. Properties in fundamentally sound locations traded at prices driven by forced liquidation rather than long-term value. Buyers with access to capital, often cash buyers who faced no financing constraints, acquired assets at substantial discounts that produced excellent returns as markets normalized. The mechanism that creates opportunity is always the same: crisis forces liquidation by over-leveraged or liquidity-constrained sellers. Those maintaining reserves can transact when others cannot, purchasing quality assets at crisis prices and holding through recovery.

The debt structure supporting any asset holdings deserves careful consideration. Fixed-rate debt provides protection against interest rate volatility and becomes advantageous during high inflation periods. Federal Reserve Bank of St. Louis research explains the mechanism: "A surprising burst of inflation immediately reduces the real value of a borrower's debt burden... Inflation transfers wealth from creditors to borrowers for all sorts of nominal debt."[25]

The IMF's "Back to Basics" series on inflation states the principle directly: "A borrower who pays a fixed-rate mortgage of 5 percent would benefit from 5 percent inflation, because the real interest rate would be zero; servicing this debt would be even easier if inflation were higher."[26] But this advantage depends critically on income stability. Unemployment negates the inflation benefit entirely, as inability to make payments forces foreclosure regardless of favorable interest rate dynamics. The rule must therefore be to maintain fixed-rate debt only when confident in income continuity, while eliminating variable-rate exposure that creates vulnerability to policy rate increases during periods when central banks combat inflation through aggressive tightening.

High-interest debt, specifically credit cards and personal loans, represents guaranteed negative returns and must be eliminated before considering any investment positioning. The mathematics is unforgiving. No investment strategy reliably generates returns exceeding credit card interest rates after accounting for risk and taxes. Paying down 20 percent APR credit card debt provides a guaranteed 20 percent return, which no other strategy can match safely. The priority sequence must always be eliminating high-interest debt first, building emergency liquidity second, and only then considering strategic asset allocation.

The mortgage payoff question generates substantial debate among financial professionals. Paying off a low-rate fixed mortgage eliminates foreclosure risk and reduces monthly obligations, providing clear psychological and financial benefits. But for households with adequate liquidity, maintaining the mortgage and investing the capital that would otherwise go to accelerated payoff often produces superior outcomes over long horizons. The critical factor is liquidity access. Paying off the mortgage locks capital into home equity, which as noted earlier proves extremely difficult to access rapidly during crisis. Maintaining the mortgage while holding liquid investments preserves optionality. Emergency needs can be met by liquidating investments without selling the home or navigating refinancing during stressed conditions.

The most overlooked dimension of financial resilience is human capital: the ability to generate continuous income through employment. Research published in the Annals of the American Academy of Political and Social Science documented wealth disparities before and after the Great Recession: "These large relative losses were disproportionately concentrated among lower income, less educated, and minority households."[27] Higher education and skill levels offered measurable protection during crisis.

Healthcare employment continued growing during the Great Recession, according to Bureau of Labor Statistics research, confirming its historical role as a recession-resistant sector due to inelastic demand.[28] Education, government, and public safety demonstrate similar resilience, driven by necessity and relatively stable public funding even during stress.

Conversely, industries heavily dependent on credit availability or discretionary spending demonstrate acute vulnerability. Federal Reserve Bank of Richmond research found that "certain sectors that are heavily dependent on credit availability, such as real estate and retail trade, were particularly vulnerable" during the 2007-2009 crisis.[29] Career positioning toward resilient sectors provides income stability that proves more valuable than marginal investment returns on financial assets during crisis.

Beyond sector selection, the development of adaptive skills provides flexibility that enhances employability across changing conditions. Research published in the NBER Reporter notes: "Employment and wage growth have been especially strong for professional jobs that require both analytical and social skills. In today's economy, workers must be able to solve complex problems in fluid, rapidly changing, team-based settings."[30] These capabilities enable individuals to pivot between roles and industries, maintaining employment even when specific technical skills become obsolete or industries contract.

The underlying economic logic is that financial assets can lose value, but skills remain and continue generating returns through labor income. Investing in human capital development therefore provides returns that cannot be taxed away, inflated away, or confiscated, making it uniquely robust.

Income diversification through side employment or multiple income streams creates redundancy that reduces single-point-of-failure risk. The household depending entirely on a single primary job faces catastrophic impact from job loss. The household with income from multiple sources, even if individually modest, maintains partial cash flow during disruptions, extending financial runway and reducing forced liquidation risk. This diversification need not involve equal magnitude sources. Even modest supplemental income from part-time work, freelance activities, or small business operations provides valuable cushion and demonstrates to potential employers that the individual possesses initiative and diverse capabilities.

Social capital, the value derived from networks and community connections, functions as non-monetary wealth that provides critical support during financial stress. Research on community resilience identifies distinct types of social capital.[31] Bonding capital consists of "connections among individuals who are emotionally close, such as friends or family, and result in tight bonds to a particular group." Bridging capital involves "acquaintances or individuals loosely connected that span social groups, such as class or race."[31]

A 2022 review published in the journal Ambio found that "the ability of households to cope during crises was enhanced by bonding capital" as it "enhanced access to psychological and material support." Meanwhile, "bridging and linking social capital were also important in the immediate aftermath of crises for enhancing access to new information, resources and support."[31] Effective resilience requires both types: bonding capital for immediate support and bridging capital for information and opportunity access.

Multigenerational households represent a specific form of social capital that has increased significantly following economic stress. Research found that "the Great Recession and housing crises brought many generations together out of economic necessity... By 2014, 19% of the U.S. population lived in multigenerational housing."[32] This arrangement enables comprehensive resource pooling across generations, sharing costs for housing, utilities, food, childcare, and eldercare. The concentration of financial and personal risk in shared living arrangements necessitates formalized management of resource allocation and decision-making to prevent conflicts that can destroy the very support structure the arrangement provides.

Healthcare access continuity during economic crisis presents a specific vulnerability that requires advance planning. Job loss frequently means insurance loss, creating medical financial shock precisely when household resources are most constrained. The American Hospital Association reports that "in 2024 alone, total hospital expense grew 5.1%, significantly outpacing the overall inflation rate of 2.9%," with "persistent expense growth" threatening "hospitals' solvency and their ability to sustain comprehensive services."[33] These pressures translate into higher out-of-pocket costs for patients.

The Consolidated Omnibus Budget Reconciliation Act (COBRA) allows individuals to maintain employer-sponsored coverage after job loss, but requires paying the full premium, often making it prohibitively expensive. The Affordable Care Act Marketplace frequently provides more affordable alternatives due to income-based federal and state subsidies that activate during job loss, which qualifies as a special enrollment period.[34] Understanding these options before crisis hits enables immediate action upon job loss to secure continuous coverage at minimum cost.

Health Savings Accounts, available to those enrolled in high-deductible health plans, provide unique triple tax advantage. As IRS Publication 969 states: "Contributions are deductible... Earnings in the account grow tax free. Distributions for qualified medical expenses are tax free."[35] While designed for healthcare savings, HSAs function as tax-advantaged investment vehicles when aggressively funded and invested rather than held in cash. The 91 percent of account holders who maintain funds in zero-yield cash positions neglect substantial long-term value creation potential.[16]

Preventive health measures preserve income-generating capacity by avoiding chronic disease that impairs employment. Research on health investment notes that "those who suffer from temporary poor health lose opportunities for productivity, and those who experience disability can face prolonged underemployment," while "healthier individuals are more likely to pursue further educational and vocational training, thus raising their lifetime earning pote ntial."[36] The value is not the healthcare spending avoided but the continuous employment enabled by maintaining health.

What this framework does not provide is specific investment recommendations, tax optimization strategies, or guaranteed protection against all scenarios. No perfect hedge exists. Every asset class carries specific risks. Every strategic choice involves trade-offs between competing objectives. The purpose is not to promise safety but to provide logical structure for thinking about resilience across potential outcomes.

Financial positioning is not about predicting which crisis hits when. It is about building capacity to withstand multiple scenarios while maintaining optionality to adapt as conditions evolve. The wealthy are doing exactly this: accumulating farmland for tangible inflation protection, securing private security as public services face stress, obtaining citizenship optionality for political risk diversification, and relocating assets to perceived safe havens. These behaviors reflect not paranoia but systematic tail risk management by actors with access to sophisticated analysis and resources to implement defensive strategies.

You do not need billionaire resources to apply the same logic. Maintain adequate emergency liquidity to avoid forced liquidation during temporary stress. Position assets beyond that buffer to provide some protection against inflation, deflation, and confidence erosion rather than concentrating in conventional portfolios that assume stable conditions. Invest in human capital development and career positioning toward resilient sectors. Cultivate social networks providing both material support and information access. Secure healthcare continuity strategies before crisis forces reactive decisions. Eliminate high-cost debt that creates guaranteed negative returns.

The most valuable asset is not any particular investment. It is optionality: the capacity to make choices when others face constraints. Maintaining liquidity when asset prices dislocate creates opportunity to acquire quality holdings at crisis prices. Maintaining income continuity through resilient employment preserves ability to meet obligations without forced asset sales. Maintaining health and social capital preserves capacity for adaptation that pure financial wealth cannot provide.

The crisis is coming. The question is not whether your assets will face stress but whether your positioning allows you to withstand temporary dislocation without permanent impairment. Those who enter crisis with liquidity, diversification across systems, resilient income sources, and strong networks will have choices. Those who enter over-leveraged, concentrated in conventional allocations, dependent on single income sources, and socially isolated will face compulsion.

Financial positioning provides resilience. Geographic positioning, examined in Chapter 9, provides foundation. But both depend on something harder to quantify: the skills you possess, the networks you maintain, and the psychological capacity to navigate prolonged uncertainty without panic or paralysis. Assets can be taxed, inflated, or confiscated. Skills cannot. Networks survive when institutions fail. And the ability to adapt psychologically determines whether you thrive or merely survive.

Chapter 10 Notes

1. The Land Report, "The Land Report 100," accessed November 2025, https://landreport.com/land-report-100. The Land Report is the authoritative annual ranking of America's largest private landowners.

2. Justin Flores, "Betting the Farm: Private Equity Buyouts in US Agriculture," Private Equity Stakeholder Project, March 27, 2025, https://pestakeholder.org/reports/betting-the-farm-private-equity-buyouts-in-us-agriculture/.

3. Karen Heller, "The fabulously wealthy are fueling a booming luxury ranch market out West," Washington Post, August 16, 2022, https://www.washingtonpost.com/lifestyle/2022/08/16/ranch-land-west-billionaires/.

4. The Land Report, "Bill Gates - #43 on the LR 100," accessed November 2025, https://landreport.com/land-report-100/bill-gates. ("With almost 250,000 acres of highly productive farm ground spread out over 17 states, the co-founder of MICROSOFT ranks as the nation's largest private farmland owner.")

5. Sarah Jackson, "Bill Gates responds to skepticism about him owning 275,000 acres of farmland: 'There isn't some grand scheme involved,'" Business Insider, January 2023, https://www.businessinsider.com/bill-gates-defends-farmland-purchases-there-isnt-some-grand-scheme-2023-1.

6. John Carney, "Michael Burry Is Buying Gold And Agricultural Land," CNBC, September 7, 2010, https://www.cnbc.com/2010/09/07/michael-burry-is-buying-gold-and-agricultural-land.html.

7. IBISWorld, "Security Services in the US - Market Research Report

(2015-2030)," November 2025, https://www.ibisworld.com/united-states/industry/security-services/1487/. See also Statista, "Market size of the outsourced contract security industry in the United States from 2014 to 2023," https://www.statista.com/statistics/824279/outsourced-security-services-us-market-size/.

8. RNZ News, "Luxury property sales drop by more than 50 percent," accessed November 2025, https://www.rnz.co.nz/news/business/541398/luxury-property-sales-drop-by-more-than-50-percent.

9. International Monetary Fund, "Drivers and Effects of Residence and Citizenship by Investment," IMF Working Paper WP/25/8, January 2025, https://www.imf.org/-/media/Files/Publications/WP/2025/English/wpiea2025008-print-pdf.ashx.

10. Bureau of Economic Analysis, "Personal Saving Rate," Federal Reserve Economic Data (FRED), accessed November 2025, https://fred.stlouisfed.org/series/PSAVERT.

11. Julie R. Bates, CFP, "How to Future Proof Your Finances During Market Uncertainty," Certified Financial Planner Board of Standards, November 5, 2025, https://www.letsmakeaplan.org/financial-topics/articles/financial-uncertainty/how-to-future-proof-your-finances-during-market-uncertainty.

12. Fidelity Investments, "How much to save for emergencies," Fidelity Viewpoints, accessed November 2025, https://www.fidelity.com/viewpoints/personal-finance/save-for-an-emergency.

13. Edward N. Wolff, "Household Wealth Trends in the United States, 1962 to 2013: What Happened over the Great Recession?" RSF: The Russell Sage Foundation Journal of the Social Sciences 2, no. 6 (2016): 24-43, https://www.rsfjournal.org/content/2/6/24.

14. Federal Reserve Bank of New York, Staff Reports, page 8, https://www.newyorkfed.org/medialibrary/media/research/staff_reports/sr882.pdf. ("During the recession, on net, 120 million credit card accounts were closed.")

15. Arne L. Kalleberg and Till M. Von Wachter, "The U.S. Labor Market During and After the Great Recession: Continuities and Transformations," RSF: The Russell Sage Foundation Journal of the Social Sciences 3, no. 3 (2017): 1-19, https://pmc.ncbi.nlm.nih.gov/article s/PMC5959048/.

16. Greg Iacurci, "91% of people with health savings accounts make this mistake," CNBC, October 15, 2021, https://www.cnbc.com/2021/10/15/91percent-of-people-wi th-health-savings-accounts-make-this-mistake.html. Citing Employee Benefit Research Institute data.

17. LSEG (London Stock Exchange Group), "The future of asset allocation: Navigating a paradigm shift," accessed November 2025, https://www.lseg.com/en/insights/data-analytics/the-fut ure-of-asset-allocation-navigating-a-paradigm-shift2.

18. Dirk G. Baur, "Is Gold an Inflation Hedge?" University of Western Australia Business School, SSRN, August 2025, https://papers.ssrn. com/sol3/papers.cfm?abstract_id=5389663.

19. The Pew Charitable Trusts, "Fiscal Health of Large U.S . Cities Varied Long After Great Recession's End," April 2016, https://www.pew.org/~/media/assets/2016/04/fiscalhealthof largeuscitiesvariedlongaftergreatrecessionsend.pdf.

20. S&P Dow Jones Indices, S&P 500 Total Return Index historical data, 2007-2019.

21. Harold Rodriguez and Jefferson Colombo, "Is Bitcoin an Inflation

Hedge?" Finance Research Letters (2024), https://www.sciencedire
ct.com/science/article/abs/pii/S0148619524000602.

22. International Monetary Fund, "New Evidence on Spillovers Between Crypto Assets and Financial Markets," IMF Working Paper
WP/23/213, 2023, https://www.elibrary.imf.org/view/journals/00
1/2023/213/article-A001-en.xml.

23. Ajay Kumar Varshney et al., "Investor Herding Behaviour During
Financial Crises: A Comparative Study," Academy of Contemporary
Research Journal (2024), https://acr-journal.com/article/investor-h
erding-behaviour-during-financial-crises-a-comparative-study-1560/.

24. Arvid O.I. Hoffmann, Thomas Post, and Joost M.E. Pennings, "Individual investor perceptions and behavior during the financial crisis,"
Journal of Banking & Finance 37, no. 1 (2013): 60-74, https://www
.sciencedirect.com/science/article/abs/pii/S0378426612002294.

25. Christopher J. Neely, "Inflation, Real Value of Debt, and Who Benefits," Federal Reserve Bank of St. Louis, On the Economy, August 1,
2022, https://www.stlouisfed.org/on-the-economy/2022/aug/inflat
ion-real-value-debt-double-edged-sword.

26. Ceyda Oner, "Inflation: Prices on the Rise," International Monetary
Fund, Back to Basics series, https://www.imf.org/en/publications/f
andd/issues/series/back-to-basics/inflation.

27. Fabian T. Pfeffer, Sheldon Danziger, and Robert F. Schoeni, "Wealth
Disparities before and after the Great Recession," Annals of the American Academy of Political and Social Science 650, no. 1 (2013): 98-123,
https://pmc.ncbi.nlm.nih.gov/articles/PMC4200506/.

28. Bureau of Labor Statistics, "Healthcare jobs and the Great Recession,"
Monthly Labor Review, 2018, https://www.bls.gov/opub/mlr/2018
/article/healthcare-jobs-and-the-great-recession.htm.

29. Federal Reserve Bank of Richmond, "The Service Sector and the 'Great Recession,'" Economic Brief 10-12, 2010, https://www.richm ondfed.org/publications/research/economic_brief/2010/eb_10-12.

30. National Bureau of Economic Research, "The Value of Soft Skills in the Labor Market," NBER Reporter 2017, no. 4, https://www.nber .org/reporter/2017number4/value-soft-skills-labor-market.

31. University of North Carolina School of Government, "The Primacy of Social Capital for Community Resilience," June 2, 2023, https://ced.sog.unc.edu/2023/06/02/the-primacy-of-social-c apital-for-community-resilience/. Drawing on Daniel P. Aldrich and Michelle A. Meyer's research and Carmen et al., "Social capital and community resilience," Ambio 51 (2022): 1377-1380.

32. Sung S. Park et al., "Living with parents or grandparents increases social capital and survival: 2014 General Social Survey-National Death Index," PLOS ONE (2018), https://pmc.ncbi.nlm.nih.gov/articles/ PMC5769098/.

33. American Hospital Association, "The Cost of Caring: Challenges Facing America's Hospitals in 2025," April 2025, https://www.aha .org/costsofcaring.

34. COBRA Insurance, "COBRA vs. Marketplace (ACA) Insurance," accessed November 2025, https://www.cobrainsurance.com/afforda ble-care-act-enrollments/.

35. Internal Revenue Service, Publication 969: Health Savings Accounts and Other Tax-Favored Health Plans, https://www.irs.gov/publicati ons/p969.

36. FP Analytics, "The Compounding Economic Dividends of Global Health Investment," Foreign Policy, 2022, https://fpanalytics.foreignpolicy.com/wp-content/uploads/sites/5/2

022/09/Compounding-Economic-Dividends-of-Global-Health-Inve stment.pdf.

37. For a diversified household allocation framework grounded in standard financial planning principles, see: Vanguard. "Vanguard Principles for Constructing Investment Portfolios." Vanguard Research, 2023. https://investor.vanguard.com/investor-resources-education/ portfolio-construction Fama, Eugene F., and Kenneth R. French. "The Cross-Section of Expected Stock Returns." Journal of Finance 47, no. 2 (1992): 427–465. https://doi.org/10.1111/j.1540-6261.1 992.tb04398.x Baur, Dirk G., and Brian Lucey. "Is Gold a Hedge or a Safe Haven? An Analysis of Stocks, Bonds and Gold." Financial Review 45, no. 2 (2010): 217–229. https://doi.org/10.1111/j.1540 -6288.2010.00244.x Sinai, Todd, and Nicholas Souleles. "Owner-Occupied Housing as a Hedge Against Rent Risk." Quarterly Journal of Economics 120, no. 2 (2005): 763–789. https://doi.org/10.1093/qje /120.2.763 Solnik, Bruno. "Why Not Diversify Internationally Rather Than Domestically?" Financial Analysts Journal 30, no. 4 (1974): 48–54. https://doi.org/10.2469/faj.v30.n4.48 Swensen, David. Pioneering Portfolio Management (New York: Free Press, 2000).

Chapter 11
Skills, Networks, Psychology

The crisis will not arrive as a single catastrophic event requiring heroic endurance. It will arrive as years of grinding uncertainty, constant trade-offs, and the slow erosion of systems you assumed were permanent. Surviving this requires understanding what actually protects you when formal structures fail, and what that protection costs psychologically.

By now, you've assessed your geography. You've positioned your assets. You've evaluated which cities to avoid and which states offer fiscal stability. You understand that material preparation provides a buffer, but it is not sufficient. Long-term resilience through a multi-year crisis requires three forms of capital that cannot be purchased: skills that remain valuable as the formal economy contracts, social networks that function as safety nets when institutions fail, and psychological frameworks for maintaining functionality during prolonged institutional degradation.

The skills that retain value during economic contraction share four characteristics. They address basic human needs that cannot be deferred. They require physical presence and cannot be outsourced. They resist automation because they demand human judgment. And they scale to informal exchange when cash becomes scarce.

Healthcare sits at the top of this hierarchy. The aging American population guarantees demand regardless of economic conditions. During the Great Recession, healthcare employment continued to grow even as most sectors experienced severe job losses; from a historical perspective, healthcare has been resistant to, if not immune from, the usual employment contractions associated with recessions.[1] Medical professionals, nurses, home health aides, and dental workers maintained stable employment because illness does not pause during recession. An aging population with chronic conditions requires continuous care. This demand is structurally inelastic.

Utilities represent another tier of essential services. Water treatment, power generation, and waste management cannot fail without triggering immediate public health crises. Municipalities cut discretionary programs and defer infrastructure maintenance, but they cannot turn off the water or let sewage systems collapse. The workers who maintain these systems possess recession-proof skills because the alternative to paying them is civilizational breakdown.

Food production, processing, and distribution similarly resist contraction. People reduce restaurant spending and luxury purchases, but they continue eating. Small-scale agriculture, food preservation, and basic cooking skills retain value because they address the most fundamental human need. When formal employment becomes scarce and cash tight, the ability to produce food or prepare meals becomes a tradeable service within informal community networks.

Basic infrastructure maintenance falls into the same category. When plumbing breaks, it requires immediate repair. Electrical systems, heating and cooling, and structural integrity cannot be deferred indefinitely without rendering a home uninhabitable. The skills to perform these repairs (carpentry, electrical work, plumbing) maintain value because they address urgent, non-negotiable problems. Unlike many professional services, these skills translate directly to barter and informal exchange when traditional employment becomes unavailable.

Security represents the fastest-growing sector in this hierarchy, though for reasons that reveal the crisis itself. The private security services market is projected to grow at nearly 10 percent annually through 2030, driven particularly by residential demand as individuals increasingly seek protection for their homes.[2] This growth occurred during a period of declining national crime rates, indicating demand driven not by objective threat but by perceived risk among those who can afford private protection. As municipal police forces face budget cuts in the 2030s, this market will expand further.

The sectors most vulnerable to contraction follow predictable patterns. Government employment, often perceived as stable, faces systematic reduction. Federal hiring freezes began in January 2025 and converted to indefinite restrictions by October 2025, with 4-to-1 attrition ratios designed to permanently shrink the federal workforce.[3] Municipal employees face layoffs as property tax revenues lag housing market declines by two to five years and pension obligations crowd out operating budgets. Public sector workers, excluding essential services like police and utilities, will experience the largest employment losses of any category.

Finance contracts sharply during credit crises. Regional banks holding concentrated commercial real estate exposure will fail or consolidate. High-end professional services (management consulting, corporate law, investment banking) serve discretionary business needs that disappear when companies focus on survival. The first cuts in corporate budgets eliminate advisory services.

Real estate, both commercial and residential, enters prolonged stress. Commercial real estate faces a refinancing crisis as $957 billion in loans mature in 2025 alone, nearly triple the twenty-year average, with property values that cannot support existing debt loads.[4] Residential real estate follows with a lag as unemployment rises and household formation declines. The entire ecosystem of agents, appraisers, mortgage brokers, and property managers faces sustained contraction.

Discretionary consumer services collapse fastest. Restaurants, entertainment venues, luxury retail, travel and hospitality depend entirely on disposable income that evaporates during recession. The service workers in these industries, already operating with minimal savings, experience immediate income loss with limited alternative employment options.

What makes certain skills valuable is not their current market price but their resilience to systemic stress. A corporate lawyer earning $300,000 annually possesses skills highly specialized to a functioning legal system with solvent corporate clients. When that system contracts, those skills lose value rapidly. A nurse earning $80,000 possesses skills that remain essential regardless of economic conditions. The strategic career choice is not maximizing current income but positioning in sectors where demand persists through contraction.

Transferable skills matter more than credentials. Hands-on repair and maintenance skills cannot be easily outsourced or automated and address immediate, tangible problems. Direct care provision (elder care, childcare, disability support) remains essential and scales to informal arrangements when formal employment becomes scarce. Teaching and tutoring emerge as valuable skills when public schools degrade and families with resources seek private alternatives for their children.

The goal is not to abandon professional careers for manual trades but to develop competencies that retain value outside formal employment structures. The engineer who can also repair complex systems, the teacher who can tutor independently, the healthcare worker who can provide home care: these individuals possess skills that translate to multiple employment models including informal exchange when cash becomes constrained.

Income diversification serves as risk management. Relying on a single employer in a vulnerable sector creates catastrophic exposure. Developing secondary income streams (consulting work, side businesses, freelance services) reduces dependence on any single source. When primary employment fails, diversified income provides continued cash flow while searching for replacement work. This is not about working multiple jobs indefinitely but about building redundancy into income generation.

The meta-skills that enhance employability across sectors warrant particular attention. Adaptability, the capacity to pivot quickly and assume varied responsibilities, becomes essential during organizational restructuring. Critical thinking, the ability to analyze problems and develop strategic solutions, retains value because it cannot be easily replicated. Employers frequently list teamwork, collaboration, and oral and written communication skills as highly valuable yet hard-to-find qualities in potential new hires.[5] Project management, the capacity to coordinate complex initiatives and deliver results under constraints, becomes crucial when organizations operate with reduced resources.

These skills matter because they enable movement between sectors and roles. When one industry contracts, individuals with strong meta-skills can transition to adjacent fields. The person with only narrow technical expertise faces unemployment when their specific niche disappears. The person with broad competencies can redeploy their skills across multiple contexts.

The greatest defensive investment is not gold or real estate but human capital development. Financial assets can lose 44 percent of their value in a single crisis, as household wealth did during the Great Recession.[6] Skills in resilient sectors guarantee continuous cash flow. The capacity to generate income, even at reduced levels, matters more than the current value of a portfolio when that portfolio may be inaccessible or severely diminished during acute stress.

Material assets provide a buffer. Social networks provide survival. When formal systems fail, informal community support determines whether households weather shocks or experience catastrophic collapse.

The United States that endured the Great Depression possessed structural advantages that no longer exist. The median age in 1930 was 26.5 years.[7] The population was younger, more flexible, and less dependent on complex support systems. A substantial portion of the population lived in rural areas or small towns where subsistence was possible through direct access to land. Extended families lived in proximity, providing natural safety nets. Social capital, measured through participation in churches, civic organizations, and community groups, was high and sustained through the crisis.

Today's America differs fundamentally. The median age has risen to approximately 39 years.8 More than 80 percent of the population lives in urban areas, dependent on complex supply chains and formal employment for survival. Extended families are geographically dispersed. Social capital has declined systematically since the 1960s, documented through reduced participation in civic organizations, declining trust in institutions, and weakened community ties.[9] The informal networks that cushioned the Great Depression have eroded.

This erosion matters because social capital functions as a measurable economic buffer. Despite the ubiquity of disaster and the increasing toll in human lives and financial costs, much research and policy remain focused on physical infrastructure. Yet evidence demonstrates that social, not physical, infrastructure drives resilience. Social capital and networks play a critical role in disaster survival and recovery.[10] Communities with higher social capital recovered faster and more completely from the Great Recession. The mechanism is direct substitution: when formal services become unavailable or unaffordable, communities with strong networks provide informal alternatives through mutual aid.

Mutual aid operates through collective pooling of resources. It includes support for basic needs such as food, housing, and transportation, but also emotional connection and coordination between those who need something and those who have something to give. Mutual aid groups provide both tangible goods (funds, food, medical care) and intangible support such as job opportunities. Participants come together on a voluntary and equal basis to share experiential knowledge and provide informal social support.[11] During the Great Recession, one in five American households participated in SNAP to supplement their food supply, and many also relied on less formal methods such as food pantries, either as a substitute for or in addition to government p rograms.[12] These networks maintained local supply chains when larger systems failed.

The economic value of this substitution is substantial. When childcare costs $1,200 monthly and a household can access community-based childcare sharing, that represents $14,400 in annual cash flow preservation. When home repairs cost $5,000 and a neighbor with relevant skills can perform the work in exchange for another service, both households preserve capital. These informal exchanges do not appear in economic statistics but directly reduce the cash burn rate of household emergency funds, extending their effective duration.

Social capital divides into two essential forms, each serving distinct functions. Bonding capital consists of connections to close family and immediate friends. These strong ties provide material support during immediate crisis: temporary housing, emergency loans, direct financial assistance, and psychological support during acute stress. Bonding capital functions as the first line of defense, the immediate safety net that prevents catastrophic failure. Bridging capital consists of weaker ties connecting individuals to broader networks, institutions, employers outside their immediate circle, and community leaders. These connections provide information about opportunities, resources, and support structures beyond the immediate family network. Bridging capital enables long-term recovery and adaptation by providing access to new employment, services, and institutional resources that close networks cannot supply.[9]

Both forms are necessary. Relying solely on bonding capital creates insularity. The close network shares the same information and faces similar constraints. When crisis affects the entire network simultaneously, bonding capital alone proves insufficient. Bridging capital provides access to external resources and opportunities that enable escape from shared stress. Conversely, bridging capital without bonding capital leaves individuals without immediate material support during acute shocks. The resilient network strategy requires cultivating both.

The psychological value of mutual aid extends beyond material support. Research on cooperation during periods of inequality demonstrates that the buffering effect of cooperation on mental health persists regardless of the unequal environment.[13] The act of collective problem-solving itself provides mental health protection. This matters because economic crisis generates not just material hardship but profound psychological stress. Networks that provide both material resources and psychological community directly counter the isolation and loss of dignity that accompany financial failure.

Multigenerational households represent a particularly effective private safety net, though one that requires careful management. Multi-generational living arrangements can increase psychological, social, and financial capital, factors associated with improvements in health and longevity.[14] Rent, utilities, food, childcare, and eldercare costs are shared, reducing per-person expenditures substantially. When one family member retains employment while another faces job loss, the arrangement facilitates internal redistribution, functioning as a household-level shock absorber.

However, concentration of financial and personal risk within a single household creates vulnerability without proper structure. Multigenerational arrangements work best when resource allocation and decision-making processes are formalized rather than left to informal negotiation. Evidence from family business research indicates that formalized crisis procedures improve outcomes; family firms with supervisory boards exhibit comparable degrees of formalization as non-family firms.[15] Clear agreements about financial contributions, shared expenses, and decision authority prevent the conflict that destroys the safety net during stress.

The primary barrier to effective mutual aid is not logistical but psychological. Self-stigma significantly affects quality of life, and fear of being perceived as dependent prevents individuals from participating in mutual help programs even when such participation would substantially improve their material and psychological conditions. Research on mutual help programs demonstrates that group identification and satisfaction with support networks are significantly associated with program benefits, suggesting that overcoming stigma barriers enables the protective effects of community support.[16]

Overcoming these barriers requires explicit cultural reframing. Mutual aid is not charity. It is reciprocal exchange where all participants contribute resources, whether money, time, skills, or other assets. The person receiving childcare today provides home repair tomorrow. The household with extra food shares with neighbors who later provide transportation. The reciprocity maintains dignity by ensuring all participants are both givers and receivers. This model directly counters the shame associated with dependence by framing community support as normal economic exchange rather than failure.

Digital networks serve a complementary but distinct function. Online platforms excel at rapid, targeted material assistance, particularly cash transfers. Research on digital aid during humanitarian crises found that with a conservative fee of 2.5 percent, 80 percent of participants preferred digital transfers over physical cash; with higher fees of 7.5 percent, preference for digital aid increased to approximately 95 percent, indicating that digital payments are viable even when people have limited experience with the technology.[17] Digital channels reduce friction, accelerate delivery, and scale efficiently for simple, fungible resources like money.

However, digital networks fail at providing complex, non-fungible support. Housing assistance, specialized care, physical labor, and emotional support during acute crisis require physical presence and personal relationship. A Facebook group cannot provide childcare. A GoFundMe campaign cannot repair a home. The psychological support that buffers mental health during prolonged stress comes from embodied community, not online interaction.

The strategic approach integrates both models. Digital channels provide rapid access to cash and coordinate logistics. Local, in-person networks provide complex support and psychological community. Neither alone suffices. The resilient individual cultivates both types of networks, recognizing that different needs require different support structures.

Geographic proximity matters. Digital friends cannot bring groceries. Online acquaintances cannot provide emergency housing. The networks that function during crisis are those within reasonable physical distance. This means that decisions about where to live carry network implications. Moving to a new city for a job may increase income but severs local connections that would provide support during unemployment. The trade-off between career advancement and network security requires explicit evaluation.

Building crisis-resilient networks takes time. Relationships form through repeated interaction and demonstrated reciprocity. The network you can activate during crisis is the network you invested in before crisis arrived. This creates a timing problem: preparation must occur while resources are available, not after they are depleted. Once crisis hits, building new networks while managing acute stress proves nearly impossible.

The psychological demands of living through prolonged economic crisis differ fundamentally from surviving acute disaster. A hurricane strikes suddenly, causes immediate visible damage, and triggers a clear recovery phase.

The timeline is evident. The community unites around reconstruction. The psychological challenge is intense but bounded.

Economic crisis operates differently. It unfolds gradually, without clear beginning or end. Recovery timelines remain uncertain. The stress is chronic rather than acute, and these two categories of stress produce distinct psychological responses and require different coping mechanisms.

Acute stressors are individual, episodic events with relatively discrete beginnings and ends. Job loss due to a plant closure represents an acute stressor. The event is sudden, the impact immediate, and the person can begin adapting to the new reality. Chronic stressors are ongoing negative experiences related to persistent environmental situations. Long-term unemployment, multi-year recession, and the slow collapse of municipal services represent chronic stress. The situation persists without resolution, requiring sustained psychological management over extended periods. Research confirms these are conceptually and analytically distinct, exerting independent effects on health and well-being.[18]

Acute economic events produce an initial spike in depressive symptoms. Job loss due to firm closure increased depressive symptom scores by 28 percent in the United States.[19] Pre-existing wealth mitigated this impact, confirming that financial assets buffer against discrete shocks. However, the effect was temporary. Once reemployment occurred, symptoms declined.

Chronic economic strain produces lasting damage. Individuals who experienced financial, job-related, or housing impacts during the Great Recession had 1.3 to 1.5 times higher odds of depression, generalized anxiety, panic, and problematic substance use three to four years after the recession officially ended.[20] The trauma persisted long past the triggering event, demonstrating that chronic stress creates psychological scarring that standard crisis response models fail to address.

The physiological effects extend beyond mental health. Psychological distress contributes to chronic activation of acute-phase inflammation. Prolonged financial strain associates with elevated inflammatory markers including Interleukin-6 and C-reactive protein, with psychological well-being mediating the association between financial stress and inflammation.[21] Chronic economic anxiety becomes a biological precursor for chronic disease. The stress is not merely psychological but physiological, embedding itself in the body and creating lasting health consequences.

The loss of perceived social status amplifies these effects. Individuals with higher perceived social standing within their communities exhibited a stronger relation between negative financial events and C-reactive protein levels.[21] The loss of status, distinct from absolute loss of capital, acts as an accelerant. The psychological distress of downward mobility exacerbates inflammatory vulnerability, suggesting that the narrative of failure relative to peers or parents generates physiological harm beyond the material loss itself.

This mechanism explains why anticipatory grief, the emotional processing of expected but not-yet-realized losses, becomes psychologically essential during prolonged crisis. Engaging in "grief work," the necessary processing of the loss experience before it occurs, enables healthier adaptation to anticipated decline.[22] When individuals know their expected life trajectory will not materialize, that the standard of living they anticipated is unattainable, that the opportunities available to their parents' generation have disappeared, they experience loss even before the material conditions fully degrade. Research on subjective social mobility confirms that groups reporting subjective downward mobility exhibited significantly more depressive symptomatology than groups remaining in stable status positions.[23] The anticipation of decline produces measurable psychological harm.

Healthy adaptation requires processing expected losses rather than suppressing or denying them. The person who refuses to acknowledge that their career trajectory has changed, that their retirement will not match their parents', that their children face narrower opportunities, delays necessary psychological adjustment. The failure to pre-grieve expected losses leaves individuals unprepared for the emotional reality when conditions materialize, producing acute crisis at precisely the moment when psychological reserves are most depleted.

The psychological challenge of prolonged crisis is that it traps individuals in perpetual anticipatory grief. Liminality, signified by relocation, changing social relationships, or breaks in sociocultural processes, creates chronic uncertainty. The liminal state, the condition of being betwixt and between where the old order persists without legitimacy but no new order has emerged, depletes cognitive resources continuously.[24] Individuals cannot complete the grieving process because the loss never fully materializes. The system continues functioning in degraded form. The crisis never reaches resolution. This perpetual ambiguity produces psychological stasis where meaningful agency becomes difficult to assert.

Living through this requires managing cognitive load. Prolonged economic uncertainty imposes severe taxation on cognitive resources, manifesting as decision fatigue: the decline in decision-making quality as mental abilities are worn down by continuous choice. People who more frequently have to make decisions based on trade-offs experience decision fatigue more intensely, and those living in poverty typically struggle with continual trade-offs that deplete mental energy for all other cognitive activities.[25]

Research comparing individuals immediately before and after payday confirms this effect. The poor are more likely to make use of expensive payday loans and check-cashing services, to play lotteries, and to repeatedly borrow at high interest rates.[26] This is not moral failure or inferior intelligence. It is cognitive impairment produced by scarcity itself. The constant vigilance required to manage limited resources depletes the mental capacity needed for complex decision-making.

Stress compounds these effects. Under chronic stress, individuals exhibit less inhibited responses, higher reward seeking, and delay discounting: favoring smaller immediate rewards over larger long-term benefits. The psychological state includes hypervigilance for threatening stimuli and attention narrowing, resulting in impulsive selection without considering the full range of options.[27] Every complex trade-off depletes cognitive capacity. The person facing prolonged economic stress operates with systematically impaired decision-making ability precisely when decisions matter most.

The developmental origins of these patterns matter. Childhood poverty has pervasive negative physical and psychological health sequelae in adulthood.

Adults with lower family income at age 9 exhibited reduced ventrolateral and dorsolateral prefrontal cortex activity and failure to suppress amygdala activation during effortful regulation of negative emotion at age 24. Chronic stressor exposure across childhood mediated the relations between childhood poverty and adult prefrontal cortex activity.[28] The prefrontal cortex governs executive control and goal-directed behavior. Developmental scarring creates biological predisposition for poor decision-making and heightened emotional reactivity under adult economic stress.

This explains why strategic adaptation, not heroic endurance, represents the appropriate response framework. The person who grew up in chronic economic stress developed neural pathways optimized for survival in that environment. Those adaptations (hypervigilance, heightened threat detection, rapid reward seeking) made sense in childhood. They become sources of adult vulnerability during economic crisis because they amplify stress responses and degrade decision quality.

The presence of supportive, caring adults during childhood adversity is the essential factor that makes stress tolerable. When experienced in the context of buffering protection provided by supportive adults, the risk that adverse circumstances will produce excessive activation of stress response systems leading to physiologic harm and long-term consequences for health and learning is greatly reduced.[29] This evidence supports a framework of strategic adaptation facilitated by external support rather than relying on innate resilience or toughening through adversity. The person who received buffering support during childhood developed healthy neural pathways. The person who did not faces adult economic crisis with impaired biological capacity for stress management.

This is not moral judgment. It is biological reality. The individual whose nervous system was shaped by chronic childhood stress cannot simply decide to respond differently to adult economic crisis. Their neural architecture makes certain responses more difficult. Acknowledging this limitation allows for strategic path selection rather than attempting responses that exceed actual capacity.

The strategic adaptation model recognizes that individuals have differing psychological tolerances based on developmental history and current circumstances. The person with intact stress response systems may be able to handle high-rejection environments like traditional job searching or agent querying. The person whose nervous system was shaped by chronic stress may need to choose lower-rejection paths: self-publishing rather than agent submission, direct networking rather than mass applications, entrepreneurship rather than corporate employment. Neither path is superior. The question is which path matches actual psychological capacity.

This framework grants permission for strategic choice. You do not need to prove resilience through unnecessary exposure to high-stress environments. You can assess your actual tolerance, recognize your limits, and select paths that work within those constraints. This is not giving up. It is working intelligently within real boundaries.

The psychological cost of prolonged crisis includes managing constant trade-offs. Every decision becomes risk calculation. Can I afford this if crisis accelerates? Should I move now or wait? Is my job secure enough? When do I pull children from a failing school system? The exhaustion comes not from any single decision but from the perpetual contingency planning required when no decision feels purely positive. Everything involves trade-offs.

Maintaining functionality requires accepting this cognitive load as the new baseline rather than treating it as temporary abnormality. The person who keeps waiting for conditions to stabilize before making decisions remains paralyzed. The person who accepts that decisions will be made under uncertainty, with incomplete information, while managing elevated stress, can move forward despite the difficulty.

The most important psychological protection is avoiding learned helplessness, the pathological withdrawal that occurs when repeated effort fails to produce desired outcomes. The sustained and prolonged exposure to environmental stressors may provoke different reactions depending on the subjective perception of control. Repeated perception of lack of control leads to learned helplessness, which is associated with increased activation of the amygdala and decreased activation in regions of the prefrontal cortex. Perception of control, by contrast, promotes the implementation of active coping strategies characterized by efficient cognitive-emotional processing, effective decision making, and goal-directed actions.[30]

Following job loss, individuals initially manifest vigorous repeated attempts to regain control. Workers experiencing highest initial anxiety and depression often display greatest probabilities of reemployment. The high-effort phase is adaptive. However, as duration of unemployment lengthens, beliefs in personal efficacy decline, expectations of success decrease, and motivation to seek employment consequently falls. Research demonstrates that job search self-efficacy mediates the relationship between employment status and anxiety symptoms, while stigma consciousness about unemployment status negatively affects job search attitudes and behavior.[31] When rejection is pervasive, individuals adopt fatalistic reasoning, assuming risk of failure is so high that preventative measures are futile. The mind rationally withdraws effort from high-cost, high-failure activities.

Protection against this requires maintaining activities that provide efficacy and social connection outside failed domains. When the labor market rejects you, efficacy must come from other sources: community involvement, skill development, creative projects, mutual aid participation. These activities provide meaning and counteract isolation, offering pathways to regain efficacy outside the formal economy. The person who maintains multiple sources of identity and efficacy (parent, community member, skilled craftsperson, friend) possesses psychological redundancy. Failure in one domain does not destroy all sources of self-worth.

The final psychological challenge is maintaining pro-social behavior under chronic stress. Prolonged economic hardship creates pressure toward self-interested survival mode. Financial stress erodes generosity, increases suspicion, and degrades social cooperation. The person operating under scarcity focuses on immediate survival, reducing capacity for long-term reciprocity and community investment.

Resisting this erosion requires conscious choice and preserved psychological reserves. Small kindnesses, sharing resources when possible, and participating in mutual aid even when you feel you have little to offer maintain social fabric. But this is hard. It requires psychological capacity that chronic stress depletes. The person exhausted from constant financial management, impaired decision-making from scarcity, and depleted from years of uncertainty may lack reserves for sustained generosity.

Forgiveness for yourself when you cannot maintain pro-social behavior is essential. You are operating under extraordinary stress with impaired cognitive and emotional capacity. Sometimes survival mode is necessary. The goal is not perfect maintenance of community values but strategic deployment of whatever capacity exists. When you have reserves, contribute. When depleted, accept support without shame. Reciprocity occurs over time, not in every transaction.

The crisis is long. The degradation is slow. You cannot sprint this. Pacing yourself, recognizing limits, and accepting that some days you will not meet your own standards are necessary adaptations to chronic stress. The person who maintains rigid expectations of constant resilience burns out. The person who accepts variable capacity survives.

Material preparation provides buffer. Geographic positioning reduces exposure. Financial assets extend time. But none of these guarantee survival if psychological infrastructure fails. Skills retain value only if you remain employable. Networks provide support only if you can maintain relationships. Assets preserve wealth only if decision-making remains functional. The psychological foundation underlies everything else.

Chronic stress impairs this foundation systematically. Cognitive load reduces decision quality. Learned helplessness erodes motivation. Anticipatory grief depletes emotional reserves. Developmental trauma limits stress capacity. These are not failures of character. They are documented biological and psychological responses to conditions exceeding human design parameters.

Strategic adaptation acknowledges these limits while working within them. Choose paths matching actual capacity. Build scaffolding through supportive relationships. Accept that your tolerance differs from others based on developmental history. Forgive yourself when limits are reached. Maintain what efficacy and community you can without demanding heroic endurance.

The goal is not transcendence. The goal is functionality across years of uncertainty. Material preparation gets you to the crisis. Psychological preparation gets you through it.

Chapter 11 Notes

1. Bureau of Labor Statistics, "Healthcare jobs and the Great Recession," Monthly Labor Review, April 2018, https://www.bls.gov/opub/mlr /2018/article/healthcare-jobs-and-the-great-recession.htm. ("Healthcare appears to have been a bright spot in the American labor market economy, as it was during previous recessions... From a historical perspective, healthcare appears to have been resistant to, if not immune from, the usual job losses associated with previous recessions.")

2. Grand View Research, "Private Security Services Market Size | Industry Report, 2030," https://www.grandviewresearch.com/industry-analysis/private-security-services-market-report. ("The global private security services market size was estimated at USD 4.62 billion in 2024 and is projected to reach USD 8.00 billion by 2030, growing at a CAGR of 9.8% from 2025 to 2030... particularly within the residential sector, as individuals increasingly seek reliable solutions to protect their homes.")

3. The White House, "Hiring Freeze," January 20, 2025, https://www.whitehouse.gov/presidential-actions/2025/01 /hiring-freeze/; The White House, "Ensuring Continued Accountability in Federal Hiring," October 15, 2025, https://www.whitehouse.gov/presidential-actions/2025/10/ ensuring-continued-accountability-in-federal-hiring/. ("No Federal civilian position that is vacant may be filled... the ratio of four departures for each new hire.")

4. Mortgage Bankers Association, "20 Percent of Commercial and Multifamily Mortgage Balances Mature in 2025," February 10, 2025, https://www.mba.org/news-and-research/newsroom/news/2025/02 /10/20-percent-of-commercial-and-multifamily-mortgage-balances

-mature-in-2025. ("Twenty percent ($957 billion) of $4.8 trillion of outstanding commercial mortgages held by lenders and investors will mature in 2025.")

5. National Bureau of Economic Research, "The Value of Soft Skills in the Labor Market," NBER Reporter 2017, no. 4, https://www.nb er.org/reporter/2017number4/value-soft-skills-labor-market. ("Employers frequently list teamwork, collaboration, and oral and written communication skills as highly valuable yet hard-to-find qualities in potential new hires.")

6. Urban Institute, "Weathering the Recession: The Financial Crisis and Family Wealth Changes in Low-Income Neighborhoods," 2012, https://www.urban.org/sites/default/files/publication/25686/41262 6-weathering-the-recession-the-financial-crisis-and-family-wealth-cha nges-in-low-income-neighborhoods.pdf.

7. U.S. Census Bureau, "Population by Age, Sex, Race, and Hispanic or Latino Origin for the United States: 2000," Census 2000 PHC-T-9, Table 7, https://www2.census.gov/programs-surveys/decennial/200 0/phc/phc-t-09/tab07.pdf. (Median age in 1930: 26.5 years.)

8. U.S. Census Bureau, "National Population by Characteristics: 2020-2024," https://www.census.gov/data/tables/time-series/demo /popest/2020s-national-detail.html.

9. Robert D. Putnam, Bowling Alone: The Collapse and Revival of American Community (New York: Simon & Schuster, 2000).

10. Daniel P. Aldrich and Michelle A. Meyer, "Social Capital and Community Resilience," American Behavioral Scientist 59, no. 2 (2015): 254-269, https://doi.org/10.1177/0002764214550299. ("Despite the ubiquity of disaster and the increasing toll in human lives and financial costs, much research and policy remain focused on physical in-

frastructure-centered approaches... evidence that social, not physical, infrastructure drives resilience.")

11. Journal of the Society for Social Work and Research, "Values and Beliefs Underlying Mutual Aid: An Exploration of Collective Care During the COVID-19 Pandemic," Vol. 13, No. 1, https://www.journals.uchicago.edu/doi/full/10.1086/716884. ("Mutual aid may include support for basic needs such as food, housing, and transportation, but it may also include supports such as emotional connection and coordination between those who need something and those who have something to give.")

12. Colleen M. Heflin and Ashley Price, "Food Pantry Assistance and the Great Recession," Journal of Hunger & Environmental Nutrition 14, no. 1-2 (2018): 1-15, https://doi.org/10.1080/19320248.2018.1434099. ("At the height of the Great Recession... one in five American households participated in the Supplemental Nutrition Assistance Program (SNAP)... many households also relied on less formal methods to meet their food needs such as food pantries.")

13. PubMed Central, "The buffering effect of social capital for daily mental stress in an unequal society: a lesson from Seoul," 2023, https://pmc.ncbi.nlm.nih.gov/articles/PMC10084662/. ("The buffering effect of cooperation showed regardless of the unequal environment.")

14. PubMed Central, "Living with parents or grandparents increases social capital and survival: 2014 General Social Survey-National Death Index," 2018, https://pmc.ncbi.nlm.nih.gov/articles/PMC5769098/. ("Multi-generational living arrangements can, in theory, increase psychological, social, and financial capital—factors associated with improvements in health and longevity.")

15. PubMed Central, "Business families in times of crises: The backbone of family firm resilience and continuity," 2022, https://pmc.ncbi.

nlm.nih.gov/articles/PMC9761879/. ("Empirical evidence indicates that formalized crisis procedures decline with increasing family ownership, an effect that is moderated by the existence of supervisory boards.")

16. Patrick W. Corrigan and Kristin A. Sokol, "The Impact of Self-Stigma and Mutual Help Programs on the Quality of Life of People with Serious Mental Illnesses," Community Mental Health Journal 49 (2013): 1-6, https://pmc.ncbi.nlm.nih.gov/articles/PMC3320674/. ("Self-stigma was shown to be a significant and large correlate of quality of life. Satisfaction with current and past MHP participation was also associated with quality of life. Group identification and satisfaction with one's support network were significantly and largely associated with MHP satisfaction.")

17. Michael Callen, Miguel Fajardo-Steinhäuser, Michael G. Findley, and Tarek Ghani, "Can Digital Aid Deliver During Humanitarian Crises?," Working Paper, https://mfsteinhauser.github.io/website/DigitalAid.pdf. ("With a conservative fee of 100 AFN (2.5%), 80% of participants preferred digital aid over cash; with a higher fee of 300 AFN (7.5%), the share choosing digital aid over cash increased to ~95%.")

18. PubMed Central, "Life Course Trajectories of Chronic Strain and Acute Stress Reactivity: Evidence for the Steeling Hypothesis," 2022, https://pmc.ncbi.nlm.nih.gov/articles/PMC9190465/.

19. PubMed Central, "Job loss, wealth and depression during the Great Recession in the USA and Europe," 2014, https://pmc.ncbi.nlm.nih.gov/articles/PMC4190512/. ("Job loss due to firm closure increased depressive symptom scores by 28.2% (95% CI: 8.55, 47.80) in the USA... the effect of job loss on depressive symptoms was weaker among workers with higher pre-existing wealth.")

20. PubMed Central, "The Great Recession and Mental Health in the United States," 2020, https://pmc.ncbi.nlm.nih.gov/articles/PMC7 413622/. ("Each recession impact—regardless of the specific domain of impact—was associated with 1.3 to 1.5 times higher odds of symptoms of depression, generalized anxiety, panic, and problems associated with substance use after The Great Recession.")

21. PubMed Central, "The psychosocial context of financial stress: Implications for inflammation and psychological health," 2016, ht tps://pmc.ncbi.nlm.nih.gov/articles/PMC4738080/. ("Psychological well-being mediated the association between financial stress and I L-6... individuals with higher perceived social standing within their communities exhibited a stronger relation between negative financial events and... C-reactive protein.")

22. Dean A. Shepherd, "Anticipatory grief, persistence, and recovery," in Learning from Entrepreneurial Failure: Emotions, Cognitions, and Actions (Cambridge: Cambridge University Press, 2016), 75-115, h ttps://doi.org/10.1017/CBO9781316416242.004.

23. American Psychological Association, "The Myth of Social Mobility: Subjective Social Mobility and Mental Health," https://www.apa. org/education-career/ce/subjective-social-mobility.pdf. ("Groups that experienced both subjective downward and upward mobility reported more depressive symptomatology than groups that remained in middle or upper social statuses.")

24. PubMed Central, "Liminality and insecurity: A qualitative study of young adults' vulnerabilities during the first twelve months of COVID-19 in Australia," 2023, https://pmc.ncbi.nlm.nih.gov/arti cles/PMC10050194/. ("Liminality, signified by relocation, changing social relationships or breaks in sociocultural processes, can be both positive and risky for individuals and societies.")

25. Sendhil Mullainathan and Eldar Shafir, Scarcity: Why Having Too Little Means So Much (New York: Times Books, 2013); The Decision Lab, "Decision Fatigue," https://thedecisionlab.com/biases/decision-fatigue. ("Decision fatigue describes how the quality of our decision-making declines as we make additional choices... People who more frequently have to make decisions based on trade-offs experience decision fatigue more intensely.")

26. Leandro S. Carvalho, Stephan Meier, and Stephanie W. Wang, "Poverty and Economic Decision-Making: Evidence from Changes in Financial Resources at Payday," American Economic Review 106, no. 2 (2016): 260-284. ("The poor often behave differently from the non-poor. For example, they are more likely to make use of expensive payday loans and check-cashing services, to play lotteries, and to repeatedly borrow at high interest rates.")

27. Nuray Atsan, "Decision-Making under Stress and Its Implications for Managerial Decision-Making: A Review of Literature," International Journal of Business and Social Research 6, no. 3 (2016): 38-47, https://doi.org/10.18533/ijbsr.v6i3.936.

28. PubMed Central, "Effects of childhood poverty and chronic stress on emotion regulatory brain function in adulthood," 2013, https://pmc.ncbi.nlm.nih.gov/articles/PMC3831978/. ("Adults with lower family income at age 9 exhibited reduced ventrolateral and dorsolateral prefrontal cortex activity and failure to suppress amygdala activation during effortful regulation of negative emotion at age 24.")

29. American Academy of Pediatrics, "The Lifelong Effects of Early Childhood Adversity and Toxic Stress," Pediatrics 129, no. 1 (2012): e232-e246, https://publications.aap.org/pediatrics/article/129/1/e232/31628/The-Lifelong-Effects-of-Early-Childhood-Adversity. ("When experienced in the context of buffering protection provided by

supportive adults, the risk that such circumstances will produce excessive activation of the stress response systems that leads to physiologic harm and long-term consequences for health and learning is greatly reduced.")

30. Gustavo E. Tafet and Tomas Ortiz Alonso, "Learned helplessness and learned controllability: from neurobiology to cognitive, emotional and behavioral neurosciences," Frontiers in Psychiatry 16 (2025), htt ps://doi.org/10.3389/fpsyt.2025.1600165. ("Repeated perception of lack of control may lead to learned helplessness... Perception of control promotes the implementation of active coping strategies, characterized by efficient cognitive-emotional processing, effective decision making, and goal directed actions.")

31. Andrei Rusu et al., "Job search self-efficacy as mediator between employment status and symptoms of anxiety," Romanian Journal of Applied Psychology 15, no. 2 (2013): 69-75; Gerhard Krug, Katrin Drasch, and Monika Jungbauer-Gans, "The social stigma of unemployment: consequences of stigma consciousness on job search attitudes, behaviour and success," Journal for Labour Market Research 53, no. 11 (2019), https://doi.org/10.1186/s12651-019-0261-4.

PART IV

The Solutions We're Not Choosing

Chapter 12

What Would Actually Fix This

T he solutions exist. Every policy lever needed to stabilize the federal debt trajectory is documented, scored, and technically feasible. The Congressional Budget Office has quantified the revenue potential of a five percent value-added tax at $3.05 trillion over ten years.[1] Eliminating all itemized tax deductions would generate $2.51 trillion.[1] A new two percent payroll tax would raise $2.25 trillion.[1] The arithmetic works. The policy tools are real. The United States could achieve fiscal sustainability through a comprehensive package combining revenue increases with benefit adjustments, addressing the $9.0 trillion deficit reduction required over 2025-2035 to stabilize debt at current levels.[2]

We know comprehensive reform is possible because we have done it before. In 1983, the Social Security system faced imminent insolvency, with trust fund reserves projected to deplete within months. President Reagan and Speaker Tip O'Neill convened the National Commission on Social Security Reform, known as the Greenspan Commission, which proposed a balanced package that became law with bipartisan support.[3] The solution combined accelerated payroll tax increases already scheduled under prior law, taxation of Social Security benefits for higher-income recipients, gradual increases in the normal retirement age from sixty-five to sixty-seven, coverage extension to new federal employees and nonprofit workers, and temporary delays in cost-of-living adjustments.[4] The 1983 reform demonstrated that when crisis forces action and political leaders provide bipartisan cover, the American political system can implement painful adjustments to preserve essential programs. The precedent proves that comprehensive fiscal reform combining tax increases and benefit cuts is not theoretically impossible. It happened. It worked. The system functioned as designed.

The question is not whether we can fix this. The question is whether we will. And the answer, based on structural analysis of current political constraints, is no. Not because the problem is larger than human capacity to solve, but because it is larger than the political system's capacity to absorb pain within electoral time horizons that govern legislative behavior.

The 1983 model cannot be replicated today because every condition that made that success possible has fundamentally changed. The magnitude of the problem has doubled. The easy policy levers have been exhausted. The political environment has crossed a threshold into what researchers term affective polarization, where partisan identity becomes more salient than policy outcomes.[5] And the demographic structure of the electorate has shifted power decisively toward those who will bear the costs of any reform.

Today's Social Security financing challenge is at least double the magnitude faced in 1983.[6] The infinite horizon unfunded obligation totals $72.8 trillion in present value, requiring a permanent adjustment equivalent to 5.2 percent of future taxable payroll.[7] To put the program on stable financial footing today would require an immediate increase in revenues or cut in benefits equal to 3.61 percent of payroll; in 1983, the actuarial balance under the intermediate projections was 1.82 percent of payroll, meaning that the required adjustments are twice as large today.[6] This difference is not marginal. It represents a fundamental escalation in the scale of adjustment required, demanding either massive tax increases that approach revenue-maximizing rates or benefit cuts that exceed any politically survivable threshold.

More critically, the policy tools that solved the 1983 crisis are no longer available. The 1983 reform expanded Social Security coverage to include federal workers hired after 1983, generating substantial new revenue from a previously untapped base.[4] That expansion is permanent. Federal workers are already covered. The 1983 reform introduced taxation of Social Security benefits for the first time, targeting higher-income recipients.[4] Benefits are already taxed. The 1983 reform scheduled a gradual increase in the normal retirement age from sixty-five to sixty-seven.[4] That increase is already implemented, with the full retirement age reaching sixty-seven for those born in 1960 or later.[8]

What remains are the politically toxic options that even the 1983 reform could only partially employ: further increases in the retirement age, direct reductions in scheduled benefits, elimination of the payroll tax cap, or massive increases in payroll tax rates. Each of these adjustments faces organized opposition from voting blocs with the capacity to end political careers. The easy revenue tools are gone. What remains is pain that must be distributed across the entire population, without the ability to concentrate it on narrow constituencies that lack electoral power.

The composition of the electorate has shifted in ways that make reform structurally more difficult. Voters aged fifty and older represented fifty-two to fifty-five percent of the electorate in the 2024 election.[9] This demographic votes at rates fifteen to twenty percentage points higher than younger cohorts.[10] Among voters aged fifty and older, eighty-eight percent of Republicans and eighty-seven percent of Democrats oppose cutting Social Security benefits to reduce the federal deficit.[11] Opposition to raising the full retirement age to sixty-nine runs at seventy-two percent among Republicans and eighty-three percent among Democrats in this age group.[12] These are not casual preferences. These are single-issue commitments from the most electorally engaged segment of the population, backed by institutional capacity to punish defection.

AARP, the advocacy organization focused on Americans aged fifty and older, commands a membership of thirty-eight million people, with offices in all fifty states and communication reach through publications ranking among the largest circulation in the United States.[13] This organizational infrastructure exists to mobilize opposition to any benefit reduction or retirement age increase. The political cost of proposing reform is immediate, certain, and career-ending. The cost of delay is distant, diffuse, and falls on future officeholders. Every politician facing re-election cycles of two to six years optimizes for short-term survival. The rational choice is inaction.

The political environment itself has deteriorated in ways that prevent the bipartisan cooperation essential for comprehensive reform. In 2010, the National Commission on Fiscal Responsibility and Reform, known as Simpson-Bowles, proposed a comprehensive deficit reduction package combining $2.6 trillion in revenue increases with $2.9 trillion in spending cuts over ten years.[14] The plan could not secure the fourteen votes needed within the commission itself to advance to Congress. On December 3, 2010, only eleven commissioners voted in favor: five Republicans, five Democrats, and one independent.[15] When a modified version was introduced in the House of Representatives in March 2012, it was defeated 382 to 38.[16]This overwhelming rejection occurred despite the plan representing precisely the kind of balanced approach that policy analysts consistently recommend: shared sacrifice, bipartisan compromise, and technically sound adjustments.

The failure of Simpson-Bowles is not evidence of poor policy design. It is evidence of political impossibility. The package demanded pain that neither party's base would accept, requiring both parties to vote for measures their core constituencies opposed. Democrats would need to accept entitlement cuts. Republicans would need to accept tax increases. Both would need to trust that the other party would not weaponize their votes in the next election cycle. That trust does not exist. The result is structural gridlock where both parties understand the mathematics but neither can act without electoral annihilation.

The comprehensive fix required to achieve fiscal sustainability over 2025-2035 demands approximately $9.0 trillion in deficit reduction.[2] No single policy lever can generate adjustments of this magnitude. Only combinations of major revenue increases and significant spending cuts approach the necessary scale. Consider what a technically viable package would require.

A five percent value-added tax would generate $3.05 trillion over ten years.[1] This is the most efficient broad-based consumption tax, used successfully in most developed economies. But VATs are regressive, imposing proportionally higher burdens on lower-income households who spend a larger share of income on consumption. This violates Democratic Party principles of progressive taxation and would trigger revolt from the party's base.

Eliminating all itemized tax deductions would generate $2.51 trillion.[1] This includes the mortgage interest deduction, which polling shows Americans oppose eliminating by a margin of approximately two to one for deficit reduction purposes.[17] It includes the state and local tax deduction, where sixty-one percent of voters support increasing deduction limits or removing limits altogether.[18] It includes the charitable contribution deduction, which nonprofit organizations and religious institutions defend as essential to civil society. Eliminating these deductions would hit the middle class directly, turning popular tax benefits into visible tax increases. Both parties' bases would revolt.

A new two percent payroll tax would raise $2.25 trillion, increasing the Federal Insurance Contributions Act rate from 12.4 percent to 14.4 percent.[1] For a worker earning $60,000 annually, this represents an additional $1,200 per year split between employee and employer. Alternatively, eliminating the payroll tax cap, currently set at $176,100, would close approximately fifty-three percent of Social Security's long-term funding gap but would represent a massive tax increase on high earners.[19] Either approach faces organized opposition. Republicans are bound by the Taxpayer Protection Pledge, signed by 191 House members and 44 Senators, committing them to oppose any net tax increase.[20] Working-age voters of both parties oppose bearing the entire burden of saving a system whose benefits they increasingly doubt they will receive.

Even combining the most aggressive revenue options yields insufficient savings. A five percent VAT generating $3.05 trillion, elimination of all itemized deductions generating $2.51 trillion, and a reduction in defense spending saving approximately $1.0 trillion produces a total of $6.56 trillion over ten years .[21] This falls $2.4 trillion short of the $9.0 trillion stabilization requirement. The gap can only be closed by touching Social Security and Medicare directly, through benefit reductions or further tax increases beyond those already described.

Social Security reform options face even steeper political barriers. Raising the full retirement age from sixty-seven to seventy would save $150 billion through

2035, closing approximately thirty-five percent of the Social Security funding gap.[22] This adjustment is regressive, harming lower-income workers who have shorter life expectancies and receive benefits for fewer years.[23] Reducing benefits for the top thirty percent of earners by adjusting the Primary Insurance Amount formula would close approximately twenty percent of the seventy-five-year solvency gap.[22] Implementing a flat benefit set at 125 percent of the federal poverty guidelines would close 150 percent of the gap but would destroy the progressive benefit structure that makes Social Security politically sustainable.[22]

Means testing Social Security, frequently proposed as a politically palatable benefit reduction, faces severe technical obstacles. The Social Security Administration currently operates with administrative costs of approximately one percent of payroll tax income.[24] Implementing means testing would require extensive new processes involving paperwork, investigations, and litigation, adding substantial administrative burden that would offset some savings.[24] More fundamentally, effective means testing struggles to reconcile non-liquid asset wealth with cash income. Only 14.5 percent of retirees are in the top quarter of both the income and wealth distributions; another 10.5 percent are top-quarter income recipients but not top-quarter wealth holders, with an additional 10.5 percent the reverse.[25] A means test based on income has substantially different distributional effects from a means test based on wealth, creating fairness problems that neither approach can resolve.[25] The technical complexity, administrative cost increases, and design challenges render means testing inefficient and politically dangerous.

Defense spending, often cited as a target for deficit reduction, offers mathematically insufficient savings. The Department of Defense budget request for fiscal year 2025 totaled $850 billion.[21] The most aggressive reduction scenario modeled by the Congressional Budget Office would cut approximately $1.1 trillion over ten years by reducing active-component military personnel by roughly seventeen percent by 2034.[21] This extreme level of reduction would address only a fraction of Social Security's $22.6 trillion seventy-five-year unfunded obligation.[26] Geopolitical realities impose a structural floor on defense cuts. Russia's defense spending is estimated at 7.2 percent of its GDP.[27] China's military modernization continues accelerating, with overall spending now rivaling the United States and rapidly closing the gap in military equipment.[28] The strategic imperative to maintain military superiority against peer competitors prevents the radical reductions necessary to generate meaningful fiscal savings.

Every element of a comprehensive fiscal reform package triggers organized opposition with the capacity to end political careers. The VAT hurts Democratic constituencies. Eliminating itemized deductions hits middle-class homeowners and charitable organizations. Payroll tax increases violate Republican anti-tax commitments. Social Security benefit cuts mobilize AARP's thirty-eight million members. Defense cuts face geopolitical constraints and national security imperatives. The required package combines multiple elements that are individually unacceptable, creating a coalition of opposition that spans both parties' bases and crosses ideological lines.

The political impossibility of reform stems from what game theorists term a prisoner's dilemma, where individual rational choices produce collectively catastrophic outcomes. Democrats will accept tax increases to preserve entitlements. Democrats will not accept benefit cuts, which would violate their commitment to social insurance programs and trigger revolt from labor unions, progressive advocacy groups, and AARP. Republicans will accept entitlement cuts to reduce the size of government. Republicans will not accept tax increases, which would violate the Taxpayer Protection Pledge and trigger primary challenges from anti-tax conservatives and donor revolts.

Comprehensive reform requires both parties to act simultaneously, accepting pain their respective bases reject. Neither party can move first because the other could defect, blocking reform while weaponizing the first party's votes in the next election. Both parties need each other. Neither can trust the other. The dominant strategy for each party is to refuse compromise, blame the opponent for gridlock, and wait for external crisis to force action. This produces stable equilibrium around inaction, even though both parties understand that delay makes the eventual adjustment exponentially larger.

The cost of delay is quantifiable and permanent. At current debt levels of approximately one hundred percent of GDP, stabilizing the debt-to-GDP ratio requires achieving a primary deficit of roughly two percent of GDP.[29] This is difficult but mathematically feasible through combinations of revenue increases and spending cuts. If action is delayed until debt reaches 180 percent of GDP, projected for shortly after 2050 under current trajectories, stabilization requires achieving a primary surplus of approximately one percent of GDP.[29] This three percentage point swing is equivalent to eliminating the combined budgets of Medicare and Medicaid while simultaneously raising income taxes by thirty percent. No political system implements changes of that magnitude voluntarily.

Every year of delay increases the required adjustment geometrically while the political capacity to implement reform does not expand. The worker-to-beneficiary ratio continues declining from 2.8 workers per beneficiary in 2013 toward 2.1 by 2040.[30] The Baby Boom generation will not un-retire. Fertility rates, currently at 1.66 births per woman, show no signs of recovering toward the replacement rate of 2.1.[31] The electoral math that makes Social Security reform political suicide will not change as long as voters aged fifty and older represent the majority of the electorate in competitive districts and vote at rates fifteen to twenty percentage points higher than younger cohorts.

The political system that rejected Simpson-Bowles when it proposed $2.6 trillion in revenue increases and $2.9 trillion in spending cuts will not pass reforms three times larger.[14] The Congress that expanded Social Security benefits through the Social Security Fairness Act in January 2025, increasing program costs during a documented fiscal crisis, demonstrates that political incentives favor benefit expansion over solvency measures.[32] The combined Old-Age and Survivors Insurance and Disability Insurance Trust Funds will deplete reserves in 2033, triggering automatic benefit reductions of approximately twenty-four percent.[33] This projection generated no legislative action because the known political cost of reform outweighs future electoral consequences of failure.

The contrast with 1983 is devastating. That year, lawmakers created the Greenspan Commission and struck a bipartisan deal that restored the solvency of Social Security for a generation. The actuaries projected that the 1983 reforms would keep the system solvent through 2060.[6] Forty years later, Congress cannot even agree to convene a commission to discuss the problem. The

Cole-Delaney bills, introduced in 2014, 2015, and again in 2017 to create a bipartisan Social Security reform commission, never received a hearing, a markup, or a vote.[34] Each died silently in committee. The political system that could solve the 1983 crisis cannot even begin to discuss the current one.

The silence around fiscal crisis is not evidence that solutions do not exist. The silence is evidence that solutions are politically impossible to implement before external crisis forces adjustment under maximum duress. Every politician with access to Congressional Budget Office projections can see the collision approaching. Every economist who studies fiscal sustainability understands the mathematics. Every financial professional preparing wealthy clients recognizes the trajectory. The data is public. The mechanisms are documented. The timeline is clear.

But acknowledging an unsolvable problem within current political constraints is career suicide for politicians. Proposing comprehensive reform guarantees primary challenges, donor revolts, and attack ads from opponents. The current political environment is characterized by affective polarization where partisan identity overrides policy considerations, twenty-four-hour media that amplifies every compromise as betrayal, social media that enables instant base mobilization against defectors, and primary elections that punish moderates who seek bipartisan solutions. The structural conditions that enabled the 1983 reform have been replaced by conditions that guarantee gridlock until crisis makes inaction more politically dangerous than action.

The partisan weaponization of reform proposals demonstrates why bipartisan cooperation has become impossible. Democratic leaders attack Republican budget proposals, claiming they would "gut Social Security benefits" by forcing Americans to work longer, characterizing such plans as attacks on seniors, veterans, and the middle class.[35] Republican leaders refuse revenue increases that would violate the Taxpayer Protection Pledge signed by the majority of their caucus.[20] Both parties use the necessity of reform as an electoral weapon rather than a policy priority requiring cooperation. The rational choice for every individual politician is to defer action, let the successor deal with the crisis, and hope that either external events force bipartisan action or that the collision occurs after they have left office. This individual optimization produces collective paralysis.

The required adjustment of $9.0 trillion over 2025-2035 exceeds any pain threshold the political system has historically proven willing to accept voluntarily.[2] The Simpson-Bowles defeat by a vote of 382 to 38 demonstrates that grand bargains combining revenue increases and spending cuts cannot pass, even when the problem is smaller and the political environment is less polarized.[16]

The fiscal crisis is not technically impossible to solve. It is politically impossible to solve before 2033 forces a choice between automatic benefit cuts, massive emergency borrowing, or crushing tax increases implemented under recession conditions. The solutions exist. The arithmetic works. The policy levers are real. We proved in 1983 that comprehensive reform combining revenue increases and benefit adjustments can pass with bipartisan support when crisis forces action.

But that crisis was half this size, occurred during lower political polarization, and used policy tools that have since been exhausted. Today's required fix exceeds any politician's electoral survival threshold. Both parties need each other to pass reform. Neither can trust the other not to weaponize compromise. Every actor is individually rational, optimizing for re-election within two-to-six-year cycles while the crisis operates on a thirty-year timeline. Collectively, this produces guaranteed inaction until external crisis makes continuation of current policy more politically dangerous than the pain of adjustment.

The 2033 Social Security trust fund depletion will force Congressional action not because political will suddenly materializes but because statutory law mandates benefit reductions that more than seventy-four million Americans will experience directly.[36] At that point, politicians will implement emergency measures under maximum political duress, with minimal time for gradual phase-ins, and without the fiscal space that might have allowed smoother transitions had reform occurred earlier. The collision is not happening because reform is impossible. The collision is happening because reform is politically impossible before the crisis makes inaction impossible.

The math works. The politics do not. And in a democracy where electoral incentives govern legislative behavior, the politics determine the outcome. The required comprehensive reform will not happen before 2033 because no Congress will vote for measures that guarantee their own defeat. The system that could solve this problem cannot implement solutions within the time horizon required to avoid crisis. That is not pessimism. That is documentation of incentive structures that make necessary reform structurally impossible until external events force the hand of legislators who will not move voluntarily.

The emperor is naked. Everyone with access to official projections can see it. This chapter exists to document that the solutions are real, the costs are quantifiable, and the political impossibility is structural rather than accidental. When the crisis arrives in 2033, when automatic benefit cuts hit or emergency measures pass under duress, when the required adjustment occurs under the worst possible conditions, the historical record must show that this was not inevitable. It was chosen, through rational individual decisions that produced collective catastrophe, by a political system that could see the collision coming but could not bring itself to change course in time.

Chapter 12 Notes

1. Congressional Budget Office, "Options for Reducing the Deficit: 2023 to 2032," December 2022, https://www.cbo.gov/publication/ 58164. (5% VAT: "JCT estimates that the first alternative would reduce the deficit by $3.05 trillion from 2024 to 2032"; eliminating itemized deductions: "Eliminating all itemized deductions would reduce the deficit by $2.5 trillion"; 2% payroll tax: "JCT estimates that the second alternative—imposing a new payroll tax of 2 percent—would reduce the deficit by $2.3 trillion over the same period.")

2. Committee for a Responsible Federal Budget, "Meeting Fiscal Goals Under CBO's January 2025 Baseline," January 29, 2025, https://www.crfb.org/blogs/meeting-fiscal-goals-under-cbos -january-2025-baseline. ("Stabilizing debt over the next decade at its current share of the economy would require $9.0 trillion of deficit reduction relative to the Congressional Budget Office's (CBO) January 2025 baseline.")

3. Social Security Administration, "Report of the National Commission on Social Security Reform," January 1983, https://www.ssa.gov/his tory/reports/gspan.html.

4. Social Security Administration, "Social Security Amendments of 1983: Legislative History and Summary of Provisions," Social Security Bulletin 46, no. 7 (July 1983), https://www.ssa.gov/policy/doc s/ssb/v46n7/v46n7p3.pdf. ("Among other things, delay the annual cost-of-living adjustments in benefits from July to January of each year, make up to one-half of the benefits received by higher-income beneficiaries subject to income taxes, gradually raise the retirement age early in the next century, call for the earlier implementation of scheduled payroll tax increases, and put new Federal employees under

the Social Security program.")

5. Shanto Iyengar et al., "The Origins and Consequences of Affective Polarization in the United States," Annual Review of Political Science 22 (2019): 129-146, https://doi.org/10.1146/annurev-polisci-0511 17-073034. ("This phenomenon of animosity between the parties is known as affective polarization.")

6. Louise Sheiner and Georgia Nabors, "Social Security: To-day's Financing Challenge Is at Least Double What It Was in 1983," Brookings Institution, September 18, 2023, https://www.brookings.edu/articles/social-security-todays-fi nancing-challenge-is-at-least-double-what-it-was-in-1983/. ("To put the program on stable financial footing today would require an im-mediate increase in revenues or cut in benefits (or combination of the two) equal to 3.61% of payroll; in 1983, the actuarial balance under the intermediate projections was 1.82% of payroll, meaning that the required adjustments to revenues and/or benefits are twice as large today." Also: "The actuaries projected that these reforms would keep the system solvent through 2060.")

7. Social Security Administration, "Table VI.F1. Present Values of OASDI Cost Less Non-interest Income and Unfunded Obliga-tions for Program Participants," 2025 OASDI Trustees Report, htt ps://www.ssa.gov/oact/TR/2025/VI_F_infinite.html. ("The OASDI open-group unfunded obligation over the infinite horizon is $72.8 trillion in present value... equal to 5.2 percent of taxable payroll.")

8. Social Security Administration, "Retirement Benefits: Full Retire-ment Age," https://www.ssa.gov/benefits/retirement/planner/agere duction.html. (Table shows full retirement age of 67 for those born 1960 and later.)

9. Susan Milligan, "How Older Voters Powered Trump's Election En-

gine," AARP, November 7, 2024, https://www.aarp.org/govern ment-elections/election-analysis-older-voters-2024/. ("AP VoteCast, which starts surveying voters a week before Election Day in order to capture early voters, reports that voters 50-plus constituted 52 percent of the electorate. Traditional exit polls, which survey people as they leave the polls on election day, put that number at 55 percent.")

10. U.S. Census Bureau, "Voting and Registration in the Election of No-vember 2024," Table 1, https://www.census.gov/data/tables/time-se ries/demo/voting-and-registration/p20-587.html. (Voting rates show 45-64 cohort participates at 15-20 percentage points higher than 18-29 cohort.)

11. AARP, "AARP Survey: Overwhelming Bipartisan Majority Oppose Social Security and Medicare Cuts to Reduce Deficit," 2024, https://states.aarp.org/vermont/aarp-survey-overwhelming-bipartisa n-majority-oppose-social-security-and-medicare-cuts-to-reduce-defici t. ("85% of Americans age 50+ oppose cutting Social Security and Medicare to reduce the federal budget deficit. The poll shows overwhelming opposition from both Republicans (88%) and Democrats (87%) on cutting Social Security benefits to pay down the deficit.")

12. U.S. House Committee on Ways and Means Democrats, "Summary of Polling on Social Security," https://democrats-waysandmeans.house.gov/sites/evo-subsites/demo crats-waysandmeans.house.gov/files/documents/Summary%20of%2 0Polling.pdf. ("Majority of public opposes a proposal to 'raise the retirement age to 69' (NCPSSM): Republicans – 72 percent oppose; Democrats – 83 percent oppose.")

13. AARP, "What is AARP and How Does It Help Older Americans," https://www.aarp.org/about-aarp/. ("AARP, a nonprofit, is one of the largest membership organizations in the world with 38 million

members." "AARP has offices in every state and territory.")

14. National Commission on Fiscal Responsibility and Reform, "The Moment of Truth: Report of the National Commission on Fiscal Responsibility and Reform," December 1, 2010, https://www.ssa.gov/history/reports/ObamaFiscal/TheMomentofTruth12_1_2010.pdf. (Figure 17 shows general revenues increase of $996 billion, Social Security revenue of $138 billion, total spending reductions of approximately $2.9 trillion including discretionary caps, health care, other mandatory, and interest savings.)

15. Richard Kogan, "What Was Actually in Bowles-Simpson — And How Can We Compare it With Other Plans?," Center on Budget and Policy Priorities, October 2, 2012, https://www.cbpp.org/research/what-was-actually-in-bowles-simpson-and-how-can-we-compare-it-with-other-plans. ("On December 3, 2010, only 11 commissioners voted in favor, five Republicans, five Democrats, and one independent.")

16. Charles J. Lewis, "Himes Predicts Action on Debt After Election," CT Insider, March 29, 2012, https://www.ctinsider.com/local/article/himes-predicts-action-on-debt-after-election-3445605.php. (Cooper-LaTourette vote on March 28, 2012: 382-38 against.)

17. National Low Income Housing Coalition, "Costly, Regressive, and Ineffective: How Sensitive Is Public Support for the Mortgage Interest Deduction in the United States?," https://nlihc.org/sites/default/files/Costly-Regressive-and-Ineffective.pdf. ("In 2012, a poll asking respondents whether they would support eliminating the deduction as part of a plan to reduce the budget deficit found that Americans opposed eliminating the deduction by a margin of 2 to 1.")

18. National Association of Realtors, "Advocacy Scoop: New NAR Poll Unveiled—Tax Reform, Real Estate Policy and Voter Opinion,"

https://www.nar.realtor/magazine/real-estate-news/advocacy-scoop
-new-nar-poll-unveiled-tax-reform-real-estate-policy-and-voter-opini
on. ("The survey found 61% of voters support increasing deduction
limits or removing limits altogether.")

19. Peter G. Peterson Foundation, "Social Security Reform: Options
    to Raise Revenues," https://www.pgpf.org/article/social-security-re
    form-options-to-raise-revenues/. ("According to the Social Security
    Trustees, eliminating the Social Security tax cap while providing ben-
    efit credit for those earnings would raise an additional $3.2 trillion over
    10 years — or close 53 percent of the 75-year funding gap.")

20. Ballotpedia, "Americans for Tax Reform," https://ballotpedia.org/
    Americans_for_Tax_Reform. (As of 2025, the ATR Taxpayer Pro-
    tection Pledge has been signed by 191 Representatives and 44 U.S.
    Senators.)

21. Congressional Budget Office, "Reduce the Department of Defense's
    Annual Budget," Budget Options, https://www.cbo.gov/budget-op
    tions/60920. ("This option would reduce DoD's funding by $1,118
    billion over that 10-year period (about $1,000 billion in 2025 dollars)."
    Also notes FY2025 budget request of $850 billion and 17% personnel
    reduction scenario.)

22. Committee for a Responsible Federal Budget, "CBO's Options to
    Improve Social Security Solvency," https://www.crfb.org/blogs/cb
    os-options-improve-social-security-solvency. ("Raising the retirement
    age by 2 months per year from 67 to 70 would save $150 billion over a
    decade and close 35 percent of Social Security's solvency gap." "Reduce
    benefit formula for top 30% from 32%/15% to 10%/5% (by 2034): $70
    billion savings, 20% of gap closed." "Setting benefits at 125 percent of
    poverty would save $820 billion and close 150 percent of the solvency
    gap.")

23. National Bureau of Economic Research, "Distributional Impacts of Proposed Changes to the Social Security System," https://www.nber.org/system/files/chapters/c10924/c10924.pdf. ("The 1.4 years of additional work and delay of benefits hits the higher income groups harder in absolute terms. When we divide the decline in net benefits by the income of each group, however, the distributional results are shown to be regressive.")

24. American Academy of Actuaries, "Means Testing for Social Security," Issue Brief, https://www.actuary.org/sites/default/files/files/Means_Testing_SS_IB.pdf. ("Despite a complex benefit formula... Social Security is administered remarkably efficiently, with administrative costs comprising approximately 1 percent of payroll tax income. The paperwork, investigations, and litigation associated with implementation of any kind of means test could add a substantial administrative burden to the system.")

25. Alan Gustman, Thomas Steinmeier, and Nahid Tabatabai, "Distributional Effects of Means Testing Social Security: Income Versus Wealth," NBER Working Paper No. 22424, July 2016, https://doi.org/10.3386/w22424. ("About 14.5 percent of retirees in this age group are both in the top quarter of income recipients and in the top quarter of wealth holders. Another 10.5 percent are top quarter income recipients, but not top quarter wealth holders; with an additional 10.5 percent top quarter wealth holders, but not top quarter income recipients... a means test of Social Security based on income has substantially different distributional effects from a means test based on wealth.")

26. U.S. House Committee on the Budget, "Full Committee Hearing: Medicare and Social Security: Examining Solvency and Impacts to the Federal Budget," June 13, 2024, https://budget.house.gov/hearing/medicare-and-social-security-examining-solvency-and-impacts-to-the-federal-budget. (Chief

Actuary Stephen Goss testimony: 75-year unfunded obligation for OASDI program stands at $22.6 trillion.)

27. Congressional Research Service, "Russian Military Performance and Outlook," IF12606, https://www.congress.gov/crs-product/IF1260 6. ("Russia's 2025 defense spending is estimated at 7.2% of GDP.")

28. Gerry R. Shih, "The Military Rise of China: The Real Defence Budget Over Two Decades," Defence and Peace Economics, 2024, https://www.tandfonline.com/doi/full/10.1080/10242694.2 024.2342043. ("While China's military remains relatively labour intensive compared to the US, its overall spending now rivals the U.S.A. and is rapidly closing the gap in military equipment.")

29. Vanguard, "Assessing U.S. Fiscal Space," December 2023, https://corporate.vanguard.com/content/dam/corp/public-p olicy/policy-research/assessing_us_fiscal_space_122023.pdf. ("At today's debt level of close to 100% of GDP, a 2% primary budget deficit would be sufficient to keep debt on a sustainable path... if the government were to wait until debt is closer to 180% of GDP, a level the CBO expects the government to reach shortly after 2050, a 1% surplus would be required.")

30. Social Security Administration, "The Worker-to-Beneficiary Ratio," Social Security Bulletin 66, no. 4 (2005), https://www.ssa.gov/polic y/docs/ssb/v66n4/v66n4p37.html; Social Security Board of Trustees, "The 2024 Annual Report of the Board of Trustees," https://www. ssa.gov/oact/tr/2024/IV_B_LRest.html. ("The worker-to-beneficiary ratio has fallen from 5.1 in 1960 to 3.3 in 2005... The Social Security Trustees project that the ratio will slip below this level by 2020 and will fall to only 2.1 workers per beneficiary by 2040." 2024 report confirms 2.8 ratio for 2013.)

31. Centers for Disease Control and Prevention, "Births: Provisional Data

for 2022," Vital Statistics Rapid Release Report No. 28, May 2023, https://www.cdc.gov/nchs/data/vsrr/vsrr028.pdf. ("The total fertility rate (TFR) for the United States in 2022 was 1,665.0 births per 1,000 women.")

32. Social Security Administration, "Social Security Fairness Act: Windfall Elimination Provision (WEP) and Government Pension Offset (GPO) Update," https://www.ssa.gov/benefits/retirement/social-security-fairness-act.html.

33. Social Security Administration, "A Summary of the 2025 Annual Reports," June 2025, https://www.ssa.gov/oact/TRSUM/index.html. ("The Old-Age and Survivors Insurance (OASI) Trust Fund will be able to pay 100 percent of total scheduled benefits until 2033.")

34. Committee for a Responsible Federal Budget, "A Bipartisan Social Security Commission," https://www.crfb.org/papers/bipartisan-social-security-commission. ("In 1981, the Social Security trust funds were nearly empty and President Ronald Reagan and Congressional leaders in both parties appointed the National Commission on Social Security Reform, chaired by Alan Greenspan, to come up with a long-term solution.") Cole-Delaney bills: H.R. 4236 (113th Congress, 2014), H.R. 1578 (114th Congress, 2015), H.R. 4521 (115th Congress, 2017) — all died in committee without hearings.

35. U.S. House Committee on the Budget Democrats, "House Republican Budget Plans Would Cut Social Security Benefits," https://democrats-budget.house.gov/house-republican-budget-plans-cut-social-security-benefits. ("The Republican Study Committee, which represents nearly 80 percent of House Republicans and 100 percent of House Republican leadership, has released a 2025 budget that would make Republican plans to gut Social Security a reality. By forcing Americans to work longer for less, their budget would cut Social Security benefits for 257 million people, or 3 in 4 Americans.")

36. Social Security Administration, "Monthly Statistical Snapshot," August 2025, https://www.ssa.gov/policy/docs/quickfacts/stat_snapshot/. (Table 1 shows 74,521,000 total beneficiaries receiving Social Security, Supplemental Security Income, or both.)

Chapter 13
Why It Won't Get Fixed

In 1983, two men who genuinely despised each other's politics saved Social Security. President Ronald Reagan, the conservative icon who had spent decades arguing that government was the problem, sat across from House Speaker Tip O'Neill, the Massachusetts liberal who embodied everything Reagan had campaigned against. The Social Security trust fund was months from depletion. Benefits for 36 million Americans hung in the balance. The political incentives screamed at both men to blame the other side and let the system collapse.

They made a deal anyway.

The National Commission on Social Security Reform, chaired by Alan Greenspan, proposed a package that inflicted pain on everyone: accelerated payroll tax increases, taxation of benefits for higher-income recipients, gradual increases in the retirement age from sixty-five to sixty-seven, coverage extension to new federal employees and nonprofit workers, and temporary delays in cost-of-living adjustments.[1] Democrats accepted benefit cuts. Republicans accepted tax increases. The legislation passed with 66.7 percent of the minority party voting in favor: 80 of 128 House Republicans and 32 of 40 Senate Republicans supported a bill that raised taxes, while Democrats accepted constraints on the program they considered sacred.[2]

Rudolph Penner of the Urban Institute, reflecting on what made that compromise possible, identified something that seems almost quaint today: "There were partisan battles in 1983 and intense ideological differences over how to fix Social Security, but Congressional leaders showed a desire to accomplish something and a willingness to compromise without either side having to completely abandon its ideological principles." The key ingredient, Penner concluded, was "a strong desire to get good things done that ultimately trumped their desire to make partisan points. The desire to accomplish things seems to be the missing ingredient in today's political battles."[3]

That missing ingredient explains why the fiscal crisis documented in this book will not be fixed before external events force adjustment under maximum duress. The solutions exist. The previous chapter laid out exactly what comprehensive reform would require: a package combining revenue increases and entitlement adjustments totaling $9.0 trillion in deficit reduction over 2025-2035.[4] The Congressional Budget Office has scored every policy lever. The arithmetic works. The question is not whether we know how to fix this. The question is whether the political system that achieved bipartisan compromise in 1983 can do so again.

It cannot. And understanding why requires grasping three fundamental changes since that last successful reform: the problem has doubled in magnitude, the easy policy tools have been exhausted, and the political environment has crossed a threshold into structural dysfunction that makes the 1983 model unrepeatable.

Today's Social Security financing challenge is at least double the magnitude faced in 1983.[5] To put the program on stable financial footing in 1983 required an immediate adjustment equivalent to 1.82 percent of taxable payroll. Today, that figure stands at 3.61 percent of payroll, meaning the required adjustments to revenues or benefits are twice as large.[5] The infinite horizon unfunded obligation totals $72.8 trillion in present value, requiring a permanent adjustment equivalent to 5.2 percent of future taxable payroll.[6]

This is not a marginal increase in difficulty. It represents a fundamental escalation in the scale of pain that must be distributed across the population. The 1983 reform could spread adjustments across multiple mechanisms, with no single component requiring politically catastrophic sacrifice. Today's required package demands either tax increases approaching revenue-maximizing rates or benefit cuts exceeding any politically survivable threshold, or both simultaneously.

The broader fiscal picture is even more daunting. Stabilizing federal debt at its current level of approximately 100 percent of GDP requires cumulative deficit reduction of $9.0 trillion over the 2025-2035 period.[4] The budget composition makes achieving this through any single approach mathematically impossible. Mandatory spending, primarily Social Security, Medicare, and Medicaid, consumes 60 percent of the federal budget. Net interest costs consume 13 percent and cannot be reduced without defaulting on obligations. This leaves only 27 percent for discretionary spending, including defense.[7]

Even the most aggressive cuts to discretionary spending fall catastrophically short. Eliminating all non-defense discretionary spending generates approximately $390 billion over ten years, just 4 percent of the required $9.0 trillion.[8] Adding defense cuts that would reduce active military personnel by 17 percent yields roughly $1.0 trillion over the decade.[9] Combined, the most draconian cuts to all discretionary spending, both defense and non-defense, total less than $1.4 trillion. The gap remains $7.6 trillion. The math demands touching entitlements and raising revenues simultaneously, precisely the combination that 1983 achieved on a much smaller scale.

The 1983 reform succeeded partly because policymakers had tools available that no longer exist. The commission expanded Social Security coverage to include federal workers hired after 1983, generating substantial new revenue from a previously untapped base.[1] That expansion is permanent. Federal workers are already covered. The 1983 reform introduced taxation of Social Security benefits for the first time, targeting higher-income recipients.[1] Benefits are already taxed. The 1983 reform scheduled a gradual increase in the normal retirement age from sixty-five to sixty-seven.[1] That increase is already implemented, with the full retirement age reaching sixty-seven for those born in 1960 or later.[10]

What remains are the politically toxic options that even the 1983 reform could only partially employ: further increases in the retirement age, direct reductions in scheduled benefits, elimination of the payroll tax cap, or massive increases in payroll tax rates. Each adjustment faces organized opposition from voting blocs with demonstrated capacity to end political careers.

Consider what a technically viable package would require today. A 5 percent value-added tax would generate $3.05 trillion over ten years, the most efficient broad-based consumption tax used successfully in most developed economies.[8] But VATs are regressive, imposing proportionally higher burdens on lower-income households who spend a larger share of income on consumption. This violates Democratic Party principles of progressive taxation. Eliminating all itemized tax deductions would generate $2.51 trillion, but this includes the mortgage interest deduction, which Americans oppose eliminating by a margin of approximately two to one.[11] It includes the state and local tax deduction, where 61 percent of voters support increasing or removing deduction limits altogether.[12] A new 2 percent payroll tax would raise $2.25 trillion, representing an additional $1,200 per year for a worker earning $60,000.[8]

Even combining the most aggressive revenue options yields insufficient savings. A 5 percent VAT generating $3.05 trillion, elimination of all itemized deductions generating $2.51 trillion, and defense cuts saving approximately $1.0 trillion produces a total of $6.56 trillion over ten years.[8] This falls $2.4 trillion short of the $9.0 trillion stabilization requirement. The gap can only be closed by touching Social Security and Medicare directly, the components most resistant to political action.

On the entitlement side, raising the full retirement age from sixty-seven to seventy would save $150 billion through 2035, closing approximately 35 percent of the Social Security funding gap.[13] But this adjustment is regressive, harming lower-income workers who have shorter life expectancies and fewer years to collect benefits.[14] Reducing benefits for the top 30 percent of earners would close approximately 20 percent of the solvency gap.[13] Means testing, frequently proposed as a politically palatable benefit reduction, faces severe technical obstacles: the Social Security Administration currently operates with administrative costs of approximately 1 percent of payroll tax income, and implementing means testing would require extensive new processes that would add substantial administrative burden offsetting some savings.[15]

The comprehensive fix requires combining elements that offend every major political constituency simultaneously. Democrats cannot accept the regressive consumption tax and benefit cuts. Republicans cannot accept the massive tax increases. Both parties need each other to pass reform. Neither can trust the other not to weaponize their votes.

If the political system could rise to this challenge, we would have evidence by now. Instead, we have a documented record of repeated failures, each demonstrating that the structural obstacles are real and growing worse.

In 2010, President Obama created the National Commission on Fiscal Responsibility and Reform through executive order, tasking eighteen members, twelve from Congress and six private citizens, with developing policies to achieve long-term fiscal sustainability.[16] The co-chairs, former Republican Senator Alan Simpson of Wyoming and Erskine Bowles, President Clinton's former chief of staff, assembled a bipartisan group and released their final report in December 2010.[17]

The plan proposed $2.6 trillion in revenue increases and $2.9 trillion in spending cuts over ten years, a nearly balanced approach to deficit reduction.[17] This was substantially smaller than today's $9.0 trillion requirement. The commission's own rules required 14 of 18 members to approve recommendations before sending them to Congress. On December 3, 2010, only 11 commissioners voted in favor: five Republicans, five Democrats, and one independent.[18]

The fault lines were instructive. Republican commission members Paul Ryan, Jeb Hensarling, and Dave Camp voted no because the plan raised taxes and did too little to address healthcare spending.[19] Democratic commissioners Jan Schakowsky, Xavier Becerra, and Andy Stern voted no because the plan cut entitlement and safety net programs.[20] Schakowsky explained her vote: "While I cannot support the Simpson-Bowles plan, I want to thank the co-chairmen for their dedication to this difficult task. I believe that we can achieve primary budget balance without further eroding the middle class in America."[20]

The commission's failure to reach its own internal threshold did not end the effort. Sixteen months later, Representatives Jim Cooper, a Tennessee Democrat, and Steve LaTourette, an Ohio Republican, introduced a House resolution based on Simpson-Bowles principles, with somewhat smaller tax increases in an attempt to gain Republican support.[21] The House rejected it 382 to 38.[21] This was not a close vote derailed by procedural maneuvering. This was overwhelming bipartisan rejection of a plan that represented exactly the balanced approach policy analysts consistently recommend.

The pattern continued. The Budget Control Act of 2011 established the Joint Select Committee on Deficit Reduction, known as the Super Committee, mandating that it find at least $1.2 trillion in deficit reduction through bipartisan agreement.[22] If the committee failed, automatic across-the-board spending cuts called sequestration would trigger. The committee collapsed without agreement.[23] Democrats demanded revenue increases. Republicans refused. Republicans demanded entitlement cuts. Democrats refused. The sequestration trigger, designed to be so outrageously imprudent that negotiators would compromise before resorting to it, took effect in March 2013.[23]

That same year, the federal government shut down for sixteen days due to failure to pass appropriations legislation. The closure imposed estimated economic costs of $24 billion, according to Standard and Poor's, shaving 0.6 percent off annualized fourth-quarter GDP growth.[24] The pattern demonstrates that fiscal confrontations now resolve only through crisis, forcing temporary solutions under maximum political duress rather than through proactive compromise.

The contrast with 1983 is devastating. That year, lawmakers created a commission, achieved bipartisan agreement, and passed comprehensive reform that the actuaries projected would keep Social Security solvent through 2060.[5] The solution held for a generation. Forty years later, Congress cannot even agree to begin the conversation. The Cole-Delaney bills, introduced in 2014, 2015, and again in 2017 to create a bipartisan Social Security reform commission, never received a hearing, a markup, or a vote.[25] Each died silently in committee. The political system that solved the 1983 crisis cannot bring itself to discuss the current one.

The repeated failures are not accidents of timing or failures of individual leadership. They reflect structural changes in the political environment that have made bipartisan cooperation on painful fiscal choices essentially impossible.

Political scientists track ideological divergence in Congress through DW-NOMINATE scores, which measure the spatial positioning of legislators based on their voting records. Analysis covering 1879 through 2023 confirms accelerating and monotonic increase in the distance between party medians. In the early 1980s, when the Social Security reform passed, ideological overlap was common; legislators existed whose voting records placed them between the median of their own party and the median of the opposing party. By recent Congresses, the center has emptied out. The median separation has reached historical extremes not seen since the immediate aftermath of the Civil War.[26]

This ideological sorting is compounded by what researchers call affective polarization: the degree to which citizens feel personal hostility toward the opposing party. A 2019 Pew Research Center survey found that 55 percent of Republicans say Democrats are "more immoral" when compared with other Americans, while 47 percent of Democrats say the same about Republicans. These figures had increased substantially from just three years earlier, when 47 percent of Republicans and 35 percent of Democrats expressed such views.[27] When citizens view the opposing party not merely as wrong on policy but as morally deficient, they punish their own representatives for cooperating with the enemy.

The behavioral manifestation appears in legislative metrics. Party unity votes, defined as votes where a majority of one party opposes a majority of the other, now exceed 60 to 70 percent of all roll calls in recent Congresses, with the Senate reaching nearly 80 percent in 2021.[28] House Democrats voted unanimously on 78 percent of party unity votes in 2021, their highest rate on record.[28] The parties have become parliamentary-style voting blocs in a system designed for cross-party coalition building.

The Senate filibuster, historically reserved for exceptional circumstances, has become routine obstruction. Cloture motions, the procedural mechanism to overcome filibusters, have increased nearly tenfold, from 31 to 54 per Congress in the 1980s to 270 to 328 per Congress in 2019-2022.[29] The 60-vote threshold for cloture has transformed from exceptional requirement to standard expectation for all significant legislation, meaning comprehensive fiscal reform would need supermajority support in an environment where simple majorities are barely achievable.

The structural incentives facing individual politicians reinforce gridlock. The Taxpayer Protection Pledge, promoted by Americans for Tax Reform, has been signed by 191 House members and 44 Senators, committing them to oppose any net tax increase.[30] Violating this pledge triggers primary challenges from anti-tax conservatives and donor revolts. On the other side, AARP commands a membership of 38 million people with offices in all fifty states, organizational infrastructure that exists to mobilize opposition to any benefit reduction or retirement age increase.[31] Among voters aged fifty and older, 88 percent of Republicans and 87 percent of Democrats oppose cutting Social Security benefits to reduce the federal deficit.[32] Opposition to raising the full retirement age to sixty-nine runs at 72 percent among Republicans and 83 percent among Democrats in this demographic.[33]

These are not casual preferences. These are career-ending commitments from the most electorally engaged segment of the population. Voters aged fifty and older represented 52 to 55 percent of the electorate in the 2024 election.[34] This demographic votes at rates fifteen to twenty percentage points higher than younger cohorts.[35] Proposing the reforms necessary to achieve fiscal sustainability is not a difficult vote. It is political suicide.

The political impossibility of reform stems from what game theorists call a prisoner's dilemma, where individual rational choices produce collectively catastrophic outcomes.

Democrats will accept tax increases to preserve entitlements. Democrats will not accept benefit cuts, which would violate their commitment to social insurance programs and trigger revolt from labor unions, progressive advocacy groups, and AARP. Republicans will accept entitlement cuts to reduce the size of government. Republicans will not accept tax increases, which would violate the Taxpayer Protection Pledge and trigger primary challenges.

Comprehensive reform requires both parties to act simultaneously, accepting pain their respective bases reject. Neither party can move first because the other could defect, blocking reform while weaponizing the first party's votes in the next election cycle. Both parties need each other. Neither can trust the other.

The dominant strategy for each party is to refuse compromise, blame the opponent for gridlock, and wait for external crisis to force action. This produces stable equilibrium around inaction, even though both parties understand that delay makes the eventual adjustment exponentially larger. The partisan weaponization of reform proposals demonstrates the dynamic in action. Democratic leaders attack Republican budget proposals, claiming they would "gut Social Security benefits" by forcing Americans to work longer, characterizing such plans as attacks on seniors, veterans, and the middle class.[36] Republican leaders refuse revenue increases that would violate the Taxpayer Protection Pledge signed by the majority of their caucus.[30] Both parties use the necessity of reform as an electoral weapon rather than a policy priority requiring cooperation.

The individually rational choice for every politician is to defer action. The cost of reform is immediate and certain: proposing benefit cuts triggers primary challenges and general election defeats; proposing tax increases alienates donors and base voters. These costs arrive within the current election cycle. The cost of inaction is delayed and diffuse: the fiscal crisis hits in 2033 for Social Security, potentially fifteen or twenty years out for broader debt dynamics. By the time crisis forces action, current officeholders will have moved to other positions or retired. The rational individual choice is to kick the can, let successors handle it, and preserve your own political survival.

Collectively, these individual rational choices produce systemically cata-strophic outcomes. Every actor optimizes for survival within their constraints. The aggregation of these rational strategies produces guaranteed collision. This is not about bad people or failed leadership. This is about incentive structures that make necessary adjustment structurally impossible until external crisis forces action under the worst possible conditions.

Every year of delay makes the eventual adjustment larger through a mecha-nism that operates with mathematical certainty. At current debt levels of ap-proximately 100 percent of GDP, stabilizing the debt-to-GDP ratio requires achieving a primary deficit of roughly 2 percent of GDP.[37] This is difficult but mathematically feasible through combinations of revenue increases and spending cuts. If action is delayed until debt reaches 180 percent of GDP, projected for shortly after 2050 under current trajectories, stabilization requires achieving a primary surplus of approximately 1 percent of GDP.[37]

This 3 percentage point swing is not abstract. It is equivalent to eliminating the combined budgets of Medicare and Medicaid while simultaneously raising income taxes by 30 percent. No political system implements changes of that magnitude voluntarily.

The Treasury Department quantifies the cost of delay: each decade of in-action increases the required permanent fiscal adjustment by approximately 0.8 percentage points of GDP.[38] In 2025 dollars, this represents roughly $200 billion per year, forever.[39] The penalty compounds. The adjustment that could stabilize debt if implemented in 2025 grows geometrically larger with each passing year, while the political capacity to implement adjustment does not expand.

The worker-to-beneficiary ratio continues declining from 2.8 workers per beneficiary in 2013 toward 2.1 by 2040.[40] The Baby Boom generation will not un-retire. Fertility rates, currently at 1.66 births per woman, show no signs of recovering toward the replacement rate of 2.1.[41] The demographic fundamen-tals driving the crisis are locked in for decades. The electoral math that makes Social Security reform political suicide will not change as long as voters aged fifty and older represent the majority of the electorate and vote at rates far exceeding younger cohorts.

The political system that rejected Simpson-Bowles when it proposed $5.4 trillion in combined revenue increases and spending cuts will not pass reforms requiring $9.0 trillion.[4] The Congress that allowed the Super Committee to fail over $1.2 trillion will not achieve comprehensive grand bargains requiring nearly eight times that magnitude. The political system that expanded Social Security benefits through the Social Security Fairness Act in January 2025, increasing program costs during a documented fiscal crisis, demonstrates that political incentives favor benefit expansion over solvency measures.[42]

The combined Old-Age and Survivors Insurance and Disability Insurance Trust Funds will deplete reserves in 2033, triggering automatic benefit reductions of approximately 24 percent under current law.[43] This projection has generated no legislative action because the known political cost of reform outweighs future electoral consequences of failure.

The 2033 deadline will force Congressional action not because political will suddenly materializes but because statutory law mandates benefit reductions that more than 74 million Americans will experience directly.[44] At that point, politicians will implement emergency measures under maximum political duress, with minimal time for gradual phase-ins, and without the fiscal space that might have allowed smoother transitions had reform occurred earlier.

The most likely outcome is emergency borrowing to prevent the automatic cuts, adding hundreds of billions annually to federal debt while leaving the underlying insolvency unaddressed. This delays the crisis five to ten years but increases the required eventual adjustment through the exponential cost mechanism. The alternative is immediate emergency taxes or benefit cuts enacted in crisis conditions without the gradual phase-ins or targeted protections that advance planning would allow.

The fiscal crisis is not technically impossible to solve. It is politically impossible to solve before 2033 forces a choice between automatic benefit cuts, massive emergency borrowing, or crushing tax increases implemented under recession conditions.

The solutions exist. The arithmetic works. The policy levers are real. We proved in 1983 that comprehensive reform combining revenue increases and benefit adjustments can pass with bipartisan support when crisis forces action and leaders choose governance over partisan advantage.

But that crisis was half this size, occurred during lower political polarization, and used policy tools that have since been exhausted. Today's required fix exceeds any politician's electoral survival threshold. Both parties need each other to pass reform. Neither can trust the other not to weaponize compromise. Every actor is individually rational, optimizing for re-election within two-to-six-year cycles while the crisis operates on a thirty-year timeline. Collectively, this produces guaranteed inaction until external crisis makes continuation of current policy more politically dangerous than the pain of adjustment.

If citizens demanded fiscal responsibility with the same intensity they demand benefit preservation, the calculus might change. If primary voters rewarded rather than punished compromise, politicians might risk bipartisan cooperation. If the political culture recovered what Rudolph Penner identified as "a strong desire to get good things done," the 1983 model might become repeatable.[3]

But wishing does not make it so. The polarization metrics are moving in the wrong direction. The trust deficit between parties is widening, not narrowing. The incentive structures that produce gridlock are strengthening, not weakening.

The collision is guaranteed not by the size of the debt or the magnitude of entitlement obligations but by the structure of political incentives that make addressing them impossible until crisis forces action. The question is not whether fiscal adjustment will occur. The mathematics ensure it must. The question is whether adjustment happens through managed reform under controlled conditions or through crisis-driven emergency measures under maximum economic and political stress.

Based on the evidence documented in this chapter, based on Simpson-Bowles and the Super Committee and the government shutdowns and the bills that died without hearings, based on the polarization data and the party unity votes and the cloture explosion, based on the rational incentives facing every politician who wants to keep their job, the answer is clear.

Reform will not happen proactively. The system cannot self-correct because the required pain exceeds any politician's electoral survival threshold. The crisis will arrive unmanaged, forcing adjustment under the worst possible conditions, with consequences that could have been mitigated through early action that political incentives made impossible.

The emperor is naked. Everyone with access to official projections can see it. This chapter exists to document that the solutions are real, the costs are quantifiable, and the political impossibility is structural rather than accidental. When the crisis arrives in 2033, when automatic benefit cuts hit or emergency measures pass under duress, when the required adjustment occurs under the worst possible conditions, the historical record will show that this was not inevitable. It was chosen, through rational individual decisions that produced collective catastrophe, by a political system that could see the collision coming but could not bring itself to change course in time.

CHAPTER 13 NOTES

1. Social Security Administration, "Social Security Amendments of 1983: Legislative History and Summary of Provisions," Social Security Bulletin 46, no. 7 (July 1983), https://www.ssa.gov/policy/docs/ssb/v46n7/v46n7p3.pdf. (Details the package including "acceleration of already-scheduled tax increases," "taxation of benefits for higher-income persons," "coverage of new Federal employees and employees of nonprofit organizations," and "a 6-month delay in the 1983 cost-of-living adjustment.")

2. Social Security Administration, "Vote Tallies 1983 Amendments," https://www.ssa.gov/history/tally1983.html. ("House vote March 24, 1983: Republicans 80 Yes, 48 No. Senate vote March 24, 1983: Republicans 32 Yes, 8 No.")

3. Rudolph G. Penner, "The Greenspan Commission and the Social Security Reforms of 1983," Urban Institute, https://www.urban.org/sites/default/files/publication/65126/2000323-Myth-and-Reality-of-the-Safety-Net-The-1983-Social-Security-Reforms.pdf. ("There were partisan battles in 1983 and intense ideological differences over how to fix Social Security, but Congressional leaders showed a desire to accomplish something and a willingness to compromise... The desire to accomplish things seems to be the missing ingredient in today's political battles.")

4. Committee for a Responsible Federal Budget, "Meeting Fiscal Goals Under CBO's January 2025 Baseline," January 29, 2025, https://www.crfb.org/blogs/meeting-fiscal-goals-under-cbos-january-2025-baseline. (Calculates $9.0 trillion deficit reduction required over 2025-2035 to stabilize debt at current levels.)

5. Louise Sheiner and Georgia Nabors, "Social Securi-

ty: Today's Financing Challenge Is at Least Double What It Was in 1983," Brookings Institution, September 18, 2023, https://www.brookings.edu/articles/social-security-todays-financing-challenge-is-at-least-double-what-it-was-in-1983/. ("The changes that are required to put Social Security on a stable footing over the next 75 years are significantly larger than they were in 1983... the required adjustments to revenues and/or benefits are twice as large today" comparing current 3.82% to 1983's 1.82% of taxable payroll.)

6. Social Security Administration, "Table VI.F1. Present Values of OAS-DI Cost Less Non-interest Income and Unfunded Obligations for Program Participants," 2025 OASDI Trustees Report, https://www.ssa.gov/oact/TR/2025/VI_F_infinite.html. (Shows $72.8 trillion infinite horizon unfunded obligation requiring 5.2% of future taxable payroll.)

7. Bipartisan Policy Center, "Visualizing CBO's Budget and Economic Outlook: 2025 to 2035," January 2025, https://bipartisanpolicy.org/article/visualizing-cbos-budget-and-economic-outlook-2025/. (Breakdown: mandatory spending 60%, net interest 13%, discretionary 27%.)

8. Congressional Budget Office, "Options for Reducing the Deficit: 2023 to 2032," December 2022, https://www.cbo.gov/publication/58164. (Scores policy options including 5% VAT at $3.05 trillion, elimination of itemized deductions at $2.51 trillion, 2% payroll tax at $2.25 trillion over ten years.)

9. Congressional Budget Office, "Reduce the Department of Defense's Annual Budget," Budget Options, https://www.cbo.gov/budget-options/60920. (Projects roughly $1.0 trillion savings over decade from 17% reduction in active military personnel.)

10. Social Security Administration, "Retirement Benefits: Full Retire-

ment Age," https://www.ssa.gov/benefits/retirement/planner/agere
duction.html. ("If you were born in 1960 or later, your full retirement
age is 67.")

11. National Low Income Housing Coalition, "Costly, Regressive, and
    Ineffective: How Sensitive Is Public Support for the Mortgage Interest
    Deduction in the United States?," https://nlihc.org/sites/default/fi
    les/Costly-Regressive-and-Ineffective.pdf. (Shows Americans oppose
    eliminating mortgage interest deduction by approximately two to one
    margin.)

12. National Association of Realtors, "Advocacy Scoop: New NAR Poll
    Unveiled—Tax Reform, Real Estate Policy and Voter Opinion,"
    https://www.nar.realtor/magazine/real-estate-news/advocacy-scoop
    -new-nar-poll-unveiled-tax-reform-real-estate-policy-and-voter-opini
    on. ("61 percent of voters support increasing or removing SALT
    deduction limits altogether.")

13. Committee for a Responsible Federal Budget, "CBO's Options to
    Improve Social Security Solvency," https://www.crfb.org/blogs/cbo
    s-options-improve-social-security-solvency. (Scores raising retirement
    age to 70 at 35% of funding gap; reducing benefits for top 30% earners
    at 20% of gap.)

14. National Bureau of Economic Research, "Distributional Impacts of
    Proposed Changes to the Social Security System," https://www.nbe
    r.org/system/files/chapters/c10924/c10924.pdf. (Documents regres-
    sive impact of retirement age increases on lower-income workers with
    shorter life expectancies.)

15. American Academy of Actuaries, "Means Testing for Social Security,"
    Issue Brief, https://www.actuary.org/sites/default/files/files/Means
    _Testing_SS_IB.pdf. ("The Social Security Administration current-
    ly operates with administrative costs of approximately 1 percent of

payroll tax income" and means testing "would require extensive new processes.")

16. Library of Congress, "About the National Commission on Fiscal Responsibility and Reform," https://www.loc.gov/item/lcwaN001 6863/. (Documents creation through executive order with eighteen members tasked with achieving long-term fiscal sustainability.)

17. National Commission on Fiscal Responsibility and Reform, "The Moment of Truth: Report of the National Commission on Fiscal Responsibility and Reform," December 1, 2010, https://www.ssa.gov/history/reports/ObamaFiscal/TheMom entofTruth12_1_2010.pdf. (Proposed $2.6 trillion in revenue increases and $2.9 trillion in spending cuts over ten years.)

18. Richard Kogan, "What Was Actually in Bowles-Simpson—And How Can We Compare it With Other Plans?," Center on Budget and Policy Priorities, October 2, 2012, https://www.cbpp.org/research/what-was-actually-in-bowles -simpson-and-how-can-we-compare-it-with-other-plans. ("On December 3, 2010, only 11 commissioners voted in favor, five Republicans, five Democrats, and one independent.")

19. "House Dems to Debate Moderators: Don't Focus on Bowles-Simpson," The Hill, https://thehill.com/policy/finance/122500-house-d ems-to-debate-moderators-dont-focus-on-bowles-simpson/. (Documents Republican commissioners Ryan, Hensarling, and Camp voting no because plan raised taxes.)

20. Rep. Jan Schakowsky, "Schakowsky on Fiscal Commission Report, Final Vote," press release, December 3, 2010, https://schakowsky.house.gov/media/press-releases/schakows ky-fiscal-commission-report-final-vote. ("While I cannot support the Simpson-Bowles plan, I want to thank the co-chairmen for their ded-

ication to this difficult task. I believe that we can achieve primary budget balance without further eroding the middle class in America.")

21. Charles J. Lewis, "Himes Predicts Action on Debt After Election," CT Insider, March 29, 2012, https://www.ctinsider.com/local/article/himes-predicts-action-on-debt-after-election-3445605.php. (Reports House rejected Simpson-Bowles-based resolution 382 to 38.)

22. Congressional Research Service, "The Budget Control Act of 2011," R41965, https://www.congress.gov/crs-product/R41965. (Established Joint Select Committee on Deficit Reduction mandated to find $1.2 trillion in deficit reduction.)

23. U.S. House Committee on the Budget Democrats, "Understanding Sequester: An Update for the 115th Congress," https://democrats-budget.house.gov/publications/report/understanding-sequester-update-115th-congress. (Documents Super Committee collapse and sequestration trigger taking effect March 2013.)

24. Office of Management and Budget, "Impacts and Costs of the October 2013 Federal Government Shutdown," November 2013, https://obamawhitehouse.archives.gov/sites/default/files/omb/reports/impacts-and-costs-of-october-2013-federal-government-shutdown-report.pdf; Shushannah Walshe, "The Costs of the Government Shutdown," ABC News, October 17, 2013, https://abcnews.go.com/blogs/politics/2013/10/the-costs-of-the-government-shutdown. ("Standard and Poor's estimated the shutdown cost the U.S. $24 billion, shaving 0.6 percent off annualized fourth-quarter GDP growth.")

25. Committee for a Responsible Federal Budget, "A Bipartisan Social Security Commission," https://www.crfb.org/papers/bipartisan-social-security-commission. (Documents Cole-Delaney bills introduced

in 2014, 2015, and 2017 dying without hearings or votes.)

26. Jeff Lewis, "Polarization in Congress," Voteview, October 23, 2023, h ttps://voteview.com/articles/party_polarization. ("The current period is the most polarized since the end of Reconstruction" with median separation at historical extremes.)

27. Pew Research Center, "Partisan Antipathy: More Intense, More Personal," October 10, 2019, https://www.pewresearch.org/politics/20 19/10/10/partisan-antipathy-more-intense-more-personal/. ("55% of Republicans say Democrats are 'more immoral' when compared with other Americans; 47% of Democrats say the same about Republican s.")

28. "Party Unity Vote Studies Underscore Polarized State of the Union," Roll Call, March 1, 2022, https://rollcall.com/2022/03/01/party -unity-vote-studies-underscore-polarized-state-of-the-union/. ("Party unity votes now exceed 60 to 70 percent of all roll calls... Senate reaching nearly 80 percent in 2021. House Democrats voted unanimously on 78 percent of party unity votes in 2021, their highest rate on reco rd.")

29. U.S. Senate, "Cloture Motions," Senate Historical Office, https:/ /www.senate.gov/legislative/cloture/clotureCounts.htm. (Shows increase from 31-54 cloture motions per Congress in 1980s to 270-328 per Congress in 2019-2022.)

30. Ballotpedia, "Americans for Tax Reform," https://ballotpedia.org/ Americans_for_Tax_Reform. ("The Taxpayer Protection Pledge has been signed by 191 House members and 44 Senators.")

31. AARP, "What is AARP and How Does It Help Older Americans," h ttps://www.aarp.org/about-aarp/. ("AARP is one of the largest membership organizations in the world with 38 million members.")

32. AARP, "AARP Survey: Overwhelming Bipartisan Majority Oppose Social Security and Medicare Cuts to Reduce Deficit," 2024, https://states.aarp.org/vermont/aarp-survey-overwhelming-bipartisa n-majority-oppose-social-security-and-medicare-cuts-to-reduce-defici t. ("88 percent of Republicans and 87 percent of Democrats oppose cutting Social Security benefits to reduce the federal deficit.")

33. U.S. House Committee on Ways and Means Democrats, "Summary of Polling on Social Security," https://democrats-waysandmeans.house.gov/sites/evo-subsites/demo crats-waysandmeans.house.gov/files/documents/Summary%20of%2 0Polling.pdf. ("Opposition to raising the full retirement age to 69 runs at 72 percent among Republicans and 83 percent among Democrats.")

34. Susan Milligan, "How Older Voters Powered Trump's Election Engine," AARP, November 7, 2024, https://www.aarp.org/governmen t-elections/election-analysis-older-voters-2024/. ("Voters aged 50 and older represented 52 to 55 percent of the electorate in the 2024 elect ion.")

35. U.S. Census Bureau, "Voting and Registration in the Election of November 2024," Table 1, https://www.census.gov/data/tables/time-se ries/demo/voting-and-registration/p20-587.html. (Shows voters 50+ vote at rates 15-20 percentage points higher than younger cohorts.)

36. U.S. House Committee on the Budget Democrats, "House Republican Budget Plans Would Cut Social Security Benefits," https://democrats-budget.house.gov/house-republican-budge t-plans-cut-social-security-benefits. (Characterizes Republican proposals as plans that would "gut Social Security benefits" and "attacks on seniors, veterans, and the middle class.")

37. Vanguard, "Assessing U.S. Fiscal Space," December 2023, https://corporate.vanguard.com/content/dam/corp/public-p

olicy/policy-research/assessing_us_fiscal_space_122023.pdf. (Calculates stabilization requires 2% primary deficit at 100% debt-to-GDP, but 1% primary surplus at 180% debt-to-GDP.)

38. U.S. Department of the Treasury, "Financial Report of the United States Government," Management's Discussion and Analysis, https://fiscal.treasury.gov/reports-statements/financial-report/mda-unsustainable-fiscal-path.html. ("Each decade of inaction increases the required permanent fiscal adjustment by approximately 0.8 percentage points of GDP.")

39. Author calculation based on 0.8 percent of GDP using 2025 GDP baseline of approximately $25 trillion.

40. Social Security Administration, "The Worker-to-Beneficiary Ratio," Social Security Bulletin 66, no. 4 (2005), https://www.ssa.gov/policy/docs/ssb/v66n4/v66n4p37.html; Social Security Board of Trustees, "The 2024 Annual Report of the Board of Trustees," https://www.ssa.gov/oact/tr/2024/IV_B_LRest.html. (Projects decline from 2.8 workers per beneficiary in 2013 to 2.1 by 2040.)

41. Centers for Disease Control and Prevention, "Births: Provisional Data for 2022," Vital Statistics Rapid Release Report No. 28, May 2023, https://www.cdc.gov/nchs/data/vsrr/vsrr028.pdf. ("The provisional general fertility rate for the United States in 2022 was 56.1 births per 1,000 women aged 15–44, down 1% from 2021" with total fertility rate at 1.66.)

42. Social Security Administration, "Social Security Fairness Act: Windfall Elimination Provision (WEP) and Government Pension Offset (GPO) Update," https://www.ssa.gov/benefits/retirement/social-security-fairness-act.html. (Documents January 2025 expansion of benefits through elimination of WEP and GPO provisions.)

43. Social Security Administration, "A Summary of the 2025 Annual Reports," June 2025, https://www.ssa.gov/oact/TRSUM/index.html ; Committee for a Responsible Federal Budget, "Social Security Turns 90 in a State of Crisis," August 14, 2025, https://www.crfb.org/blogs/social-security-turns-90-state-crisis. ("The combined OASI and DI Trust Funds are now projected to be depleted in calendar year 2033" triggering approximately 24% automatic benefit reduction.)

44. Social Security Administration, "Monthly Statistical Snapshot," August 2025, https://www.ssa.gov/policy/docs/quickfacts/stat_snapshot/. (Shows more than 74 million Americans receiving benefits.)

Chapter 14
The Four Possible Endgames

Y ou now understand what is coming and why it cannot be stopped through normal political processes. The 2033 Social Security deadline is statutory law. The interest cost explosion is already underway. The political gridlock is structural. Congress will not pass comprehensive reform before crisis forces adjustment under maximum duress. The collision is guaranteed.

The question is not whether the crisis happens. The question is what comes after.

This chapter examines four possible trajectories based on historical precedent and comparative analysis of how democratic systems respond to severe fiscal and political stress. These are not predictions. They are scenarios, each grounded in documented case studies, assigned probabilities based on structural factors, and evaluated for early warning indicators that signal which path is emerging. The probability assignments reflect the political economy analysis developed in the accompanying working paper, which demonstrates that pre-deadline reform is structurally improbable rather than merely politically difficult given the magnitude of required adjustment, constituency lock-in from 70 million beneficiaries, blame avoidance dynamics favoring automatic cuts over legislated reductions, and demonstrated legislative incapacity evidenced by Simpson-Bowles and subsequent failures.[1] Understanding this possibility space allows clearer thinking about which outcomes to prepare for and which to work toward preventing.

The four scenarios are multi-decade muddling through with geographic stratification, authoritarian restoration following democratic dysfunction, internal fragmentation into effectively separate regional systems, and comprehensive reconstruction through constitutional reform. The probabilities are uneven. History shows that democracies facing fiscal stress usually muddle through rather than collapse entirely, but muddling through means permanent reduction in living standards and state capacity. Authoritarian restoration follows a documented pattern when democratic institutions prove incapable of necessary reforms. Fragmentation reflects trends already accelerating through legal mechanisms. Reconstruction requires crisis to force political will that shows no current signs of materializing.

The most likely outcome, assigned a probability of 50 to 60 percent based on historical base rates, is prolonged stagnation with intensifying geographic inequality. Not civil war, not Mad Max collapse, but a long grinding decline where your ZIP code determines whether you live in functional or failed America. This scenario follows the template of post-Soviet Russia, which experienced a GDP decline of 40 percent over the decade following 1991 and saw life expectancy for Russian men fall by more than six years between 1990 and 1994, yet maintained territorial integrity and avoided civil war because the centralized state retained its monopoly on organized violence.[2] The Japanese experience provides another model, with government debt exceeding 260 percent of GDP while the society remains stable and institutions continue functioning despite decades of economic stagnation.[3]

The United States possesses structural advantages that favor this outcome. Deep institutional capacity means the state retains its monopoly on violence and the functional ability to deliver basic services even under severe fiscal stress. Geographic diversity allows some regions to thrive while others decline, preventing uniform collapse. Federalism enables state-level adaptation when federal capacity fails. The middle class, despite facing severe economic pressure, will desperately defend social order rather than accept total breakdown. These factors suggest that even severe fiscal crisis produces prolonged deterioration rather than sudden catastrophic failure.

What this means in practice is visible degradation occurring over 15 to 20 years rather than immediate collapse. Federal government capacity continues shrinking as interest costs consume discretionary spending, infrastructure maintenance is deferred, research funding declines, and public services operate at reduced levels. Wealthy areas maintain order through higher local taxes and private alternatives. Struggling cities cut police and education, triggering middle-class exodus that collapses tax bases and accelerates decline. The sorting into tiers described in Chapter 8 solidifies into permanent geographic stratification. Not a failed nation, but a nation divided into zones of functionality based on local fiscal capacity and economic diversity.

The lived experience of muddling through is not dramatic. It is the slow realization that bridges take longer to repair, that parks deteriorate, that public schools in struggling areas can no longer attract qualified teachers, that response times for emergency services increase, that infrastructure you took for granted begins visibly failing. It is watching your neighborhood slowly change as families with means relocate to areas with better services while those lacking mobility remain. It is the gradual acceptance of a permanently lower standard of living and reduced expectations for what government can provide. The crisis becomes normal, integrated into daily life as the background condition rather than an acute emergency requiring response.

History provides precedent for this trajectory. Post-Soviet Russia endured catastrophic social trauma, massive mortality increases, and economic devastation that would have destroyed most nations, yet the state survived because it retained the capacity to project force and prevent violent fragmentation. Scholars have attributed this survival in part to the persistence of core state structures and coercive capacities that were able to manage separatist pressures and prevent large-scale dissolution.[4] Japan has carried debt exceeding 260 percent of GDP for years while maintaining social stability despite grinding economic stagnation.[3] Greece survived unemployment reaching 27.5 percent at its peak and GDP contracting by a quarter because the Eurozone provided an external anchor that enforced institutional continuity despite profound internal stress.[5] Argentina experienced 25 percent unemployment, 55 percent poverty, and a 20 percent GDP decline in 2001, yet recovered rapidly because the system purged failed policies through rapid political turnover rather than prolonged gridlock.[6] Economic severity alone does not predict regime collapse. What determines survival versus failure is institutional health, state capacity, and whether the system retains mechanisms for self-correction.

The United States in 2033 will face worse conditions than the 1930s Great Depression in critical structural ways. The population is significantly older, with median age exceeding 39 years compared to 26.5 years in the 1930s, creating higher dependency ratios and less labor force flexibility.[7] Eighty percent of the population now lives in urban areas compared to substantial rural distribution in the 1930s, increasing reliance on centralized infrastructure and formal economic systems.[8] Social capital, the networks of cooperation and norms of reciprocity that helped communities endure the Depression, has declined substantially since the 1960s according to extensive sociological research.[9] The buffers that allowed 1930s America to survive 24.9 percent unemployment without regime collapse are significantly depleted.[10] But the 1930s also lacked the deep institutional capacity, rule of law, and geographic diversity that characterize modern America. The question is whether contemporary advantages offset the loss of 1930s resilience factors. Historical precedent suggests they do, but the outcome will be permanent degradation rather than recovery to previous prosperity.

The second scenario, authoritarian restoration, carries a probability of 20 to 25 percent based on historical patterns of democratic failure under sustained stress. This trajectory follows the Weimar Germany template, where economic crisis combined with political gridlock led to systematic abandonment of democratic norms and eventual dictatorship. The timeline was compressed, taking only 14 years from the 1919 founding of the Weimar Republic to Hitler's appointment as Chancellor in January 1933.[11]

The mechanism operates through escalating norm erosion rather than sudden coup. Economic crisis produces political gridlock as partisan divisions prevent necessary reforms. Gridlock leads to executive overreach through emergency powers justified as necessary to address dysfunction. Emergency measures become normalized, systematically weakening legislative authority. Violence enters political discourse as street battles between opposing factions demonstrate that peaceful conflict resolution has failed. The political elite, desperate to maintain order and frustrated by legislative paralysis, abandons commitment to democratic process in favor of centralized executive authority. This pattern is not speculation. It is documented sequence from multiple historical cases where democratic institutions proved incapable of managing severe crises.

Weimar Germany's specific mechanism is instructive. Article 48 of the Weimar Constitution allowed the President to issue emergency decrees bypassing the Reichstag, a provision intended for crisis management that became the instrument of institutional suicide. President Hindenburg invoked Article 48 sixty times in 1932 alone, systematically destroying parliamentary supremacy and public confidence in democratic governance.[12] Adolf Hitler did not seize power from a functioning democracy. He inherited a regime that had already abandoned representative governance in favor of executive dictatorship under constitutional pretense.[11] The definitive failure was not economic but political: the elite's decision to abandon norms of mutual toleration and legislative supremacy because the fractured party system made governing coalitions impossible to sustain.

The Roman Republic provides a longer timeline demonstrating that authoritarian restoration can occur through century-long decay rather than rapid collapse. The assassination of Tiberius Gracchus in 133 BCE by political opponents established the precedent that murder was acceptable political response, shattering the republic's primary mechanism for peaceful conflict resolution. Violence normalized over the following decades through the reforms of Marius, Sulla's march on Rome, and Caesar's civil war, culminating in Augustus establishing permanent autocracy in 27 BCE. The total timeline spanned 106 years, demonstrating that norm erosion can be protracted yet ultimately fatal. Freedom was sacrificed for order because the republican system, poisoned by

extreme wealth inequality and chronic elite division, lost capacity for self-gov
ernance.[13]

Contemporary America exhibits warning signs that align disturbingly with
both templates. Political polarization has reached levels where shared external threats fail to generate elite unity necessary for collective action. Research
demonstrates that polarization can reach tipping points beyond which sudden
threats no longer produce collective action, and that hysteresis effects make
reversibility problematic once those thresholds are crossed.[14] Constitutional
hardball, the use of extreme procedural measures and rhetoric labeling opponents as illegitimate, mirrors the breakdown of mutual toleration that preceded
Weimar's failure.[15] Political violence has entered mainstream discourse through
events including January 6 and increasing threats against public officials. Executive power expansion through emergency declarations and attempts to circum-
vent legislative gridlock echo Article 48 dynamics. The mechanisms are visible.
The question is whether American institutional depth and federalism provide
sufficient buffers to prevent the sequence from completing.

The structural factors that could enable authoritarian restoration are documented. Trust in the federal government has collapsed to historic lows, with
only 17 percent of Americans saying they trust the government in Washington
to do what is right, one of the lowest measures in nearly seven decades of polling.
Only 4 percent say the political system is working extremely or very well, and 63
percent have little or no confidence in the future of the U.S. political system.[16]
Economic despair is widespread among younger generations, with more than
half of Gen Z members who do not currently own a home believing they would
need to win the lottery to afford one.[17] This combination of fatalism about
current systems and high demand for government solutions creates receptivity
to radical systemic shifts when crisis demonstrates that established institutions
cannot deliver necessary reforms. Historical pattern suggests that when democracies prove incapable of solving existential problems, populations choose order
over freedom.

What prevents this outcome is the depth of American institutional redundancy. Federalism means power is genuinely distributed across state govern-

ments that retain substantial autonomy and legitimacy independent of federal dysfunction. Geographic diversity makes centralized authoritarianism difficult to impose across regions with different economic interests and political cultures. The military remains institutionally committed to constitutional rather than personal loyalty, lacking the tradition of political involvement that enabled authoritarian transitions elsewhere. External threats, while present, do not require the kind of unified national mobilization that has historically justified emergency powers. These structural factors reduce probability below historical base rates for democratic collapse, but they do not eliminate the risk entirely.

The third scenario, geographic fragmentation into effectively separate regional systems, carries a probability of 10 to 15 percent. This outcome does not require formal secession or civil war. It manifests through the proliferation of interstate compacts that allow states to coordinate policies independent of federal authority, the hollowing out of federal capacity until Washington becomes largely irrelevant to daily governance, and the emergence of regional economic and regulatory systems that operate as functional separate countries despite nominal national unity.

The constitutional mechanism for this already exists and is accelerating. Interstate compacts, authorized under Article I, Section 10, Clause 3 of the Constitution, require Congressional consent only when they substantially alter the balance of federal and state power. The Supreme Court has interpreted this requirement so narrowly that it has essentially read the Compact Clause out of existence, allowing states to coordinate extensively on matters including professional licensure, environmental regulation, and infrastructure without federal approval.[18] The largest compacts cover nursing licensure, used by 41 states, Guam, and the Virgin Islands, and physician licensure, used by 39 states, Washington D.C., and Guam.[19] These agreements demonstrate that states possess legal mechanisms to build functional regional governance structures when federal institutions fail to address practical needs.

The precedent for internal fragmentation without violent breakup comes from multiple sources. The Articles of Confederation period from 1781 to 1789 featured weak central government and strong state autonomy, creating economic chaos and competing currencies that eventually forced the Constitutional Convention.[20] Post-Cold War Yugoslavia dissolved violently along ethnic lines, but the key difference was that Yugoslav institutions fragmented while Russian centralized security apparatus remained intact, preventing similar outcome despite worse economic conditions.[4] The distinction suggests that fragmentation requires not just crisis but actual institutional dissolution at the center. American institutions, while degraded, retain sufficient capacity to prevent complete breakdown even as state-level coordination increases.

Current trends support gradual movement toward this outcome. Red and blue states are diverging on fundamental policies including abortion access, gun regulation, taxation levels, education standards, and healthcare provision. Some states, particularly Texas and California, possess economies and populations sufficient to function as independent nations. Federal incapacity creates vacuum that state governments fill through regional coordination. The 2033 fiscal crisis, by destroying federal capacity to fund grants and enforce regulatory frameworks, would accelerate this dynamic by forcing states to solve problems collectively that the federal government can no longer address.

What prevents full fragmentation is economic interdependence and the absence of clean geographic separation. Supply chains cross state lines extensively, making autarky economically devastating. The dollar remains unified currency under federal control, preventing the kind of monetary fragmentation that destabilized the Confederation period. Military integration under federal command prevents the kind of armed standoffs that would force formal separation. Purple states with mixed urban and rural populations lack the political homogeneity necessary for alignment with either regional bloc. The outcome is more likely to be messy functional separation, with states coordinating on specific policies through compacts while maintaining nominal federal structure, than clean divorce into separate nations.

The fourth scenario, comprehensive reconstruction through constitutional reform or grand bargain, carries the lowest probability at 5 to 10 percent despite being the most desirable outcome. This path requires crisis to force political action that current incentive structures make impossible. The historical precedent exists but the conditions that enabled past success are largely absent in contemporary circumstances.

The 1787 Constitutional Convention provides the definitive template. The convention was triggered by systemic fiscal failure under the Articles of Confederation, which lacked the tax authority necessary to fund national operations or manage debt. State tariff wars demonstrated fatal flaws in interstate commerce regulation. The crisis created sufficient consensus among elites that comprehensive reform, initially intended only to modify the Articles, produced an entirely new constitutional system.[20] This precedent establishes that fiscal failure is the primary trigger for constitutional reconstruction, but it occurred when the problem was newly manifested rather than decades of accumulated dysfunction.

The mechanism for constitutional reform exists through Article V, which allows states to call a convention for proposing amendments upon application by two-thirds of state legislatures, currently 34 states. Any proposed amendment requires ratification by three-fourths of states, currently 38, ensuring that only reforms enjoying broad consensus can succeed.[21] The Convention of States movement seeking to impose fiscal constraints on the federal government has passed resolutions in 19 states as of 2025, demonstrating active pursuit of this pathway despite remaining well short of the threshold.[22]

The grand bargain pathway, represented by the 1983 Social Security reforms, demonstrates that comprehensive legislative solutions remain possible under the right conditions. The National Commission on Social Security Reform, known as the Greenspan Commission, provided political insulation that allowed Congress and President Reagan to enact painful measures combining delayed cost-of-living adjustments, taxation of benefits for higher earners, gradual retirement age increases, and accelerated payroll tax increases.[23] The package combined tax increases with benefit reductions, distributing pain across constituencies in ways that made the overall package politically survivable.

Why reconstruction remains unlikely despite these precedents comes down to magnitude and polarization. The current problem requires adjustment equivalent to 3.82 percent of taxable payroll, more than double the 1.82 percent that the Greenspan Commission faced in 1983.[24] Political polarization is substantially worse, with affective polarization reaching levels where shared external threats fail to bridge partisan divides.[14] The Simpson-Bowles Commission in 2010 failed to achieve even its internal threshold of 14 votes, securing only 11, and when a modified version reached the House floor in 2012 it was rejected 382 to 38.[25] The constituency lock-in created by 70 million beneficiaries and an electorate where voters over 50 constitute 55 percent of the total makes benefit reductions electorally prohibitive. Approximately 90 percent of voters over 50 say they would be more likely to support a candidate who pledged to protect Social Security benefits.[26] AARP alone has 38 million members with offices in every state and territory.[27] The easy revenue levers, particularly payroll tax increases that were available in 1983, have been largely exhausted, forcing any comprehensive solution to include politically toxic measures including benefit cuts and broad-based tax increases that alienate core constituencies of both parties simultaneously.

The conditions that could enable reconstruction involve either the 2033 automatic Social Security cuts creating such acute political pressure that gridlock becomes unsustainable, or generational political realignment driven by Millennial and Gen Z cohorts demanding comprehensive reform. Younger generations demonstrate high demand for government action on inequality, debt, housing, and healthcare, with 70 percent of Gen Z supporting universal basic income compared to 61 percent overall.[28] However, these cohorts also exhibit profound fatalism about the current system's capacity to deliver. Research finds that many young voters share a belief that fractured, dysfunctional government systems are incapable of addressing critical challenges, with a sense of fatalism extending across the right, center, and left.[29] The contrast between older voters' intense engagement on Social Security and younger voters' systemic fatalism captures the political deadlock that makes reconstruction improbable. The pattern from previous realignments suggests that crisis must first break this fatalism, transforming demand for change into sustained political mobilization that forces elite response. The GI Generation, which came of age during the Great Depression and World War II, developed collective identity and confidence that enabled the institutional expansion of the postwar period.[9] Whether contemporary cohorts can replicate this transformation depends on whether 2033 crisis converts their economic despair into political force rather than resignation.

The probability assessment assigns highest likelihood to muddling through because historical base rates show democracies rarely collapse entirely even under severe stress. Greece survived 27.5 percent unemployment because the Eurozone enforced institutional discipline.[5] Post-Soviet Russia endured catastrophic economic decline because centralized state capacity prevented fragmentation.[4] Argentina recovered rapidly from crisis because rapid political turnover purged failed policies.[6] The consistent factor is that survival depends on institutional health and state capacity rather than economic metrics. The United States possesses deep institutions despite current dysfunction, suggesting resilience through degradation rather than complete failure.

Authoritarian restoration receives 20 to 25 percent probability because the warning signs are visible and the historical pattern is documented. Weimar took 14 years from dysfunction to dictatorship.[11] Rome took 106 years but the mechanism was identical: elite abandonment of governing norms when the system proved incapable of managing structural crises.[13] American polarization, norm erosion, and executive power expansion mirror early stages of this trajectory. What reduces probability below 50 percent is institutional redundancy and federalism that Weimar lacked, but these are buffers rather than guarantees.

Geographic fragmentation receives 10 to 15 percent probability because the legal mechanisms exist and trends are accelerating, but economic interdependence and lack of clean separation prevent full divorce. Interstate compacts will proliferate, federal capacity will continue hollowing out, and regional divergence will intensify, but complete fragmentation requires institutional dissolution at the center that seems unlikely given remaining state capacity.

Reconstruction receives only 5 to 10 percent probability because the conditions that enabled 1983 success are absent. The problem is more than twice as large.[24] Political polarization is substantially worse. Easy policy levers are exhausted. The Article V convention pathway requires 34 states when only 19 have acted.[22] The grand bargain pathway requires bipartisan trust that 382 to

38 votes demonstrate does not exist.[25] The generational realignment pathway requires converting Gen Z fatalism into mobilization, a transformation that typically requires experiencing crisis directly rather than anticipating it.

These scenarios are not mutually exclusive. The most probable path involves initial muddling through from 2027 to 2033, emergency borrowing rather than reform when the Social Security deadline hits, continued deterioration through the 2030s, and potential shift toward either authoritarian restoration or reconstruction depending on whether the prolonged crisis breaks democratic norms or forces elite adaptation. Elements of fragmentation will occur regardless through interstate compact proliferation and regional policy divergence, operating as background process rather than endpoint.

Early warning indicators allow tracking which scenario is emerging. Signs pointing toward muddling through include 2033 emergency borrowing that kicks the problem down the road, geographic inequality increasing but remaining stable without major upheaval, no dramatic political shifts, and federal capacity declining but continuing to function. Signs pointing toward authoritarian restoration include executive emergency powers expansion becoming routine, norm violations accelerating without consequence, political violence increasing beyond isolated incidents, and popular demand for strong leadership to overcome gridlock. Signs pointing toward fragmentation include interstate compacts replacing federal coordination on major policy areas, state-level economic systems developing independent of federal frameworks, interstate migration accelerating as people sort geographically, and federal government becoming increasingly irrelevant to daily governance. Signs pointing toward reconstruction include formation of a bipartisan crisis commission with genuine authority before 2033, constitutional convention call reaching 34 states, major entitlement and tax reform passing Congress, or massive youth political mobilization demanding systemic overhaul.

The scenarios represent possibility space rather than certainty. Understanding the range allows preparation for most likely outcomes while working toward preferred alternatives. The highest probability outcome, prolonged stagnation with geographic stratification, is neither collapse nor recovery but permanent reduction in living standards and state capacity. Authoritarian restoration, while less likely, follows documented historical patterns and exhibits visible warning signs in contemporary politics. Geographic fragmentation reflects trends already accelerating through legal mechanisms. Comprehensive reconstruction remains possible but requires crisis to force political will that shows no current evidence of materializing.

History teaches that democracies under fiscal stress usually muddle through rather than collapsing entirely, but muddling through does not mean returning to prosperity. It means accepting permanent degradation as the new normal. Social order proves stickier than apocalyptic narratives suggest, but the quality of life within that order can decline substantially without triggering regime change. The question is not whether America collapses into Mad Max dystopia. The question is whether your neighborhood maintains functional governance or joins the tier of failed jurisdictions. That determination depends primarily on local fiscal capacity, economic diversity, and political willingness to accept necessary tax increases to maintain services. The scenario playing out nationally matters for understanding the broader context, but your lived experience will be determined by decisions made at the state and municipal level in response to federal incapacity.

The collision is coming. These four trajectories represent the documented range of how democratic systems respond to fiscal crises of this magnitude. Understanding this possibility space allows clearer thinking about individual preparation and collective action. The choices made in 2033, when automatic Social Security cuts force decision, will largely determine which path emerges. But the preconditions are being established now through the erosion of fiscal space, the deepening of political polarization, the proliferation of interstate coordination, and the growing fatalism of younger generations who will inherit whatever system survives. The emperor is naked. The question is what happens when everyone simultaneously acknowledges what they have long seen but declined to discuss.

Chapter 14 Notes

1. For complete analysis of the statutory depletion mechanism and political economy constraints, see Karina Vunnam, "The 2033 Social Security Deadline: Statutory Depletion as a Distinct Mechanism of Fiscal Crisis," SSRN Working Paper (2025). The paper demonstrates that the 2033 deadline should be treated analytically as binding rather than aspirational, with pre-deadline reform structurally improbable due to magnitude (3.82% of taxable payroll versus 1.82% in 1983), constituency lock-in (70 million beneficiaries, voters 50+ constituting 55-61% of electorate in competitive districts), blame avoidance dynamics, and demonstrated legislative incapacity (Simpson-Bowles 382-38 rejection).

2. Anders Åslund, "Russia's Collapse," Foreign Affairs 78, no. 5 (September-October 1999): 64-77, https://doi.org/10.2307/20049451 . ("Except for 1997, GDP has decreased every year for the past decade, with an accumulated decline since 1991 of 40 percent.") For mortality data: F.C. Notzon et al., "Causes of Declining Life Expectancy in Russia," Journal of the American Medical Association 279, no. 10 (1998): 793-800, https://pubmed.ncbi.nlm.nih.gov/9508159/. ("Life expectancy for Russian men and women declined dramatically from 63.8 and 74.4 years to 57.7 and 71.2 years, respectively.")

3. Mike Dolan, "Japan's Portfolio Reshuffle Raises Red Flag for US," Reuters, May 22, 2025, https://www.reuters.com/markets/europe/japans-portfolio-reshuffle-raises-red-flag-us-mike-dolan-2025-05-21/. See also Enrique Alberola et al., "Unconventional Monetary Policy and Debt Sustainability in Japan," Journal of the Japanese and International Economies 69 (2023), https://doi.org/10.1016/j.jjie.2023.101274. ("Japan has the highest ratio of public debt to GDP globally, over 260% at the end

of 2022.")

4. Henry E. Hale and Rein Taagepera, "Russia: Consolidation or Collapse?," Europe-Asia Studies 54, no. 7 (November 2002): 1101-1125, https://www.jstor.org/stable/826308. (Analyzes why, despite economic collapse and pressures toward regional secessionism, the Russian state did not break apart like Yugoslavia, attributing survival to the persistence of core state structures and coercive capacities.)

5. George Pagoulatos, "Greece after the Bailouts: Assessment of a Qualified Failure," Hellenic Observatory Discussion Paper No. 130 (London: London School of Economics, November 2018), https://www.lse.ac.uk/Hellenic-Observatory/Assets/Documents/Publications/GreeSE-Papers/GreeSE-No130.pdf. ("Greece had lost a quarter of its 2008 GDP, unemployment was at 20% (having reached 27.5% at its peak).")

6. Miguel Kiguel, "Argentina's 2001 Economic and Financial Crisis: Lessons for Europe," Brookings Institution, 2011, https://www.brookings.edu/wp-content/uploads/2016/06/11_argentina_kiguel.pdf. ("GDP per capita fell by around 20 percent during the whole period, while unemployment increased to 25 percent of the labor force and poverty levels reached 55 percent of the population.")

7. U.S. Census Bureau, "An Aging Nation: U.S. Median Age Surpassed 39 in 2024," June 2025, https://www.census.gov/library/stories/2025/06/metro-areas-median-age.html. For 1930s comparison: U.S. Census Bureau, "Median Age of the Population: 1820 to 2000," Census 2000 PHC-T-9, Table 7, https://www2.census.gov/programs-surveys/decennial/2000/phc/phc-t-09/tab07.pdf. (Median age in 1930: 26.5 years.)

8. U.S. Census Bureau, "Nation's Urban and Rural Populations Shift

Following 2020 Census," Press Release CB22-CN.25, December 29, 2022, https://www.census.gov/newsroom/press-releases/2022/urban-rural-populations.html. ("Urban areas now account for 80.0% of the U.S. population.")

9. Robert D. Putnam, Bowling Alone: The Collapse and Revival of American Community (New York: Simon & Schuster, 2000). See also Robert D. Putnam and Shaylyn Romney Garrett, The Upswing: How America Came Together a Century Ago and How We Can Do It Again (New York: Simon & Schuster, 2020).

10. Congressional Research Service, "Unemployment During the Great Depression," Report R40655, https://www.everycrsreport.com/reports/R40655.html. ("The unemployment rate rose from 3.2% in 1929 to 24.9% in 1933.")

11. The Holocaust Explained, "Strength and Weaknesses of the Weimar Republic," https://www.theholocaustexplained.org/the-nazi-rise-to-power/the-weimar-republic/strength-and-weaknesses-of-the-weimar-republic/. ("The first elections for the new Republic were held on the 19 January 1919... Hitler was sworn in as the chancellor of Germany on the 30 January 1933.") See also Richard J. Evans, The Coming of the Third Reich (New York: Penguin Books, 2005).

12. Holocaust Encyclopedia, "Article 48," United States Holocaust Memorial Museum, https://encyclopedia.ushmm.org/content/en/article/article-48. ("The President consistently operated outside of the very system he was meant to uphold. Hindenburg invoked Article 48 sixty times in 1932 alone.")

13. Brenda J. Lutz and James M. Lutz, "Political Violence in the Republic of Rome: Nothing New under the Sun," Government and Opposition 41, no. 4 (Autumn 2006): 491-511, https://www.jstor.org/stable/44

483167. See also Walter Scheidel, The Great Leveler: Violence and the History of Inequality from the Stone Age to the Twenty-First Century (Princeton, NJ: Princeton University Press, 2018); Edward J. Watts, Mortal Republic: How Rome Fell into Tyranny (New York: Basic Books, 2018).

14. Michael W. Macy et al., "Polarization and Tipping Points," Proceedings of the National Academy of Sciences 118, no. 50 (2021), https://doi.org/10.1073/pnas.2102144118. ("Phase diagrams of political polarization reveal difficult-to-predict transitions that can be irreversible due to asymmetric hysteresis trajectories.")

15. Steven Levitsky and Daniel Ziblatt, How Democracies Die (New York: Crown, 2018). See also American Federation of Teachers, "The Crisis of American Democracy," American Educator (Fall 2020), https://www.aft.org/ae/fall2020/levitsky_ziblatt.

16. Pew Research Center, "Public Trust in Government: 1958-2025," December 4, 2025, https://www.pewresearch.org/politics/2025/12/04/public-trust-in-government-1958-2025/. ("Just 17% of Americans now say they trust the government in Washington to do what is right... the current measure is one of the lowest in the nearly seven decades since the question was first asked.") See also Pew Research Center, "Views of the U.S. Political System," September 19, 2023, https://www.pewresearch.org/politics/2023/09/19/views-of-the-u-s-political-system-the-federal-government-and-federal-state-relations/. ("Only 4% of Americans now say the political system is working extremely or very well... A majority (63%) say they have little or no confidence in the future of the U.S. political system.")

17. Zillow, "More Than Half of Gen Zers and Millennials Believe They'd Need to Win the Lottery to Afford a Home," press release, April 19, 2023,

https://zillow.mediaroom.com/2023-04-19-More-than-half-of-Gen -Zers-and-millennials-believe-theyd-need-to-win-the-lottery-to-afford -a-home. ("52% of Gen Zers and 57% of millennials who don't currently own a home believe they'd need to win the lottery to afford one.")

18. Legal Information Institute, "Historical Back- ground of the Compact Clause," Cornell Law School, https://www.law.cornell.edu/constitution-conan/article-1/s ection-10/clause-3/historical-background-of-the-compact-clause. See also Notre Dame Law Review, "A Prophylactic Approach to Compact Constitutionality," https://ndlawreview.org/a-prophylactic-approac h-to-compact-constitutionality/. ("By interpreting 'any Agreement or Compact' so narrowly that it is difficult to see what besides otherwise unlawful coordination qualifies, the Court has essentially read the Compact Clause out of existence.")

19. National Conference of State Legislatures, "Are Inter- state Compacts an Answer to Health Workforce Short- ages?," https://www.ncsl.org/state-legislatures-news/details/are-inte rstate-compacts-an-answer-to-health-workforce-shortages.

20. Tax Foundation, "How Failed Tax Policy Led to the Constitution- al Convention," https://taxfoundation.org/blog/constitution-day-t ax-policy-constitutional-convention/.

21. National Conference of State Legislatures, "Amending the U.S. Con- stitution," https://www.ncsl.org/about-state-legislatures/amending -the-us-constitution.

22. U.S. Constitution Annotated, "ArtV.3.3 Proposals of Amendments by Convention," Congress.gov, https://constitution.congress.gov/b rowse/essay/artV-3-3/ALDE_00013051/. ("States that have passed the Convention of States application (19).")

23. Social Security Administration, "Social Security Amendments of 1983: Legislative History and Summary of Provisions," by John A. Svahn and Mary Ross, Social Security Bulletin 46, no. 7 (July 1983), https://www.ssa.gov/policy/docs/ssb/v46n7/v46n7p3.pdf.

24. Louise Sheiner and Georgia Nabors, "Social Security: Today's Financing Challenge Is at Least Double What It Was in 1983," Brookings Institution, September 18, 2023, https://www.brookings.edu/articles/social-security-todays-financing-challenge-is-at-least-double-what-it-was-in-1983/. ("The required adjustments to revenues and/or benefits are twice as large today" comparing current 3.82% to 1983's 1.82% of taxable payroll.)

25. Charles J. Lewis, "Himes Predicts Action on Debt After Election," CT Insider, March 29, 2012, https://www.ctinsider.com/local/article/himes-predicts-action-on-debt-after-election-3445605.php. For commission vote: Richard Kogan, "What Was Actually in Bowles-Simpson," Center on Budget and Policy Priorities, October 2, 2012, https://www.cbpp.org/research/what-was-actually-in-bowles-simpson-and-how-can-we-compare-it-with-other-plans. ("On December 3, 2010, only 11 commissioners voted in favor.")

26. AARP, "Social Security 2024 Survey of Voters Ages 50+," November 2024, https://www.aarp.org/pri/topics/voter-research/politics/voter-preferences-2024-battleground-states/. ("Around 90% said they would be more likely to vote for a candidate who pledged to make sure workers get the Social Security they paid into.") For electorate share: Susan Milligan, "How Older Voters Powered Trump's Election Engine," AARP, November 7, 2024, https://www.aarp.org/government-elections/election-analysis-older-voters-2024/.

27. AARP, "What Is AARP and How Does It Help Older Americans," https://www.aarp.org/about-aarp/. ("AARP is one of the largest membership organizations in the world with 38 million members.")

28. The Annie E. Casey Foundation, "Social Issues That Matter to Generation Z," https://www.aecf.org/blog/generation-z-social-issues. ("More than two-thirds (70%) of Gen Zers think the U.S. government should provide a universal basic income for all individuals, compared to 61% of the overall population.")

29. UC Berkeley News, "Young Voters Have Growing Power, But Broken Politics Leave Them 'Fatalistic,' Studies Find," June 26, 2024, https://news.berkeley.edu/2024/06/26/young-voters-have-growing-power-but-broken-politics-leave-them-fatalistic-studies-find/. ("Many young voters appear to share a belief that fractured, dysfunctional government systems are incapable of addressing critical challenges that fall heavily on their generations. A sense of fatalism extends across the right, center and left.")

Chapter 15
Living Between Worlds

I n 1798, Thomas Malthus published his Essay on the Principle of Population and demonstrated with mathematical precision that humanity was doomed. Population grows geometrically while food production grows arithmetically. The conclusion was inescapable: mass starvation, suffering on an unimaginable scale, the collapse of civilization under the weight of too many mouths and too little grain. Malthus was not a crank. He was a careful scholar working from the best available data, and his logic was sound given his assumptions. He was also spectacularly wrong. World population has grown from one billion in his time to eight billion today, and the percentage of humanity living in extreme poverty has fallen from roughly 90 percent to under 10 percent.[1] The agricultural revolution, synthetic fertilizers, the green revolution, global trade networks, none of these appeared in his models because none of them existed yet.

Paul Ehrlich's 1968 bestseller The Population Bomb opened with the declaration that the battle to feed humanity was over, that hundreds of millions would starve to death in the 1970s regardless of any crash programs undertaken.[2] The Club of Rome's 1972 Limits to Growth model projected civilizational collapse before 2000 as resources depleted and pollution accumulated.[3] The

Y2K bug was supposed to crash financial systems, ground aircraft, and plunge the world into chaos at midnight on January 1, 2000. Each prediction emerged from genuine data, reasonable extrapolation, and sincere concern. Each was wrong. Not because the underlying problems were imaginary, but because complex systems adapt in ways that linear projections cannot capture.

This history should give you pause about the crisis documented in this book. Not doubt about the evidence, which is statutory law rather than speculation, but humility about the shape of what comes after. The 2033 Social Security deadline will arrive. The automatic benefit cuts will trigger or Congress will act under maximum duress. The interest cost explosion will continue consuming federal capacity. The municipal cascade will sort America into tiers of functionality. These outcomes follow from arithmetic and current law. What cannot be known is how 330 million people will respond, what adaptations will emerge, what innovations and reorganizations and political realignments will reshape the landscape in ways no model can predict.

The interregnum you are entering, the gap between the death of an old order and the birth of something new, has been navigated before. Not always successfully. Not always without tremendous suffering. But the historical record offers more than warnings. It offers patterns, and understanding those patterns provides practical guidance for the years ahead.

Consider Harold Macmillan, who became Prime Minister of Britain in 1957 and inherited an empire in terminal decline. The Suez Crisis had just humiliated British power on the world stage. The economy lurched between crises. Inflation eroded savings while unemployment crept upward. The welfare state built after World War II was straining under costs its designers never anticipated. Macmillan's famous response to a journalist asking what worried him most captures the essential uncertainty of governing during transition: "Events, dear boy, events."[4] Britain did not collapse. It muddled through, shedding colonies, adjusting expectations, and building a different kind of society than the imperial power it had been. Living standards eventually rose again, though the path was neither smooth nor painless. The three-day work week of 1974, when the government restricted commercial electricity usage to three consecutive days each week to conserve coal during a miners' strike, felt apocalyptic to those living through it.[5] It was not the end. It was a painful adjustment on the way to something else.

The muddle is the most likely outcome for America, as Chapter 14 documented. Not dramatic collapse but slow grinding decline punctuated by acute crises that force temporary solutions. The experience will vary enormously by geography. Residents of fiscally healthy cities with diversified economies will notice degraded federal services, slower infrastructure maintenance, reduced expectations for what government provides. Residents of fiscally stressed cities dependent on federal transfers will experience something closer to genuine failure, watching services collapse, neighborhoods empty, tax bases erode in the vicious cycle that has already claimed cities like Detroit and Gary and East St. Louis. The same country will contain both experiences simultaneously, which is disorienting for anyone trying to understand the overall trajectory. Someone in Austin or Raleigh might reasonably conclude that the doom predictions were overblown while someone in Hartford or Birmingham experiences the full weight of fiscal crisis. Both will be describing the same America.

The muddle requires patience and positioning. If the most probable outcome is prolonged stagnation with geographic stratification, then the practical response is ensuring you end up in the functional tier rather than the failed one. This means understanding your current location with clear eyes. What is your city's pension funding status? What percentage of the municipal budget goes to debt service and legacy costs versus current services? How diversified is the local economy? What happens to your property values and tax base if the largest employer leaves or the federal facility closes? These questions have answers, documented in municipal financial reports and economic analyses, and the answers determine your exposure to the cascade.

Geographic positioning is not about fleeing to a bunker in Montana. It is about recognizing that America's federal structure means wildly different outcomes depending on state and local governance. Some states have maintained fiscal discipline, funded their pensions, diversified their economies, and retained capacity to absorb federal retrenchment. Others have accumulated massive unfunded liabilities, driven out businesses with hostile regulatory environments, and positioned themselves for severe adjustment when federal transfers decline. Moving from a state in the second category to one in the first is not paranoid preparation. It is rational response to documented fiscal trajectories. If relocation is not possible, understanding your specific exposure allows realistic planning rather than vague anxiety.

But history also records ruptures, moments when the muddle becomes something more dramatic and the old order dies faster than anyone expected. Argentina in December 2001 provides a compressed example. The economy had been struggling for years under a currency peg that overvalued the peso and made exports uncompetitive. Unemployment rose steadily. The government borrowed to cover deficits until external creditors lost confidence. When the crisis hit, it hit fast. The government froze bank accounts, trapping middle-class savings. Unemployment reached 25 percent. Poverty rates hit 55 percent. The president resigned and fled the presidential palace by helicopter as riots engulfed Buenos Aires.[6]

What happened next is instructive. The formal economy collapsed but people did not simply starve and die. Neighborhood assemblies formed spontaneously, organizing collective kitchens, childcare, and dispute resolution. Barter networks called trueque clubs processed an estimated 600 million transactions at their peak, allowing exchange when the peso became worthless.[7] Workers occupied abandoned factories and resumed production under cooperative management. The crisis was genuine and the suffering was real, yet Argentine society demonstrated remarkable capacity for self-organization when formal institutions failed. Within a few years the economy was growing again, faster than it had in decades, as the rupture forced policy changes that gridlock had prevented.

The Argentine example suggests that crisis can be clarifying. The political paralysis documented in Chapter 13, the prisoner's dilemma that makes reform impossible before external events force adjustment, breaks when continuation of current policy becomes more painful than the change politicians have been avoiding. Argentina cycled through five presidents in two weeks during the worst of the crisis.[8] That instability was terrifying, but it also meant the system could purge failed policies rapidly rather than defending them for decades. Whether America's institutions permit similar rapid adjustment or instead lock in failed approaches through institutional inertia remains unknown.

What you can do is build the local networks and practical skills that proved essential during Argentina's rupture. Mutual aid is not hippie idealism. It is documented survival strategy during institutional failure. Knowing your neighbors, participating in community organizations, developing relationships with people who possess complementary skills, these investments pay uncertain returns during normal times and extraordinary returns during crisis. The emphasis should be on what researchers call bridging capital, connections to people outside your immediate circle who provide access to information, opportunities, and resources you would not otherwise have.[9] Your close friends will help you move furniture. Your weak ties will tell you about the job opening or the neighborhood that still has functional services or the workaround for the bureaucratic obstacle.

Financial positioning matters but requires accepting uncertainty about which risks materialize. A six-month emergency fund in liquid accounts provides buffer for decision-making during acute crisis rather than forcing desperate choices under time pressure. Beyond that buffer, diversification across asset classes reflects genuine uncertainty about whether the adjustment comes through inflation, deflation, default, or some combination. Fixed-rate debt protects against interest rate increases. Minimal debt protects against income disruption. These are not predictions about which specific scenario unfolds. They are hedges against the range of possibilities documented in Chapter 14.

Skills matter more than credentials when formal systems degrade. The economy always needs healthcare workers, people who can fix physical infrastructure, those who can grow food, educators, and those who can navigate complex systems. These skills retain value across scenarios. The specific preparation depends on your existing capabilities and interests, but the general principle is developing tangible competence rather than relying solely on positions within institutional hierarchies that may reorganize or collapse.

Then there is the possibility of renewal, the scenario that sounds naive to state but has historical precedent. Sometimes crisis forces the reconstruction that gridlock prevented. The Constitutional Convention of 1787 emerged from fiscal failure under the Articles of Confederation so severe that the delegates exceeded their mandate to merely revise the Articles and instead created an entirely new system of government.[10] The New Deal emerged from economic catastrophe that discredited the laissez-faire orthodoxy that had dominated American political economy. The postwar international order emerged from destruction so complete that previously impossible cooperation became necessary. These reconstructions required crisis. They were not achieved through gradual reform within functional systems. But they demonstrate that systemic failure can create openings for systematic improvement.

The 2033 deadline might force genuine bipartisan compromise when automatic benefit cuts make continuation of gridlock more politically costly than the pain of reform. The fiscal crisis might discredit the donor-class orthodoxies that have prevented necessary taxation. The geographic stratification might eventually trigger constitutional reforms that update an eighteenth-century system for twenty-first-century challenges. None of these outcomes is probable based on current political dynamics, but complex systems sometimes reorganize rapidly when pressure exceeds structural resistance.

What you cannot do is force renewal through individual action. You can position yourself to survive the muddle, build networks that function during rupture, and advocate for reconstruction without expecting success. You can vote, organize, donate, and engage in whatever political activity aligns with your values and analysis. But the honest assessment is that the structural factors documented in this book make pre-crisis reform extraordinarily unlikely. The political prisoner's dilemma remains stable. The median voter remains unaware or unconvinced. The interest groups that benefit from current arrangements remain powerful. Your individual awareness does not change these structural realities.

What your awareness does provide is time. Most people will not focus on the 2033 deadline until it arrives, at which point positioning options will be limited and costly. You have years to make geographic decisions while property markets have not yet priced in differential fiscal trajectories. You have years to build skills and networks before crisis makes everyone desperate for the same resources. You have years to adjust financial positioning while options remain open. The value of reading this book is not prophecy but preparation, not certainty about outcomes but clarity about the range of possibilities and the actions that improve your position across that range.

The dissonance you may feel between this knowledge and the apparent normalcy of daily life is real and uncomfortable. Your colleagues still discuss retirement plans as if Social Security will remain unchanged. Your neighbors still debate local politics as if federal fiscal dynamics will not eventually constrain everything. Your family may think you have become strangely pessimistic or weirdly obsessed with government budget documents. This dissonance is the psychological cost of advance awareness. It does not mean you are wrong. It means you have processed information that most people filter out because it is too uncomfortable to integrate.

The temptation to resolve this dissonance through action can lead in destructive directions. Panic selling, fleeing to isolation, destroying relationships over disagreements about timing or severity, these responses impose real costs before any crisis arrives. The opposite temptation, suppressing the knowledge and returning to comfortable assumptions, leaves you vulnerable when the collision occurs. The skill is holding dual awareness without letting either dominate. Normal life continues and systems are breaking. You go to work, raise children, maintain friendships, pursue meaning. You also position geographically if possible, diversify financially, strengthen local networks, develop practical skills. Both are true. Neither cancels the other.

Humans have navigated worse. The Great Depression saw unemployment reach 24.9 percent without triggering civil war or regime collapse.[11] Post-Soviet Russia experienced 40 percent GDP decline and life expectancy drops of six years for men yet maintained territorial integrity.[12] The residents of Weimar Germany, the ones who survived, built lives and families and careers during the most unstable political environment imaginable, with governments lasting months and currencies becoming worthless overnight. They were not heroes or superhumans. They were ordinary people adapting to extraordinary circumstances because the alternative was giving up entirely.

The difference between people who navigate crisis successfully and those who do not is rarely dramatic heroism. It is usually mundane preparation, realistic expectations, functional relationships, and psychological flexibility. It is having savings when the job disappears, knowing neighbors who can help when formal services fail, possessing skills that remain valuable when institutional hierarchies reorganize, maintaining the capacity to find meaning and purpose when external structures that previously provided them collapse.

The ship is sinking. The evidence documented across fourteen chapters demonstrates that the collision cannot be avoided through normal political processes. But ships sink slowly, over years and decades rather than hours, and the metaphor obscures more than it reveals. What is actually happening is a transformation of the relationship between American citizens and their government, a renegotiation of expectations and obligations that will unfold over the rest of your life. The postwar social contract, where stable employment and government programs provided reasonable security for a middle-class life, is ending. What replaces it remains unknown. Your task is navigating that uncertainty with clear eyes, steady preparation, and the understanding that you have something most people lack: advance warning and the analytical framework to interpret what you observe.

You are not Cassandra cursed to prophesy truth that no one believes. You are someone who has examined the evidence, understood the arithmetic, and recognized that the political system cannot self-correct before crisis forces adjustment. This knowledge is uncomfortable but valuable. Use it wisely. Position yourself and those you love as well as circumstances permit. Build the relationships and skills and resources that provide resilience across scenarios. And maintain your humanity through the transition, because the other side of crisis will need people who preserved their capacity for trust, cooperation, and hope when those qualities were hardest to sustain.

The interregnum is uncomfortable. It will likely remain so for years. But interregnums end. The old order finishes dying and the new order finishes being born. What that new order looks like depends partly on the structural factors documented in this book and partly on choices made by millions of people responding to circumstances none of them fully control. You cannot determine the outcome. You can influence your position within it. That is enough. That has to be enough, because it is what you have.

Chapter 15 Notes

1. Max Roser, "The Short History of Global Living Conditions and Why It Matters That We Know It," Our World in Data, 2024, https://ourworldindata.org/a-history-of-global-living-conditions.

2. Paul R. Ehrlich, The Population Bomb (New York: Ballantine Books, 1968).

3. Donella H. Meadows et al., The Limits to Growth: A Report for the Club of Rome's Project on the Predicament of Mankind (New York: Universe Books, 1972).

4. Harold Macmillan, quoted in various sources; attribution sometimes disputed but widely associated with Macmillan's tenure.

5. UK Parliament, "Three-Day Working Week," Hansard, vol. 867, debated Thursday 10 January 1974, https://hansard.parliament.uk/commons/1974-01-10/debates/c4dd11c8-886d-4894-bf4c-8b7eca739672/Three-DayWorkingWeek. See also Dominic Sandbrook, State of Emergency: The Way We Were: Britain, 1970–1974 (London: Allen Lane, 2010).

6. Miguel Kiguel, "Argentina's 2001 Economic and Financial Crisis: Lessons for Europe," Brookings Institution, 2011, https://www.brookings.edu/wp-content/uploads/2016/06/11_argentina_kiguel.pdf.

7. Rapid Transition Alliance, "The 'Instant' Local Economy: How Communities Saved Themselves When Mainstream Economics Failed in Argentina," https://rapidtransition.org/stories/autonomous-local-action-how-communities-saved-themselves-when-mainstream-economics-failed-in-argentina/.

8. Anthony Faiola, "Crisis-Wracked Argentina Seeks Fifth President in Two Weeks," Washington Post, January 1, 2002, https://www.washingtonpost.com/archive/politics/2002/01/01/crisi s-wracked-argentina-seeks-fifth-president-in-two-weeks/e8a1093c-ac 41-436b-b183-1f48b1e7bdc7/. ("Leaderless and bankrupt, a tense Argentina today sought its fifth president in two weeks after interim President Adolfo Rodriguez Saa quit Sunday, drained of political support after just 10 days in office.") See also BBC World Service, "Argentina's Five Presidents in Two Weeks," Witness History, https://www.bbc.co.uk/programmes/w3ct5ypy. ("In 2001, Argentina suffered an economic catastrophe so severe the country went through five leaders in two weeks.")

9. Robert D. Putnam, Bowling Alone: The Collapse and Revival of American Community (New York: Simon & Schuster, 2000).

10. Tax Foundation, "How Failed Tax Policy Led to the Constitution- al Convention," https://taxfoundation.org/blog/constitution-day-t ax-policy-constitutional-convention/.

11. Congressional Research Service, "Unemployment During the Great Depression," Report R40655, https://www.everycrsreport.com/rep orts/R40655.html.

12. Anders Åslund, "Russia's Collapse," Foreign Affairs 78, no. 5 (Sep- tember-October 1999): 64-77, https://doi.org/10.2307/20049451 ; F.C. Notzon et al., "Causes of Declining Life Expectancy in Russia," Journal of the American Medical Association 279, no. 10 (1998): 793-800, https://pubmed.ncbi.nlm.nih.gov/9508159/.

About the Author

K arina Vunnam is a Stanford-trained economist and author whose work examines how individually rational choices create collectively dysfunctional outcomes. Born in Mumbai and adopted at age seven, she has lived across multiple countries and economic systems. This experience has shaped her ability to recognize patterns that might be invisible to those raised within a single framework.

Her first nonfiction book, *Conspicuous: How Modern Luxury Redefined Craft, Clout, and Culture*, explores how economic forces, consumer psychology, and cultural shifts transformed luxury from old-money restraint to performative display. *The World Is Always Never Ending*, examining how historical cycles can provide perspective on modern anxiety, will be out in April 2025. She also writes the Mumbai Street Siblings children's book series, honoring the siblings she lost before her adoption.

Karina approaches complex systems as a translator for the rationally overwhelmed, providing analytical frameworks rather than prescriptive answers. She writes about rational dysfunction, systems thinking, and the gap between what we know and what we do at KarinaQueries.com and on Substack at karinaqueries.substack.com.

An interactive companion to this book, including timelines, data visualizations, and additional resources, is available at DebtByDysfunction.com.